imPERFECT 10

First published in the United Kingdom in 2022 by Vertical
Editions, Unit 41 Regency Court, Sheffield, S35 9ZQ

www.verticaleditions.com

Cover Design by Sam Turner. Cover images
by Shutterstock/Colorsport (front), Colorsport (back)

ISBN 978-1-908847-27-0

A CIP catalogue record for this book
is available from the British Library

Printed and bound by CMP, Poole

*im*PERFECT10
THE MAN BEHIND THE MAGIC

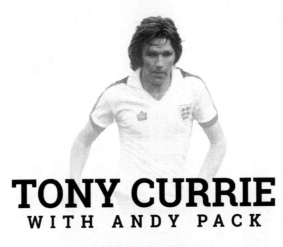

TONY CURRIE
WITH ANDY PACK

VERTICAL
editions

To the best Mum in the world; Bert and Jim, for always being there; Elizabeth, who has given me so much help over the last 20 years or so; My whole family, who are so important to me ... and to all the fans who appreciated the way I played the beautiful game.

CONTENTS

PREFACE

C live White blew his whistle. And he blew it because I had made a desperate challenge.

Like me, the referee had seen Spurs' defender Graham Roberts run almost unchallenged through our half and into the penalty area. The danger he posed had been obvious to concerned QPR fans – and thrilling to the Tottenham faithful – but there was danger also in my attempt to stop him from inflicting maximum damage.

As I had tracked back trying to get in a position to halt his progress, I'd anticipated teammates blocking Roberts by now. I wasn't really close enough to put in a proper tackle with any degree of certainty of winning the ball. He was in the area and I lunged, more in hope than anticipation, trying to push the ball away. As soon as I failed, but caught Graham, I knew the almost inevitable outcome – that horrible, guilty feeling that players have known since the game was invented.

But this was the biggest stage. Wembley. An FA Cup Final replay on May 27, 1982, and it was only six minutes into the game. Plenty of time to get back into it, but sickening all the same – especially given the power and pedigree Spurs had at their disposal.

After around 15 years as a professional footballer, had it all come down to this? A childhood dream of playing in an FA Cup-winning team. Of winning a trophy. Of representing England. Of being fulfilled and happy with what I had achieved in the game I was obsessed with; promotion, First Division glory days, England caps.

Within an instant of making that challenge, I could see this was almost certainly my last opportunity on a big stage, to achieve that part of my dream. At 32 years old, with a knee injury that was rapidly worsening, it was a wonder I was even playing at all. I knew there could be no future in which winning something at this level might ever happen again.

I would never give up on the match while there was still breath in my body, but the internal questioning was so strong again. Why does this always happen to me? Negative thoughts had clouded my life virtually all the way through – but never on football pitches. There I was, the King of Confidence, able to express myself; have an influence and above all be someone I found so difficult to be away from a football pitch. The two Tony Curries were virtually opposites.

Self-doubt eats away at you and inhibits your ability to make good decisions. It affects your relationships, limits you socially and affects your whole life. I wasn't hampered by these problems between three and five o'clock on Saturdays, when I was so often painfully plagued by them away from the pitch. Don't ask me why. Because I don't know either ...

1

NATURE OR NURTURE?

Have you ever wondered why your life has turned out as it has? What would have happened if your parents had been, for example, richer or poorer? Are you more like your mum or your •a•, an• how has your life been affecte• by people and circumstance? I'm not a deep thinker, but my own life has seen enough contradiction and frustration to make me wonder...

Edgware General Hospital in the Borough of Hendon, north-west London and just three miles from Wembley, was the venue for my first-ever 'debut' on January 1, 1950. In those days – before sophisticated scans – women often relied on long and well-established signs or signals during pregnancy which they believed were accurate enough to pre-identify the sex of their forthcoming child.

Presumably the forecasts were based on observations of the baby's size, shape and position and so on. Whatever they were, they couldn't have been very reliable. Mum was convinced I was going to be a girl, so everything acquired in advance of my arrival was pink!

Four years later my father – I can never call him Dad – left us for another woman, called Mary. He was an army man and had been a prisoner of war, but Mum never talked about him because he had obviously hurt her so much. When he left, I was four years old and my brother Paul was two. Basically, my father had been living a double life. He and Mary also had two sons, Billy and David, at virtually the same time as Paul and I were born. (Many years later, in 2008, Paul won an 'inventor of the year' award for his design for a riot shield that was used by the police and prisons).

I could never forgive my father for what he had done and for failing to have any positive part in my growing up, but I do believe I inherited some of his sporting skills; he was talented enough to have represented the Army at football, rugby and boxing. But without him, Mum and her two boys moved in with my maternal grandparents on Cricklewood Lane in a very roomy townhouse.

It needed to be – there were 12 of us in our family, including various aunties and three uncles all living there. Mum, one of my aunts, Paul and I all slept in the attic because my nan and grandad lived on the ground floor. On the one above, uncles Bert, Jim and Terry all shared one small room while auntie Eileen, husband Harry, a religious scoutmaster, and their daughter Sandra, who was like a sister to me, occupied a larger one. It was very much an extended family!

Unfortunately, my father was the love of my mum's life, which is why she never took up with anyone else after he had walked out. Astonishingly, years later in the 1960s, after Mary had died and my father was still looking after his other two boys, she forgave him and began seeing him while he was living in Finchley and working for Simms Motor Units. She used to visit him on Saturday nights and creep back home early on a Sunday morning because, for obvious reasons, she didn't want her brothers to know. He never came back to our house. Probably because my uncle told him that if he did, he would "get his bleedin' head kicked in!"

But he was back on the scene and actually took Mum, Paul and me out occasionally in his works van on an evening when Paul and I were in our early teens. The 'new' relationship was still under wraps, but in 1966 they had another son, Peter. Despite not being big, nobody had noticed Mum was pregnant, especially because a lot of women often wore pinafore dresses then.

Again the relationship didn't last which meant Peter never knew him as a dad either. Mum wouldn't say boo to a goose, but she did admit to me that once she had thrown a brick through Mary's window when she knew my father was in there! Because my parents had never divorced in a legal sense, they remained married until they died.

I loved our part of London in those days. The family had bought the house from the council and it became, I suppose, lower middle class. When it was compulsorily purchased in 1971, they gave us £4,000. But it was worth much more than that. Before Mum had us, she had worked in Lipton's, the grocer, but while we were all living together at Cricklewood Lane she packed that in and took on the role of chief cook and bottlewasher for everyone else who was working. I suppose she was a kind of 'whole family' housekeeper – and a bloody good one as well.

***

My father figures growing up were instead my three uncles, Bert, Jim and Terry. In fact, and ironically, Bert would have been an ideal pairing for my mum as far as I was concerned. If they hadn't been brother and sister! He virtually took over the role of Dad in my life and played a big part in my growing up.

For Bert and Jim, watching me play in London for Sheffield United or Leeds was like a home game for them because they didn't have to travel across the capital to catch a train north every other week to see our home games. Bert had kickabouts in the garden with me, took me to play matches and to training twice a week when I was a kid at QPR. And much more.

In many ways the fallout from my father leaving didn't affect Paul and me too much and I had a happy childhood. We were always out in the garden, which was just the right size for us to play football against each other; taking turns at being in goal or shooting in. Bolton were a top team in those days so he was goalkeeper Eddie Hopkinson or centre-forward Nat Lofthouse, while I was a Chelsea fan and would fancy my-self as Reg Matthews or Peter Bonetti in goal, and Jimmy Greaves or Bobby Tambling when I was shooting. But basically I was always Jimmy Greaves!

I had my fair share of scrapes and scares like any lad would have done in those years. Working people were still trying to reconstruct their lives after the war, and health and safety issues had not even been considered. Two little episodes spring to mind. When I was seven years old, I was sent to the attic to fetch something, but it was dark up there and when I went to press the light switch – which was in the lampshade – I didn't realise that there was no bulb in place.

I put my fingers in and got such a big electric shock it knocked me across the bed to the floor. It was one hell of a fright which sent me run-ning and screaming for my mum. She checked me out and found that my fingers were singed. Pity I wasn't clever enough then to ask who had taken the bulb out…

We had whole family holidays every year, normally at Deal, Bognor or Hayling Island and, although Mum often wasn't keen on going, our relatives would look after Paul and me. On one occasion we went to Brighton and its pebble beach for the day, but I don't recall why we kids wanted to go in the sea because I hate it. Thankfully uncle Bert ignored my protestations about wearing a rubber ring and insisted that I did, because the waves were pretty rough.

After just a few seconds of walking into the sea up to my knees, the beach shelved a bit sharpish and I dropped down with it, my head naturally going under. When I bobbed back up in a panic, I looked down at my rubber ring, which had hardly any air in it and was deflating. I could swim, but I was panicking and somebody had to dive in and drag me out. I had cheated death for a second time!

My days were basically football, football, football, until the park-keeper locked the gates at about 8pm. The never-changing routine was to come home from school, go down the park to play football, then come home to eat dinner which would be in the oven, probably burnt, but with the gravy on. It was great. I'd just keep licking away at it. I loved my food, even back then.

On the rare occasions we weren't playing football, it was Test cricket in the back garden where a strip of concrete with little cracks in it ran slightly downhill. We used it as the pitch and our games would be England against whoever were touring at the time; normally India, the West Indies or Australia. The wicket was about 10 yards long and although we used a tennis ball, you wouldn't believe the number of windows that were put through.

We soon learned how to use the bat and ball and both of us went on to represent Hendon Boys at cricket. We often used the tennis ball to kick around as well because we were lucky to have even a football at times. Our home had a slate roof and Paul and I used to throw the ball up so it would bounce off at strange angles, which was dead handy for testing our anticipation and ball skills. The potential problem was that if one of those slates had come down, it would have chopped our heads off like a guillotine!

Playing the ball off the wall also tested us out because it could rebound to hit the edge of a stone and misbehave. That also encouraged us to play with both feet. I loved those make-believe Bolton v Chelsea contests with Paul and would commentate on them, therefore ensuring I was always Greaves. Playing in the park often meant playing about 30-a-side and having to beat about five men before passing the ball off. Yeah, I did pass it. Occasionally...

There was a common school of thought for quite a while that Paul would do better than me in the game. Naturally he was smaller than me in the early years, but eventually outgrew me and played for London Schoolboys at centre-forward. He played decent level non-league football all his life, including for Dagenham in the 1976 FA Trophy Final. They were leading Scarborough 1-0 with a minute to go, only to lose 2-1.

Our infant and junior school, Childs Hill, was literally just across the road from our house and at lunchtime Paul and I would play a bit of football before nipping home for something to eat. On one occasion when I was about eight, I went home at playtime by mistake, got caught and was sent to the head, Mr. Robertson, who didn't believe my story. He was adamant that I was lying and kept on at me until I cried and blurted out what he wanted me to say, even though I had been telling the truth. School life was very different in the 1950s.

Another teacher, Mrs. Waite, made the most gorgeous fudge and would bring it in occasionally for us to share. But if you got the wrong side of her, she would rap your knuckles with a ruler. Not with the flat side, but with the edge. Believe you me, it really hurt. I later went to Whitefields Secondary Modern School, which was great; particularly for sport. Both boys and girls teams regularly won everything they entered. Although I was well-behaved, like so many kids who weren't academically inclined I regularly received school reports suggesting I would do better if I concentrated more.

It was true. We had a lot of exams throughout the year and they frightened me to death. In a two-hour exam I'd spend the first 45 minutes just reading the first question because I was scared, probably about not doing well. I was always like that and still am, to an extent. I take after my mum for that. She was a born worrier and I'm the same. Worry, worry, worry all the time, about all manner of things. This nature or nurture question is nagging me again...

In 1961, as I was leaving junior school, I was awarded the prize for best sportsman in the year. I was given a medal, plus Peter Dimmock's *'Sportsview Annual.'* In it was written: "Presented to Anthony Currie by Mr. J Robertson, headteacher". Because I was always the fastest there, when I switched to senior school, I thought, as you do: 'Well, I'll be all right here.' But, of course, you find out that there are always others who are better and I came down to earth with a bump – finishing last on sports day!

Dave Bedford, who went on to become a world-class distance runner, was in the same year as Elizabeth, my future wife, and I. There were six classes in each year and David – the brainy bastard – was in 1.1 while Elizabeth and I were in 1.5, one above the bottom. When we were 14 years old, he entered the 800 yards, as did I and the rest of the football team, and he beat us by about half a lap.

None of us could believe it because he never really played sport and we didn't know he could run that way. But he took to it from there and by the time he was 21 he was a star and an international. For those too young to remember David Bedford, but old enough to recall the much more recent *'118, 118'* television adverts, the two characters in running gear and headbands were based on David – who apparently tried to sue as a result. Our paths have crossed occasionally since and it has been lovely chatting to the great man who has a dry sense of humour.

That hammering on the track apart, I was a pretty decent sportsman and maybe could have made something of a cricketer. I had a good eye, but the trouble was we didn't have much coaching at school and played only about five matches a year. I tried a bit of slow bowling, could keep wicket and always smash a quick 50 with some aggressive batting. Les Hill, our PE teacher, sent my best mate Bob Turpie and me for a couple of Middlesex Schools under-15 trials, which came to nothing. I would have liked to have played more cricket, but my involvement fizzled out when football took over.

Starting life at Whitefields Secondary meant meeting Elizabeth for the first time. I liked her a lot and for me it was probably love at first sight, although I wasn't really aware of that at such a young age. We went out a few times, the first occasion being to the Golders Green Hippodrome to watch Bob Hope in 'The Road to Hong Kong.' She might have asked me first, I can't remember, but I do know she paid for sixpence worth of chips at Lyons' teahouse before we went. Come to think of it, she probably paid for the cinema tickets as well!

Undoubtedly she was the toughest girl in the school, but a protector not a bully. Her brothers had taught her to box and she would stand up for the underdog, even at night. If someone was being picked on, she would confront the bullies – even once sticking one of them, Margaret Lee, in a bin!

Elizabeth was good at sport, too, being the borough high-jump champion and also excelling in the long jump, hurdles and sprinting. We were friends really because we were too young for it to be a relationship and by the time I reached 13 I had a girlfriend called Linda, who was to become my first wife. In any event football was the number-one priority in my young life and I thought of very little else.

I wouldn't change that for the world because there were thousands of us across the country absolutely consumed by it at every opportunity; we were out in the open air, not under our parents' feet, relatively safe, active, acting out our dreams in all weather. Surely modern generations can't possibly benefit as much from their admittedly more sophisticated pastimes?

Football devotion logically led to collecting cigarette cards featuring players whom the sweet manufacturers very cleverly included in their products. They attracted the attention – and eventually more importantly the custom – of the football-mad young lads in every street in the land. When you had a few 'fag' cards, you could then enter the bartering world of 'swaps' which might even have encouraged some budding young entrepreneurs to take their first empire-building steps as well.

Christmas was always about ripping off the wrapping from football annuals, usually the famous Charles Buchan version. We are used to having pictures, articles and statistics at the touch of a button today, but in my childhood there was precious little for young fans to get their hands on apart from those once-a-year books. Even television coverage of football was still in its infancy. I reckon it made reading them and seeing opposition stars in picture form even more exciting. We had little idea of what they even looked like, never mind how they played.

My own football development was steadily advancing and there were signs that I might be above average. I played centre-forward for the school's under-11 team when I was eight and by the age of 11 I was the captain of Hendon Boys, playing wing-half. We reached a couple of finals and lost one of them 3-0 to East London, which was a large area. They had a future professional in Paul Went in their team and he was physically a giant compared with everyone else. Mr. Goliath virtually won the game on his own.

But we had a good team; virtually all the Whitefields team in fact. Playing representative games and finals for several years at the Hendon FC ground, when they were the best amateur side in the country, was just fantastic for us kids. Sometimes the whole school would get off early to watch us and uncle Bert always manipulated his work hours to turn up.

I'm sure that in this period I would wonder for the first time in the back of my mind if I could go on to become a professional footballer, but it would have been entirely down to the love of the game. It certainly would not have been for the money. There wasn't a lot of it in football until Jimmy Hill came along and successfully campaigned to change the landscape in terms of professional players and their wage expectations.

Whitefields School continued to mop up all the competitions in the Hendon region, including six-a-side tournaments, even though other boroughs were bigger and stronger. My best mate Bob, Micky Waterman and I were head and shoulders the best lads in the team, which really was built around us. That was what usually happened in school teams when physical development also played its part. Bob and Mick scored goals for fun so I balanced it by playing at centre-half. We had a very good goalie in Bob Sands, too, and were fortunate to be encouraged by our PE teacher Les Hill.

He first recommended me and taught me so much about football and cricket during training after school. He ended up as a selector for London Schoolboys and subsequently sent Bob and I for under-15 trials for both Middlesex and London and later England Schoolboys. There were so many boys in attendance – maybe about 100 – that organising them so that they could all be given a fair chance must have been nigh on impossible.

As a result I was handed a shirt to play right-back or somewhere, certainly out of position. I was normally captain and centre-back, to the overall benefit of the school team, and if I had been more assertive on the day, I might have questioned the fairness of it. Even at that age. But all my life I have never confronted decisions and those who make them. I had clearly been stuck at right-back because there were just too many youngsters there at one time. The selectors had to make up teams and it became a bit of a lottery if you were unfortunate enough to be out of position.

At 13 Bob and I had trials together at QPR and although they didn't sign me, Bob – who was a very good player – was taken on. He didn't quite make it to being a regular in the first-team and three years later I was representing England Youth. It just proves that sometimes it is just about getting the breaks and developing at the right time. I had four trials at Chelsea at centre-half, but I had no chance because I wasn't big for my age.

Uncle Bert had a dodgy heart which had prevented him from joining up for National Service and he had to be careful what he did, but he had a lovely left foot and taught me a lot about football and cricket. He would take Paul and me round the corner to Brondesbury Cricket Club, to watch and have a knockabout with some decent players. One of them was Steve Gatting, whose brother Mike later became England Test captain.

I was always a Chelsea fan – and I even played against my idol Jimmy Greaves on my debut for Sheffield United – and Bert took us to Stamford Bridge. And from when I was about six, we also supported Hendon. They were in the Athenian League before it was changed to the Isthmian League in 1961 and they were probably the top amateur team in the country between 1960 and 1965. The three of us even travelled to away games to places such as Enfield and Grays Athletic on the supporters' coaches and it was a special experience.

People were allowed to smoke on the coaches and every time we went to such as Carshalton and Hounslow, some punter would shout for the coach to stop because they felt sick! I recall in 1964, when Team Spirit became the smallest horse to win the Grand National, I had bet a pound on it at 14/1 – courtesy of uncle Bert, of course. It really made my day. While the race was being run, I was at Enfield FC and you will understand why I will always remember that occasion. I am happy to report that my Hendon link still remains; my cousin is on the club committee and I still follow their progress.

But at league level it was always Chelsea for me and Bert took us to Stamford Bridge, even though it took an hour and a half to get there. It was only about eight miles away, but getting there would involve different combinations of walking, bus, train or tube and as a kid, it seemed to take forever. It was worth every second to me, though, because I basically lived to watch all those wonderful players such as Greaves and another favourite of mine, Bobby Tambling, who also scored plenty of goals. Not forgetting the Sillett brothers, Brabrook, Bentley, Bridges, Blunstone and many more.

Bert made sure Paul and I never wanted for anything, especially where sport was concerned. It cost him 1/3 each for us and 2/6 for himself to stand in the Shed at the Bridge and I remember watching Stan Matthews playing for Stoke against us in 1961. Stoke won the old Division Two and Chelsea were runners-up, winning promotion to the top-flight.

There had to be a bit of ducking and diving for us to get a little place to see from, but you could always manage it and I liked to be a bit higher up so that I could see more of the pitch. I could never be a manager watching from the touchline, where you can see naff all. When Stoke beat us 2-1 in that big promotion battle, I watched Matthews from up the tree just back from the corner flag – it was bloody brilliant! There were so many people there that Bert helped me up and, although I laugh about it now, today's health and safety brigade would have a field day with that one.

My own progress in the game continued slowly, despite feeling sore about what I perceived had been a raw deal in trials at QPR and Chelsea. The experience had taught me a lot about defensive play and I thought I was a decent defender even though I always harboured hopes of becoming a striker. Being honest, I don't think I had any real expectations of being successful in the trials. They were like exams to me, so it seemed likely that I would underperform anyway. It didn't lessen my disappointment, though.

Bert used to take me twice a week to a place called Heston near London Airport for training with QPR on schoolboy forms. There was a lot of dribbling and passing and so on, which I loved, and I couldn't wait to go, especially for the small games at the end. I was kicking a ball about and there wasn't anything else I wanted to do in all the world. In fact, that obsession once got me into trouble in a bizarre way, which sort of summed up my upbringing – as well as demonstrating what a different world school was back then.

In 1963 England took on the Rest of the World in a match at Wembley. I'm pretty sure that it took place against a backdrop of national power cuts, so it was to be played on a Wednesday afternoon when kids were still at school. Even so our favourite teacher Les Hill, who did so much for our development, very kindly obtained match tickets for Bob and me.

Imagine what a thrill that was, especially because it was down to a helping hand from a teacher. We trotted off and enjoyed ourselves. But when we turned up for school the day after, Les asked us: "Where were you two yesterday? You weren't in my lesson."

"What do you mean, sir?" we asked. "You got us tickets for the match?"

"Yes," he replied. "But I didn't say you could go!"

Then it was, *whoosh*… Six of the best! He loved his bit of fun, did Les – and we loved him for it, too.

2

PERSISTENCE PAYS OFF

By the time I reached school-leaving age, there was never a question of staying on. I wanted to leave even though I'd had a great time and been quite popular because of my sports ability. That was just as well because I didn't really shine at anything else. During my final year I even ▪i▪ some gar▪ening lessons an▪ regularly pumped up footballs for Les Hill's PE classes. There weren't too many lessons in the classroom!

But leaving was one thing and finding a job was another entirely. I had no idea what I wanted to do. School careers nights didn't clarify things because I totally hated going to each of the little booths to talk with staff about what I might go on to do.

Eventually I ended up at Roberts Brothers at Childs Hill, a small building firm in the Hampstead area, and what an experience that was. I did everything apart from bricklaying and a two-month spell putting in ink pipes at the *Croydon Advertiser* meant getting up at 6am and leaving at 7am to start at 8am. They were long days, but I enjoyed it and it taught me a lot about plumbing and painting and decorating. I did 49 hours a week – which I was later told was illegal for a 15-year-old – for five quid before getting a small pay rise.

The job meant working on Saturday mornings, but I must have had some time off for football. I played mainly on Sunday mornings for Kiwi United and my mate Bob Turpie even turned out for us despite being with QPR. This was a men's league, at places such as Hackney Marshes and Regents Park and although most of our side were under 20, we were good. By now I could see tackles coming and ride them pretty easily, which was a useful transition for me into a more physical type of football.

By now I was going out with a girl called Linda, who had been at school with Liz for a year before switching to a girls' school. She was now work-ing at John Barnes – not him, but a branch of John Lewis – which was situated in a lovely big building in Finchley. She'd visit me after work and later I'd see her on the bus home or go with her and walk the two miles back from West Hendon.

One night, as a 15-year-old, I had another much more adult and sin-ister scare after seeing her as usual. I was walking back when a bloke in a car stopped and offered me a lift, which I naively accepted. He started asking me pervy questions, such as: "Have you been with your girlfriend then? Have you f****d her?"

I thought: "Hello, what's going on here then?" There was nothing like that going on for me at that time and, although it was only a short trip, it seemed to take half an hour. I was very frightened and regretted getting in the car in the first place. When we stopped at traffic lights halfway back, I took the chance to jump out and probably broke the world record for running home. Remember, I was no budding man of the world at this time, compared with some of my contemporaries, and I had no interest in beer and pubs, preferring to go home to my uncles. And believe it or not, I didn't even have an alcoholic drink until I was 21 years old. But more of that later ...

My four trials with Chelsea had been at their training ground, which was then at the Welsh Harp, right at the bottom of the M1, near where I lived in Hendon. There was a large reservoir nearby which was a bit of a go-to destination for regattas and garden parties. That didn't hold much interest for me, but going along to the South-East Counties League fix-tures and watching Peter 'Ossy' Osgood, and later Alan Hudson, play-ing for Chelsea juniors was definitely up my street. 'Ossy' was already a Chelsea apprentice so he would be at the training ground with players such as Jimmy Greaves, although you couldn't see the first-team training because it was kept private.

Those trials were all separate matches and being played out of posi-tion at centre-half against some big Scottish boys didn't exactly allow me to show my potential. I was only about five feet nine inches tall, much smaller than the strikers, and more of a Bobby Moore-type of defender than a Jack Charlton.

As a Chelsea fan I can't tell you how disappointed I was at this second rejection at joining a league club. But although I was pretty down and wondering if I would ever make it, I still kept playing games with the same attitude of trying to be the best player on the pitch. I was always that way whether I played in the local park or at Wembley: 'If it's in you, it's in you' is how I look at it, and I couldn't be any different.

***

By now my father had reappeared in our lives and would take my brother and me out once a week in his firm's Ford Anglia, but there was too much resentment and lack of trust from me for it really to mean anything. There was no real warmth in the relationship and the only thing Paul and I gained was a day out with somebody who might just as well have been a distant uncle we didn't particularly want to be with.

The whole rather bizarre domestic situation took another surprising twist after a year or so when my parents produced another child, Mum giving birth to Peter. Even assuming that the pregnancy had been an accident, it is still difficult to try to make sense of it. I can think only that the study of human relationships and the motives and emotions involved must be truly fascinating.

When my father left initially, he had to pay my mother £1 per week in maintenance and often he elected to stay a night in the clink rather than pay it. He'd also borrow money from one of my aunties, so it isn't difficult to understand the resentment I built up during the years, not to mention sympathy for Mum who obviously must have been besotted with the man.

I was really enjoying playing for Kiwi United and remained hopeful of being spotted, so you can imagine what a boost it was to be asked by Frank Grimes, Watford's junior scout-coach, to train with them. This time, though, it wasn't a case of the odd one-off trial, a route which had already afforded me little opportunity to do myself justice on an ongoing basis. Now I had the chance to train on two or three nights a week, with others on amateur forms and the already-contracted apprentice professionals.

That environment obviously suited me because one day Frank told me that the club manager Ken Furphy wanted me to attend for six weeks as an apprentice. He didn't sign me as one, but it meant I travelled every day by bus to Watford and did what all the other apprentices did. I was over the moon to get another crack at it, but to be honest we didn't get as much training as I expected. Club apprentices would be given jobs to do at the ground so I got to know a lovely bloke called Les Simmons, the groundsman whom I helped to harrow, fork and mark out the pitch at Vicarage Road. There were loads of other tasks we all had to muck in with and I'm pretty sure today's academy products aren't required to paint railings, clean baths, sweep terraces, clean boots and so on.

I won't harp on about today's youngsters having it easy in comparison so I'll just say it must have been character-building… but more training and coaching would have been good! Les didn't have any ground staff to help him and we were his helpers all day, every day from Monday to Friday. It meant that in terms of developing as footballers, we had training only after work on Tuesday and Thursday nights, plus the occasional match.

But every night after working at the club, another youngster, Mickey Packer, and I used to play each other at head tennis and I can't tell you how bloody good at it we became. So when Furphy decided to organise a head-tennis competition for all the players at the club, Mickey and I won every time, absolutely stuffing even top players and future Blades such as Keith Eddy and Stewart Scullion.

We had developed specific skills, imparting swerve, spinning the ball before we served and generally making things difficult for our opponents. It did us no harm in terms of getting ourselves noticed and it was obvious that we had put in extra hours of skills practices after work – not for head-tennis competitions specifically, but just to improve. I'm convinced that kicking balls against the uneven-edged tiles at home, playing head tennis and practising bending the ball and so on helped me to develop accuracy and control.

If the truth be told, training, even at first-team level back then, was pretty much the same old, same old, with repetitive drills before finishing with five-a-side. My stint was a first-year apprentice wage of £7 per week, effectively for doing ground-staff work every day with just a couple of nights of training. No wonder it took Furphy so long to make his mind up about me because there was little opportunity of seeing me train or play for the juniors in the South-East Counties League.

The best bits, and the nearest we ever came to really testing ourselves, were when, every other week or so, the first-team might need an extra player or two from our group to make up the numbers in training or a reserve team to play against. That was a massive thrill and a good yard-stick as to how you might cope at a higher level, even though personally I was still walking a tightrope and waiting for a decision.

Eventually I was old enough and good enough to play against more experienced opposition in reserve games in the old Football Combination League against sides such as Charlton Athletic, Millwall, QPR and Leyton Orient. The extensive travelling involved around the south-east contributed to the demise of the league, which was eventually replaced by the London Midweek League, and by now I wasn't playing centre-half any more.

I was scoring goals regularly in midfield for Watford juniors and up top for the reserves. When the Watford 'trial' began, I had simply walked away from my existing little job – too scared to let my employers know formally – and put everything into making the grade. It was a different workplace to get used to and the football world of the 1960s was a tough environment for young lads to negotiate. Senior professionals would take the proverbial and rituals were a regular part of the induction. Many a lad had his testicles blackened with shoe polish, which was embarrassing for some. And although I didn't have to endure that experience, another I did suffer brought an out-of-character response from me.

There was a Scottish winger called Hamilton who regularly stuck his leg out to trip me when I, a callow 16-year-old, would carry a tray of steaming tea into the dressing-room for the professionals. I knew I would have the job of cleaning it up if it dropped and although I invariably managed to stay balanced and save it, one day I decided I'd had enough. I turned round and gave him a hard kick to the shins. I probably surprised myself because I didn't really have a temper in those days. But I learned that I had a trigger point. And he never did it again.

Mostly it was all in good fun and we had characters such as Terry Melling, who was only small, but would run through a brick wall; Duncan Welbourne, a good full-back and a tough man; and Tom Whalley, who became a very good coach. No doubt I was given some good-natured stick by those good guys when I messed up during one of the days spent working on the ground.

I was driving the club tractor once through the gates, up a slope to the turnstiles, and must have accidentally pressed the accelerator too hard. It resulted in a completely demolished turnstile and buckled tractor wheels!

Mickey Packer and I were always up to tricks and one day after a snowy and freezing night he bet me a quid – a seventh of my weekly wage – that he could climb to the top of a floodlight pylon with just his shorts on and not even any shoes. It was just bravado, but Mickey was very daring and that was the sort of daft thing we did. And I lost my pound.

Growing up during this period, I was often bored although I didn't mingle and wasn't comfortable in group get-togethers. While at Watford I was seeing less of Linda, but I was in no way into drinking, smoking or gangs because I was training twice a week and spending most of the rest of my time at home. My focus was football, football, football. Linda, Linda, Linda. Even though our opportunities to spend time together had become more limited, I always wanted to get married and have kids early so that I could grow up with them. It was all planned, in a way, in my own head.

The six-week arrangement with Watford had gradually extended to six months as Furphy deliberated about signing me. I had started to worry and it may have been, of all people, my father's ultimatum that they signed me or I was off that led to the decision. But another driving mishap on that very day might have derailed the whole thing.

Furphy used to give Mickey Packer and me a lift into training in his gleaming, new Humber Sceptre Gold, and consequently we were often given the job of cleaning it. The vehicle was parked up at the ground and while Mickey was spraying water on it, I jumped in. I switched the engine on and was either messing about or moving the car slightly to make room for the clean. The inevitable happened and it suddenly lurched forward and hit the railings ... *crump!*

Mortified, I went straight to George Aitken, Furphy's right-hand man, and owned up, almost in tears. "You f*****g idiot," he said. "You're supposed to be signing on today, aren't you, Tony? Well, you're going to have to tell him."

It didn't exactly make me feel better, but after the initial shock of being told what had happened, Furphy seemed as calm as you like. "Hmmm, right," he said. "You can give me your first England cap or England fee."

I suppose he must have recognised I might have a big future in the game and although I got to know him much better later in my career, he never asked for that favour to be returned. In truth I have to say that I didn't find him a nice man. After all, he was the one who labelled me with the 'lazy' tag. It followed me around later in my career and, in my opinion, was grossly unfair.

I had broken into the Watford team as a 17-year-old, scored nine goals in my first six games and was getting noticed by the newspapers in the London area. But when the *Watford Observer* did a piece about me, in which Furphy said he wouldn't be playing me if I wasn't scoring because I was lazy, it really upset me. I wasn't a cocky, confident youth who could take that sort of thing in my stride and brush it off.

But he did eventually offer me that six-month apprentice contract and not long after, on my 17th birthday, I signed as a professional on £16 per week. Leading up to it, I had very little idea of whether it would happen or not despite being awarded three England youth caps and playing alongside Peter Shilton, Wolves' Alun Evans and Gary Scothorne, of Sheffield Wednesday. I would have achieved further recognition at that level, but, with a few others, I missed out on selection for an international youth tournament in France because we were in our clubs' first-team set-ups.

That first professional contract came out of the blue really, and that's how little I actually knew about the procedures and formalities. It just happened and, like any other 17-year-old, I was elated. I probably thought I'd made it. As a kid I had watched the Chelsea ball boys in their tracksuits, with CFC on their backs, and wanted to be one so badly.

When that didn't happen, I wanted to be an apprentice, and after that maybe go on to sign full-time – the same dreams as thousands of other starry-eyed kids up and down the land. Now it wasn't just a dream. I had signed my first proper contract and achieved what I had always wanted to in becoming a professional footballer. I was on the ladder.

3

A GIANT LEAP

You know how, when you are a kid, every year seems like a really long time? It takes ages for Christmas to come around, the six-week summer holiday seems to last for months and you don't ever feel that you will one day become an adult. That was what it was like for me until my sheltered world was well and truly shaken from the day I turned 17. The next 12 months or so heralded such significant changes in my life.

Looking back now, at the shy teenager I was with very little life experience, I don't honestly know how I managed to survive it. They were different days with fewer social pressures. But equally there was no established support network for a boy – and I wasn't much more than that – starting Third Division football, moving three hours north and playing in the top-flight. Oh, and getting married. Here goes ...

Without a doubt signing as a professional has always been a huge deal and I was as thrilled as it's possible to be. To be rewarded with that privilege, I had dedicated every day to making myself better and made great strides in the juniors and then reserves. After countless rejections, or because of them, I had a fierce ambition and had really worked hard to improve. That was put in context for me long afterwards when Alan Ball told me that he had never had to do that. Hearing that only confirmed my belief that things usually worked against me and that my awkward social skills had somehow contributed.

Playing for Watford was probably the limit of my ambition when I started at Vicarage Road. Training was every day at Croxley Green, which boasted just one pitch: we had to get changed first at the ground, which was 10 minutes away. There were maybe 20 professionals all on the pitch together from 10am until 12.30pm, mainly doing lots of running and ball work. That was it really, apart from a sort of hard standing area where we and the staff played head tennis or five-a-side games. It wasn't great, but better than doing odd jobs with the groundsman. I was usually first there and last to leave.

I had the enthusiasm of a kid and that didn't ever leave me. I loved training throughout my career. We had some tough boys in the squad; both Ron Saunders and Sammy Chung were both there and went on to become coaches and managers in their own right. Dennis Bond was Watford's stand-out player about that time, until he was picked up by Spurs just before I got in the team.

That summer of 1967, six months into my first contract, I went to France and played against Ireland and France for England Youth, which didn't do my or the club's reputation any harm. I had fitted in comfortably during first-team training and although some of the players were always trying to kick me up in the air, that was par for the course for most youngsters.

The first week of my first proper pre-season was spent at Dunstable Downs, near Luton, and after that it was back to the ground. I couldn't wait for it to start and even though we knew that a lot of running was on the agenda, it was always a shock to the system after a period of relative inactivity. In later years I had often been away with England squads during the summer, which did slightly reduce the impact, and when I was at Sheffield United I used to run occasionally with local international athlete Ken Wood, whom some people might remember from the Derek Ibbotson and Gordon Pirie era.

The 1967/68 season began with me playing up top for Watford reserves alongside former West Ham man Brian Dear in a line-up including, I think, Brian Owen, Micky Block and George Harris. As a striker I wasn't tall and didn't play with my back to goal, so my game had to be about movement, anticipation and finding space. Terry Garbutt, who also eventually made a move to Bramall Lane, was with me then and he was another who didn't fit the stereotype of the big man upfront. Neither of us was above medium height and we didn't run in behind defenders.

If I were to move up the pecking order as a forward for the senior squad, it was clear that I would have to get past regulars David Carr,

Jim Lawton – who was a big lad – and Garbutt. A League Cup fixture at Stoke City was my first opportunity and I couldn't believe it when I saw my name on the teamsheet, albeit at number 12 as the only substitute. At least that meant there was a great chance of getting on even if it was because someone had been injured.

Stoke were a high-profile team and the great Gordon Banks was in goal for City when I came on after about 70 minutes. I would certainly have spent the period before that being nervous and worrying about letting myself down. That is how I still am, even doing something such as a question-and-answer session with an audience. The difference was that those early nerves would have evaporated as soon as I stepped on the pitch because I was supremely confident in myself with a ball at my feet.

It might have cost me a goal to remember. When a chance came my way, I rounded Banks and directed the ball towards the net, but it was cleared off the line by John Marsh. Maybe I should have shot instead of taking the ball on, but I will always remember going round Gordon that night. It was my method and a few months later, playing West Ham in Dave Carr's testimonial, I went round the goalie and walked the ball in from a few yards out. I did that a few times in my career – not to be clever, but because it was second nature to me and gave me the best chance of scoring. If you shoot, the ball can always hit somebody and I had the confidence to try to remove any potential barrier.

A week after the Stoke game I was given my full debut at home to Bristol Rovers in the Third Division. It turned out to be a dream day for me because I netted twice in a 4-0 victory, the first a diving header level with the near post from a right-wing cross that Stewart Scullion eventually put in after beating his man about six times. Timing that run took some doing and I got another at the same end, so it was a great start.

I can't explain just how it felt, but 50 years on I still get that shivery feeling whenever I recall those moments. It was a nice, fresh sunny September afternoon, the biggest crowd I'd played in front of and it remains a magical moment in my life.

One week on we played at Barrow and to this 17-year-old it seemed to take about a week to get to where we stayed in Kendal. I hit the post in a 0-0 draw and it got even better on the following Tuesday when I scored a hat-trick as we beat Peterborough United 4-1.

Scoring a 'perfect three' – one header and one with each foot – just made it even more special and I still have the match ball in my possession. This was a purple patch of goalscoring that I would not equal again throughout my career. I then grabbed another three in a seven-goal demolition of Grimsby Town, taking my total to nine goals in my first six games. It was astonishing and as well as boosting my own personal pride and generating a bit of interest, they helped the team to points which were really needed after a poor start.

That sort of scoring run would create big headlines now, but there wasn't much publicity. In fact, there was very little media coverage at all; no score updates from all over the country, no instant goal clips, no pre-match analysis in the paper. No instant post-match reaction, no internet, no player interviews, very little radio and television coverage.

Instead I would just go home after games and carry on training as usual although the good start did attract some attention from big, hard defenders determined to keep me in my place. To me at 17, they seemed about 40 years old. At least, I thought, there was a good chance that scouts would have noticed my arrival on the scene.

We had a fair old team and it's surprising that Watford did nothing in my short time there, given that we had the calibre of Keith Eddy, Scullion, Duncan Welbourne and Tom Whalley. Tom in particular was a great influence on me and although he was a hard bastard, you knew he meant well. And you took notice. It has given me great pleasure to have had Tom as my guest at Bramall Lane on a couple of occasions.

Incidentally there's a distinct possibility that I may have created a bit of history during my short Watford career, but it took a particularly bizarre piece of refereeing to put me in the spotlight. We were playing at Swindon and the man in the middle was Roger Kirkpatrick, a rather round, Dickensian-looking character whom many players regarded as an arrogant exhibitionist, although his exaggerated manner often amused supporters.

Furphy had substituted me and my replacement took to the field. As I was sitting in the dugout, Kirkpatrick came over, brandished a yellow card in my face and snapped: "You left the field without my permission." It might have been the first caution of its type. I was confused and unhappy with it and we were all mystified as to what was going on. But I suppose Roger enjoyed making a fuss.

My goals dried up as quickly as they had arrived. After those nine in six, I went 11 without another and don't really know why. I wasn't doing anything different because it hadn't gone to my head: I was just happy to be in the team. I'll always be grateful to Furphy for giving me that opportunity, but I never felt that he was altogether happy with me.

I had ability and was scoring for fun with head and feet, but he was always on at me about work-rate. He was only 36 then, very confident in his own ability and quite tactical for a manager in that era. It must have been difficult for him to play and manage at the same time and I don't want to run him down too much because he was a good manager.

But senior players used to answer him back and although he seemed to take it on the chin, he would have them in the office later if he thought they were out of line. He could be quite arrogant and in my opinion, man-management wouldn't be at the top of the list of his personal qualities. However, he was playing me and I was earning good reviews while just getting on with my job. I certainly wasn't thinking of leaving.

In the FA Cup second round we beat Hereford at home – the great John Charles marked me – and were subsequently pitched against Sheffield United in the next round at Vicarage Road. There was a full house that day and United won 1-0, but I was left out of the side altogether. Naively I just wondered what I had done wrong. I had no idea how things might work in the game with regard to transfers and the agreements around them. Four days later I signed for United.

Obviously John Harris, the United manager, and Furphy had agreed the move in advance with the proviso that I couldn't play in that game. United were a bigger club and I had been devastated not to face them, but I wouldn't dare say anything. Even now I hope it was a hush-hush deal because at first I was disappointed that a London club hadn't come in for me, especially because Sheffield was 160 miles up the road. There were no whispers, nothing, and I was just called in and told what was happening. It scared me stiff.

But at least Sheffield United were in the old First Division and I signed for them on February 1, 1968, for a fee of £26,500. There was no discussion about it; I simply went home and said to my mum: "Bloody 'ell, Sheffield United want to sign me." She was chuffed for me because I was only 18 years old and was about to achieve my ambition of playing in the top-flight against my idols such as Greaves, Denis Law and Bobby

Charlton. Little did I know that we would go down that season and that, in about a six-month span, I would have played in all three top divisions!

Furphy didn't stand in my way, telling me that he had always said I would go on and do well and that this was a big chance for me. He could have hung on and got a lot more money for me – not too long afterwards Alun Evans, who I played with in the international set-up as we progressed, went from Wolves to Liverpool for £100,000. Watford, however, did have to pay for the lease of Vicarage Road so had little option but to sell players. My sale would have enabled that debt to be settled. Although I didn't have any particularly hard feelings about the fee, it did mean that my 10 per cent of it was a lot less than Evans got!

I was on 16 quid a week at Watford and didn't negotiate when I moved to United, which pretty much became a pattern for the rest of my career. I didn't have the stomach to play hardball over the worth of a contract, unlike the older players who knew the ropes. For example, when Ted Hemsley came to United a few months later, he got the club to buy him a house. Len Badger was similar to me, in that I think he signed blank contracts every time rather than stick out for more money, while John Flynn maintains that he was always on 35 quid a week throughout his time at the Lane. Many players were taken advantage of at clubs because they wouldn't give pay rises. As a result, players would leave and then clubs would have to replace them with someone else and pay them more anyway. Crazy.

The excitement about going to the top division quickly overcame any disappointment about not going somewhere more local, but I was a bit worried because I was far from being a confident lad off the grass. I knew very little about my new team other than they were way 'oop north' and some of their older players, including Joe Shaw, Alan Hodgkinson and Cec Coldwell, had featured in my fag-card collection.

A few days later I got off the train in Sheffield on a wet, cold and grey afternoon and was met by John Short from the coaching staff. He took me to Montgomery Road in Nether Edge, not far from the ground, where I was placed in digs with Mrs. Lowes and her family with Scotsman Paddy Buckley, a winger who had signed for the Blades a few months earlier.

It was a lovely little house; the food was great and my first experience of using an electric blanket was an eye-opener. But the change from living at home with my family was pretty frightening. That doesn't mean

I was unhappy because the family really looked after me and I stayed friends with the Lowes for years after.

Seeing Bramall Lane – then still a three-sided ground because it was also used by Yorkshire County Cricket Club – was a huge thrill and an amazing sight. I was such a devotee of football at that stage of my life and I was absorbing everything about the game, such as club nicknames and the names of their grounds, so I was aware that only United and Northampton had that set-up. But it was the first time I had seen it and of course it looked so large. I still recall trying to take in the old flood-lights, the pavilion that had stood there for so long and the massive expanse of turf that accommodated the summer's cricket.

I am sentimental, a traditionalist and instinctively appreciate the history of things. Personally – and I realise a lot of fans might be shocked – I wish it had remained three-sided despite appreciating the sound reasons why it was developed into the wonderful stadium it is today. You can't beat the old rose-coloured spectacles, can you?

It was a top-flight club and the ground seemed like Wembley to me. Although the new Bramall End had been built only three years earlier, the Kop was fabulous, often bursting with fans, and the old John Street Stand had all sorts of nooks and crannies. It all seemed so unique, absolutely steeped in history, and I could almost feel the presence of the old ghosts of former greats of United and Yorkshire CCC.

Training was held a mile away at the nearby Ball Inn Ground, which had a couple of changing-rooms, some old showers and a bath that was just as unwelcoming. I spent eight-and-half-years training on the one pitch up there, although late in my stay we did start changing at Bramall Lane, where the dressing-rooms were just so incredibly dark and dingy. Even Vicarage Road was all nice and bright; Bramall Lane had a coal cellar with a lid beneath the dressing-room floor!

Len Badger, a Sheffielder born and bred, might well have been the first senior player I met when I arrived and he straightaway went out of his way to be welcoming and friendly with any new arrivals. I settled in immediately at all my clubs and didn't make any enemies – although things were understandably a bit frosty at United with Mick Hill, whom I eventually replaced.

My flatmate Paddy Buckley became a close pal and was a bit of a betting man so for something to do on a Friday night before a home game, we'd go to the greyhound meetings at Hyde Park and then 10-pin bowling at the Silver Blades on Queens Road. We would always be back by 11pm, mind you – even though I was always a bad sleeper and would lie awake at night, worrying about something or other.

Inevitably for a youngster making a big jump up the divisions, I was eased in with a couple of reserve fixtures and my style of play probably helped me to settle, too. United were all about passing. The first-team lads befriended me when they realised I was a young, shy lad and not a cocky Londoner, for which they respected me. Socialising wasn't my scene, apart from those innocent evenings with Paddy. Especially after the first month when Linda came up for good.

Although I had scored my first United goal at Bolton Wanderers in a reserve fixture three weeks after signing, I hadn't been even as close to the team as being on the bench. But I was training with the seniors and knew I was good enough.

Then I was selected to start at the Lane on a Monday night against a still-great Tottenham team. They had Pat Jennings in goal, Dave Mackay at the back, plus Gilzean, Chivers and... Jimmy Greaves. It was a fabulous debut occasion for me and although people tell me I had a good game, I don't know how they remember! I do recall scoring with a near-post header from a deep cross from the right from David Munks in a 3-2 win.

That encouraging start was immediately interrupted because I was unavailable for selection for the next fixture, a trip to Leicester City on March 2. I got married. I had always wanted an early marriage and then kids so, while I was still at Watford, Linda and I had made all the necessary arrangements for a ceremony at St Mary's Church in Hendon.

John Harris knew I was getting married and pulled me after the Spurs game. He told me he wanted to put on a fast car for me, so I could be at Leicester within an hour of kick-off and in time to play. He tried hard to get me to agree, but for once I stood firm. It was Linda's big day. I was grilled in his office for about an hour and in the end, he gave in. Probably just before I would have done if he had carried on for just a bit longer.

My father wasn't invited to the wedding, but all our relatives were there and the reception was held at South Harrow church hall, where my uncle was caretaker. We had ham and pease pudding. Imagine that now?

There was no time for a honeymoon, of course; that had to wait for the summer, when we spent a red-hot week in Margate and got sunburnt. I was red raw.

Linda and I got together when we were about 13 years old and within a year were seeing each other on most nights when she came round for tea. Even by the time we were due to marry, we were still kids really and she was six months younger than I was. She never liked the idea of uprooting and was disappointed to have to pack in her job in the deli department at a large department store. When Linda came up to Sheffield, she didn't work; I was old-fashioned and wanted to be responsible for her. It was a mistake on my part. I shouldn't have said it and although I didn't actually stop her from working, we had kids early which had the same effect anyway.

Two days after the marriage I was back training and we were moved into a club house on Bishopscourt Road in Meersbrook, where United legend Joe Shaw had lived. We were there for four years, paying 12 and six a week, and on reflection I should have bought it. Sadly, Linda soon suffered a miscarriage but when Sharon was born a year later, in November 1969, board member John Hassall put central heating in for us. There was still no telephone, though!

I played more or less every game until the end of the season, apart from when I was cup-tied, and the quality of our players was excellent despite what was later to happen. There were so many ups and downs during our fixtures and two games that stood out for me were Easter clashes with Liverpool, both of which I scored in. We drew with and beat them, effectively ending their title hopes.

During the away win I replicated Pele's goal in the 1958 World Cup final in Sweden when I lobbed the ball over Ron Yeats and volleyed it in, luckily through Tommy Lawrence's legs. We played on Good Friday, Saturday and Easter Monday – yes, three games in four days! – and I absolutely loved it.

Against that, we were 2-0 up on Fulham at the Lane with 20 minutes to go only to capitulate and lose 3-2. It was a part of a poor late run of form that relegated us when one more point would have saved us. Who eventually sent us down? Chelsea, my boyhood team. Peter Osgood scored the winner and even though our goalkeeper Alan Hodgkinson was yelling at him to miss it, it was a chance so unmissable that he wouldn't have got away with it even if he had tried. The team's demise had been sudden, having been in the top-flight for seven years and finishing 10th the previous year.

It had been a whirlwind six months for me and a massive life-change in a little more than a year, but I was happy with where I was. There were no regrets about moving and I thought we were unfortunate to go down, one point behind Coventry and two behind Sheffield Wednesday. Relegation was a disappointment I could cope with, but there was a different factor that was starting to cloud the relationship between Linda and me and it was to have a destabilising effect on us for years.

We went 'home' for the summer because she was homesick from day one. I don't know what was on her mind, but she probably hadn't wanted to come up in the first place. She didn't like to go out much either, although she did come with me to the Penny Farthing nightspot on a Saturday night when we had a babysitter. Eventually, if ever there was any chance of nipping back down to London, we took it and on one occasion I even talked her off a train back home after running all the way to Sheffield station to stop her. It wasn't her fault; living away from London just didn't suit her. The circumstances we found ourselves in were to cause a lot of distress for both of us.

4

CALL-UPS AND LACE-UPS

As a lad dreaming of being a footballer in my formative years, the twin fantasies were playing in an FA Cup Final and being selected for England. I lived those dreams out hundreds of times, not knowing I would be given hopes of one of them coming true pretty early on in my career ...

During the 1967/68 campaign the England youth manager was Pat Welton, who had been a player at Leyton Orient and Spurs. This was the season I joined Sheffield United in February 1968; if I recall correctly, I won one youth cap while I was at Watford and the rest while in Sheffield. Welton was a nice bloke, a gentleman, but he was experienced, really knew his stuff and had a good squad in the tournament in France. Quite a few of us went on to much bigger things, which probably wasn't a great surprise because so many were already playing in their clubs' first-teams.

We were all confident players, even as youngsters, and had been to the national training centre at Lilleshall two or three times for training get-togethers. Peter Shilton was much the same then in terms of style and ability as he was when he became established; it was pretty obvious that he was special. His competition then was Sheffield Wednesday's Gary Scothorne and Reading's Steve Death, whom people also may remember.

Spurs' right-back Ray Evans, Jeff Blockley of Coventry City, 'Chico' Hamilton and Alun Evans all played in that tournament, while Alan Foggon of Newcastle and Rotherham's Dave Bentley were also in the squad. All went on to have successful careers, a high proportion in anyone's book – even in the days when foreign players were not adding to the competition for first-team places.

On occasions some of us weren't allowed to play for England if our clubs needed us when potential relegation was an issue – 'Shilts' and I both experienced that. In fact, switching between England Youth and the professional game was okay in those days, but became more difficult later when comments such as "He's got to do more work" and being labelled "lazy" muddied the waters.

Those youth games were less physical and there was more freedom to play than in the league, which I enjoyed immensely. It was an honour to be selected and I was grateful for it, but I must confess that there was also an element of wanting to prove a point to QPR, Chelsea and the London schoolboys' set-up who had all rejected me. I felt ecstatic to be honest, really vindicated – even if it really wasn't big news to most punters. After all, there wasn't much Press coverage of sport back then, often just a back page with another inside.

I was up-front with Alun Evans at that time and within a few months I had joined the Blades for £26,500, before Liverpool spent a whopping £100,000 on Alun. The disparity in the size of the fee did needle me, perhaps a bit more than it should have, but I went on to acquire full international honours and Alan drifted away a bit after his big move. I don't blame him at all; it was just about circumstances over which we had no control. We weren't big, speedy strikers, but we could hold the ball up, dribble a bit and score our goals.

It amuses me to reflect on how things have changed in the game at every level and how the experience of being selected for England, even at youth level, will differ today. We received a small package in the post which contained cards of information and lists about where we were staying, who was who on the staff and England board and the itinerary for the stay. Me being me, I didn't really care about get-togethers and meeting new people – it was always something I'd be a bit apprehensive about.

So it might have been a good thing that I roomed on several occasions with Chico, who was a character even then. He never changes and he was called Chico even at 16 years old at Chelsea, although his real name is Ian. I don't know why; it might have been because of Chico the clown! We got along well and took it on ourselves to practise an indirect free-kick routine to use in the penalty area; I would touch the ball to Chico and he would toe-poke it into the roof of the net. Lo and behold, that morning we had a practice match, I think against a team from Wolves, and he scored from it! Funnily enough Ian eventually ended up at Bramall Lane – after I had left – and all the boys loved him. He now lives in Spain.

I look back on those England youth days with great fondness and have kept my caps. As a quirk of the times, when you went on tour you were presented with only the one cap, complete with the names of the other teams embroidered on it, rather than one for each game played. The whole episode was one of learning and gathering experience ... of different styles of football, of players, of travelling, of other young players talking about their clubs. It all helped to broaden my knowledge of the game and the industry I was trying to make my way in.

A year later when I was still only 19, I was called up to the England under-23s and although it was a big transition from the youth scene, it was nothing I couldn't cope with. I went on to get 13 caps at that level, plus three more for the Football League against the Scottish League. If you are young enough to be puzzled about the inter-league games, they were a regular fixture back then!

Now I was up alongside Joe Royle, who was a bloody good striker at Everton. He was massive, not surprisingly great in the air, and we went on to oppose each other many times in our careers. There was Chris Garland around as well, plus Dave Thomas – a wonderfully tricky winger – and the bustling, powerful Steve Kindon, who became very successful on the after-dinner circuit. Less well-known, but a nice little player who had a good career, was Norman Piper of Plymouth Argyle – I certainly recall him in our team when we played an England under-23 game at Home Park, probably because he was a local player. Also in and around the squad at that time were Mike Bernard of Stoke City, Wolves' Derek Parkin and a good friend of mine, Dennis Mortimer of Villa.

We would be aware of the representative games coming up and be looking out for the envelope from the FA with a call-up letter inside. There were tours in Poland and Russia, places lads of my age would never have dreamt of getting to in those days. Travel in eastern Europe wasn't very common then and it was an eye-opener to see a very visible security presence outside every lift on every floor of our hotels. And, believe me, they wouldn't just have been a brooding presence if the need arose.

I still have a photograph of the lads outside a hotel in Kiev and they look pretty well, considering that the country seemed to be living most of the time on red cabbage soup! It was similar in Warsaw as well while the Poles were having a troubled time. The whirlwind changes in freedoms and expression of 'the swinging sixties' still in full swing back in England made the contrast with how things were over there even more stark.

I think I had already won a full England cap when I was given the captaincy of the under-23s because I was still eligible for both squads. It was a great feeling, but I don't really know why I was the lucky one. By that point I had been switched to midfield, playing alongside Alan Hudson, who became a great pal, and Alf Ramsey – who had led England to World Cup glory a few years earlier – managed the under-23s as well as the senior squad. Harold Shepherdson was his assistant on those under-23 trips while the Sheffield United chairman Dick Wragg was also on our international ruling body.

Early in his reign Alf had introduced 4-3-3 as his preferred system of playing and a good pre-World Cup victory against France had inspired a famous newspaper headline referring to his 'wingless wonders.' It was a system he stuck with and I always liked it. I had more or less been brought up on it and if I'd been a manager in the 1980s, I would have favoured playing it, too.

I had also been brought up with football boots with leather studs, which wasn't quite so innovative. The studs were hammered into the soles with the help of a hobbing foot as well and if we knew the pitch would be hard, we'd change them to 'nail studs' for grip. Predictably the nails started poking through the bottom of the boot before long and you can imagine the injuries.

When boot design finally started to develop – I can't believe it took so long – rubber studs moulded into the soles appeared, as well as screw-ins. They enabled players to replace worn studs and also change the type of stud to adapt to the conditions. How modern was that? It would take a while longer to deviate from the standard colour of black, though.

When I was about 11 years old and playing for Hendon Boys, there was a sports shop close to the bus stop I used to wait at with uncle Bert. I was like the proverbial image of a little boy, gazing through the shop window at something he could never afford. Like many lads across the country, I stared wistfully at the shiny Adidas or Puma boots while having to be content with some cheap ones with four red lines on. Never mind. Not having those boots was probably character-building...

Time, and I, moved on and we all progressed to the next stage. We tended to refer to the sleek, cutaway versions that did without the cumbersome ankle support as 'continentals' and there's no doubt Europe and South America were way ahead of us for years in developing and modernising boots and strips. The UK might have given football to the world, but we could have learned a thing or two from the rest much more quickly if we hadn't been so stuck in our ways.

At Watford, and during my early years with Sheffield United, I had no boot sponsor. That wasn't really unusual because only the top players, mainly internationals, did and at United we got two pairs per season. One pair had rubber studs, which we rarely used and if a pair needed some stitching or replacement tacks, we enlisted the help of the club's maintenance man to get them repaired at Archer's, the local sports shop. Big time, eh?

But you fared better if you were an England player and I believe I was the first pro in the country to get Patrick boots. Adidas always gave the international players a small envelope with 100 quid inside, even if you didn't use their boots; to solve the issue they would blacken out, for example, the Puma logo and put Adidas stripes on. Being seen wearing non-Adidas boots if you were on the telly was just a complete non-starter – understandably so, too, if your company were paying for boots rights.

I would imagine today's boots are more comfortable than ours were and don't require so much breaking in. We couldn't wear new ones within a week of the next game in case they caused blisters. The answer for some players was to hand them to the juniors who would soft-soap them and then wear them for at least a fortnight first. Believe it or not, unless the whole sole came off, you would never get another pair!

Ex-United players and I still regularly laugh at some of the tatty stuff we wore for the club, even in the top-flight – we called ourselves 'Rag-arse Rovers!' There were socks that had been stitched up, socks that varied in length, different shades of colour, shorts without laces in the waist. It reminded us of playing amateur football when the kitbag was emptied on to the floor and you had to be quick and dive in to get the best stuff!

5

BUILDING BLOCKS

The immediate aim has to be to return to the First Division at the first time of asking and although investment in team strengthening wasn't as essential as it is in the same circumstances today, planning for promotion was still on the agenda. It was to involve a change of manager...

During the season we went down we had worn white shorts instead of our traditional black and I hadn't been aware at the time of the superstition among Unitedites that they were unlucky. To many of them, going down was proof positive of the folly of making the change, so it wasn't surprising that one year on we were back to the familiar black ones.

I have a really nice photograph of some of us on the John Street side of the ground and remember thinking how good the white version looked. They probably looked better than the black ones, especially if we had white socks with them, although I'm well aware that mine wouldn't have been a popular view.

Relegation, although disappointing, didn't seem to carry the same weight of gloom it does today and there was absolutely not the same clamour for a manager's head. Harris had been there a long time and was well-respected. He was a teetotal, devout Scotsman who didn't smoke or swear either, but got his point across with alternative phrases that players could understand equally well.

Responsible for my transfer to Sheffield, he was also really good to me, almost a father figure, and as far as playing was concerned, he gave me the freedom to do what I could do. However, the board decided that a new man in charge would be beneficial so John became general manager with Arthur Rowley appointed as team manager.

Arthur had enjoyed a career as a very effective striker and built an enviable scoring record. Like many a player in those days he loved a bet on the horses and, as with Furphy, was much closer to us in terms of age. He did have our respect and demonstrated an eye for a player with some good acquisitions, including Ted Hemsley, a midfielder with Shrewsbury Town, Eddie Colquhoun from West Brom as captain, striker John Tudor and Welsh defender Dave Powell.

They all became regulars and helped to form the basis of the side that eventually won promotion. Powell smoked like a trooper – mind you, so did Alan Woodward – and Eddie did, too. But both were like lightning across the pitch. The fact that they were wiry, especially Powell, probably helped them to be so fast and it was a great asset for defenders to have. I know Eddie had a slightly ungainly run, with high steps which might not have looked quick, but he certainly was. A tough-as-teak Scotsman, he took no prisoners and led the team by example.

We had a decent squad that was so defensively strong that we conceded only 15 goals at home in the league. But losing busy midfielder Willie Carlin to Derby, who wrapped up promotion relatively early in the season, was a big mistake and the goals dried up. I was up-front but nobody scored a big, season-defining total and only Woodward, with 12, reached double figures.

We lacked creativity in midfield that season, with Frank Barlow more of a destroyer, Barry Wagstaff essentially a defender and Hemsley yet to be re-discovered as a fine left-back. It was ironic that Rowley, who as a player was involved in scoring so many goals, produced a side that fell down in that department and yet was so frugal in keeping the ball out of the net.

But training was enjoyable, led by John Short, a hard, tough man and a great motivator in the way Don Howe would be at Leeds United. It was quite varied with attack-versus-defence drills, free-kicks, the occasional practice match and shooting. Arthur joined in with that – he loved showing us what he could still do.

We would have been favourites to go back up, but we finished ninth – terrible, really, considering the players we had. I'm amazed that we finished where we did. I was out injured for November and December, my first experience of being on the treatment table for a prolonged spell, and my return coincided with what was to become an all-too-familiar shock dismissal in the FA Cup to a lower-ranked club. This time Mansfield beat us 2-1 at Field Mill in the third round and in the eight seasons I was at United, apart from my first half-season, we never got past the fourth round.

At least there was a bit of a silver lining at the end of the season, for me at least, because I really enjoyed our three-friendly game trip to Italy. I'm convinced that this was the forerunner to the Anglo-Italian Cup, but what is certain is that we drew 3-3 with Napoli and 0-0 with Bologna before winning 2-0 in Verona. At one point in that first match the great Italian international José Altafini produced outrageous skill as he seemed to go from one side of the pitch to the other while keeping the ball up in the air. Our hosts then snatched the draw with a last-minute equaliser, but it was a great trip overall; we had half a day on the beach during a trip to Rimini, visited Pompeii when we played in Naples and went through Sorrento on the beautiful, but expensive Amalfi Coast.

Back home I was pleased to be still playing at a level higher than I had with Watford and was now very settled. Len Badger, whose death in 2021 hit me hard, was the life and soul of the party and although Ted Hemsley was a bit older, wiser and more thoughtful, the pair formed a fantastic relationship which existed for so many years. Our first child, Sharon, had been born so Linda and I had a family unit, but I still hadn't got into going out much and we were doing those regular trips to London.

Two incidents in particular increased the need for us to go back down south more regularly. Linda's mother was randomly attacked in London and thrown over a wall in pouring rain – the despicable incident was even covered by the local Sheffield sports 'paper – and then suffered a broken nose when the bus she was travelling on crashed. We stayed with our mums when we went back to London and mine had by that point moved into a flat, still on Cricklewood Lane.

It helped the trips that I was now driving... legally! I had bought my first car from Frank Grimes at Watford, a Ford Pop 704 PPP which I still had when I went to join Sheffield United. I hadn't even passed my test and used to drive teammate Paddy Buckley's car without L-plates! I hadn't told him I had failed my first driving test at West Hendon – mainly as a result of answering a question wrong – and I didn't pass at the second attempt until a year later, with flying colours this time.

I'd had loads of lessons with my uncle Alf in his column change Vauxhall Cresta and he'd been good to me in another way, too. He was a bus driver and if ever I was walking along and saw his bus, he and his conductor mate would let me ride for free. All in all, he must have saved me a few quid!

It came as a shock on August 6, 1969 – so close to the new season starting – to hear that Rowley had been sacked after just a year in charge. Clubs weren't as trigger-happy back then and I can only surmise what prompted the board to curtail his services, but the change wouldn't have registered too much in my thinking. I was young and just wanted to kick a ball about, not really worrying too much about which manager was in charge, whereas experienced players such as Len and Ted would have thought about the reasons and repercussions.

Perhaps the board considered that they had underestimated John Harris's qualities because they handed him back his old role, this time with former long-serving captain Cec Coldwell as coach. It meant that the lads played in a more off-the-cuff way again although still within the loose structure that we were comfortable with.

Defender John Flynn came in from Workington for a nominal fee and what a bargain he proved to be for many years. Flynny, a lovely bloke and all-round good player, was very reliable in the air and although he didn't have any speed, he read the game very well. His biggest drawback was that he would get very nervous, so he was more than happy when I told him just to give me the ball whether I was marked or not!

Geoff Salmons, Frank Barlow and I made up the midfield on most occasions, with Woodward wide right, while Colin Addison and John Tudor played up top for the majority of time. My eventual switch to midfield had come about because we weren't creating. I went to Harris and told him that I was finding myself going back to help to create and felt more like a midfielder. I enjoyed making goals and felt confident doing that because it was a big part of my game. John wasn't daft and I think he knew it might be the right thing to do. As things turned out, it was absolutely the correct decision, both for the team and for my career.

Huddersfield Town had a good team that year, including Trevor Cherry, Frank Worthington, Jimmy Lawson, Bobby Hoy and Geoff Hutt, and although our games with them that season finished in 2-1 home wins, they won the title while we finished sixth. It represented some progress from the season previous, but it was easy to see where we were lacking. At home we scored 50 goals and conceded only 10.

We didn't go up because of our away form, losing 12 games on the road, and for better or worse it had become our style to play attacking football and never sit back, whatever the state of the game. We just enjoyed playing that way. But it cost us dearly on our travels and we didn't have the players or tactical knowledge to adapt a more pragmatic approach when we should have done.

One of the highlights of the season for me was the opportunity of facing Watford for the first time since I had left because they had now won promotion to Division Two. They still had Keith Eddy, Tom Whalley and Stewart Scullion in their ranks, but we beat them 2-1 at Vicarage Road with goals from Frank Barlow and, still playing up-front, me. Of course, I was desperate to do well on my return, even though there had been no fall-out when I left, and Colin Addison got our goal at the Lane when we drew 1-1 in the return.

We were in contention until March, but after a run of six wins in nine, we lost four times on the spin, scoring only once. With only four fixtures left, the three wins we got were never going to make up the lost ground and we finished sixth. Only nine players scored all season although four of us managed double figures. Woodward led the way with 18 and Gil Reece added 14, with John Tudor notching 10 and me chipping in with 12. I thought that was pretty respectable for someone who was now dropping deeper and starting to become a midfielder. Although we had improved on the previous campaign, I was disappointed after two seasons of not getting back up.

Going down in the first place had been unexpected. But we were getting stronger and starting to establish a bunch of lads who were showing signs of gelling into a promotion-chasing side. And an entertaining one at that. There were wingers with degrees of power, pace and trickery. Woodward, now a consistent threat, had a dry sense of humour and liked a laugh in the dressing-room and Gil Reece was tricky and very quick.

He might have sometimes lacked a little concentration, but he was really good in the air for a small man and for the team in general. Geoff Salmons was rangy with pace to burn and he could frighten defenders to death when he took off down the flank. Little partnerships and links across the areas of the field were beginning to emerge naturally.

As the season ended with only friendlies to fulfil, Harris signed a couple of strikers, a move that was to prove very significant in completing a promotion-winning jigsaw. John Barnwell was 31 years old and by now injury-prone, but had experience on his side. He at least had a decent profile and pedigree in the game, whereas the slightly-built 26-year-old winger brought in from Chester for £10,000 was a new name to most. He had cartilage problems to boot, but what a player Billy Dearden turned out to be. His arrival didn't inspire the fans at first, but he proved an inspirational signing – and one Harris rated as his best.

Promotion had eluded us, but Harris was back in charge, the signs were promising from an evolving squad of players and on a personal level international recognition was continuing through the age groups. I was 19 and after being paired up-front with Joe Royle for my first England under-23 cap, I went on to complete a 13-game stint by the time I was 22. All were under Sir Alf Ramsey and I captained the side for the last five of them.

Alf had a high regard for me and made some nice comments about my ability and potential, which I am still very proud of. Things had started to change when I had gone into midfield. I was demanding the ball all the time, getting it more and I knew what I could do with it. Part of the discipline of playing in midfield is keeping the team shape and being confident enough to pull people about even though back then I would have been selected on the right. The team often included players such as Colin Todd, Jeff Blockley, Peter Shilton and Derek Parkin and I still played for the under-23s even after I had made my debut for the full senior side.

By the time the summer of 1970 had ended I was optimistic again, both for United and my prospects as a future full international. It proved to be the end of my 'professional apprenticeship.'

6

PROMOTION IS SOON...

Our prospects at the beginning of 1970-71 would probably have made us a sound bet for the top six again, but not one of the two favourites. Our signings had been low-key, the away form needed addressing and promotion back then, before the play-offs ha• been intro•uce•, coul• be achieve• only by a top-two finish.

John Harris was still in charge and included one of his summer acquisitions, John Barnwell, in the starting 11 at Orient on opening day. But a 3-1 loss was a shock start and one that also ended with John Flynn being taken out of the firing line – virtually until the final month of the campaign – allowing Dave Powell to become Eddie Colquhoun's partner in central defence.

Although we won at home to Swindon Town next, another defeat and two draws, albeit one from three down at home to Bristol City, weren't in the least encouraging. By now Billy Dearden had won a place, scoring his first United goal in the 3-3 thriller, and his energy and immediate impact soon forced Barnwell into taking more of a back seat. Our biggest boost was knocking a tremendously strong Leeds United team out of the League Cup when I managed to score the only goal before almost 30,000 at Bramall Lane. The nature of the goal – a run and shot from range – really pleased me and the scalp seemed to galvanise us in the league.

Although Spurs ended our cup hopes narrowly at White Hart Lane, we put together a great run which included a Woodward hat-trick in a third successive five-goal mauling of Portsmouth. A week later we beat Sheffield Wednesday 3-2 with a last-minute winner from John Tudor and 40,000 fans packed in at Bramall Lane. The team had begun to settle down with Dearden particularly and Tudor forming a free-scoring partnership.

A 16 league-game run without defeat ended at Luton at the beginning of December and if we had managed to turn some of the nine draws into wins, we would have been sitting even more comfortably than the usual seventh or eighth. We were scoring regularly, but clean sheets, despite an overall respectable defensive record, were a bit too thin on the ground.

We weren't quite clicking and when we hit an inconsistent spell at the turn of the year, which included five successive losses on the road – including a friendly at Chesterfield and an FA Cup defeat – Harris made what seemed some uncharacteristic and bold moves in the transfer market. There was no hint as far as the players were concerned that it was in the offing and it seemed a mistake to a lot of onlookers.

A fee of £40,000 was invested in the Birmingham City winger Trevor Hockey, who was almost immediately transformed into a busy, aggressive central midfield player and brought character and steel into the centre of the park. But it was the decision to move Tudor on to Newcastle United, in exchange for ex-Wednesday striker David Ford and the relatively-inexperienced goalkeeper John Hope, which prompted some head-scratching.

Tudor had gained popularity with the crowd for his scoring exploits over a few months, but goalkeeper Alan Hodgkinson had enjoyed legendary status at Bramall Lane for almost 20 years. Whether or not the manager had decided that the great man had been single-handedly responsible for some of the goals conceded, I don't know. But Hope's arrival signalled the end of Hodgy's career and put huge pressure on his young successor.

Yes, Hodgy was coming to the end of a brilliant career for United and England, but it was still a shock to see him sidelined and I didn't know what the manager had seen in Hope at the time. I was very surprised and thought it absolutely ridiculous to get rid of Tudor. He was a top striker in his own right, as he proved by going on to enjoy more success alongside Malcolm 'Supermac' Macdonald with the Magpies. But Harris liked pace and Fordy, a lovely lad who fitted in with the lads straightaway, was another speed merchant, a tricky winger who was a good addition for us.

I'd love to know how John Harris worked out these changes in personnel and just how confident he was that they would make us stronger. If he was, it was a masterstroke. After I'd hit the bar with a penalty against Luton and had another one saved at Charlton the following week, I decided I'd had enough and gave up the job after missing two of five. But the misses didn't matter because those games were won as we put together four victories on the bounce to get us right back on track.

Fresh faces can inject interest and momentum into a squad, but the new players have to prove themselves, too, or it soon wears off. The new lads played their part in the surge, but I maintain that the rest of the players deserve some credit as well; three new players suddenly thrust into a settled team takes some adjustment, for everyone.

It was great to play with Hockey. He gave me more freedom because his role was to win the ball and give it to me, plus he brought real personality. His long hair, headband and love of a tackle soon made him a favourite of the crowd, who chanted "Hockey is a werewolf" at every appropriate opportunity! He was originally a winger like Billy Dearden, but Harris converted both – Billy to centre-forward and Trevor to a combative, dynamic midfielder.

Hock was hyper and you half-expected him to be on pills or something because of the way he got everybody going before we came out. He would be kicking doors, punching fists and shouting encouragement to the rest of us and, most importantly to me, he and I hit it off straightaway on the pitch. We became roommates and he really was a lovely bloke, not always as exuberant as you might have thought; he had a piano at home and ran a sporty Triumph Herald in a flash, bright colour. You couldn't miss his car wherever he was driving!

But Trevor wasn't one of the boys who would go out regularly about the time when we'd have our Monday nights out. They couldn't often attract him, Eddie Colquhoun or Woody for various reasons. Hock also had the smelliest feet in the world – probably because he always wore suede Hush Puppies!

Despite my initial concerns, or maybe just my lack of knowledge about what he could do, I was soon glad that John Hope had been brought in. Not only for what he achieved in that season, but also for his role in a 22-match undefeated run in league and cup that straddled that season and the next.

He was tall and imposing enough to pluck stuff out of the air as he commanded his area, but he was also extremely brave and regularly dived into a penalty-area melee of legs, often emerging with painful cuts and bruises. He was a good last line of defence for a more than handy back-four and most of the best teams rely on having a top goalkeeper and a strong backline. Ask Sir Alex Ferguson.

When we had forwards-versus-defence in practice, it was the hardest job to get the better of ours even though they were outnumbered. John took some stick at times because, like most goalies, he was prone to mistakes, but he was a very good goalkeeper and was highly popular with the rest of the lads. We both lived in Dronfield on the outskirts of Sheffield and he became my best mate.

Hope set a record of seven clean sheets in a row during March and April of 1971, beginning only seven games after his debut. That record stood alone until Mark Howard eventually achieved eight 43 years later. Incredibly John played in the final 17 games of that promotion season, keeping 10 clean sheets and conceding just nine goals.

After four straight wins we stuttered through a run of results that might have ended our promotion hopes, but we gained enough from them to use as inspiration to turn things back in our favour. The 1-0 loss at Carlisle United at the end of February might have been seen as just a hiccup because they had a decent side. We had only drawn with them earlier in the season, and they went on to finish fourth. But hosting Hull City 10 days later had greater significance; we were at home and needed to bounce back.

Despite being right in the running for going up, Hull opted not to take us on in a footballing contest and made the game scrappy, physical and cynical. Their midfielder Ken Knighton was clearly instructed just to stop me from playing and the referee kept letting it go, even early on when he should have stamped his authority on such an important contest. I tried to get protection, but it didn't happen and I think even neutrals from that night would agree that Knighton should have been sent off.

City stopped our flow, did a job on us and ironically the referee saw fit to call both teams together in an attempt to calm things down. That was bizarre because it was obvious what each team's intentions were. Ours was definitely to let our football do our talking, but City drove off with both points because, despite Gil Reece's goal, we lost 2-1.

We'd had a massive and expectant crowd and both we and the supporters were shell-shocked at what had happened. Perhaps we should have just left it to Hock and Knighton to sort it out! I wasn't a softie by any means and wasn't wanting special treatment for fair, but strong tackling, but the sort of attention I got was a forerunner of the days of the tough man-markers of the 1970s such as Tommy Smith, Ron Harris and Peter Storey.

Four days later, when we were two goals down at QPR with only two minutes left, our promotion challenge looked to have stalled again – only for a Woodward penalty and a last-gasp equaliser by Hemsley to earn us a point. There were 10 games left and we lost none of them although three successive goalless draws, admittedly tough fixtures, slowed our progress at one stage.

Consecutive home games against Millwall and Birmingham City were won without conceding and Hockey, who rarely ventured much out of the centre-circle, made a rare, but invaluable appearance on the scoresheet when he bundled one in against the Londoners. Then a creditable 1-1 draw at Middlesbrough put us in a very good position with just two fixtures remaining, both at Bramall Lane. Win them and we would be up.

Cardiff City were well-placed with us and were a real threat, but, backed by a fantastic crowd of 42,963, we were unstoppable. After going in at the break with a 2-1 lead, we added three without reply afterwards, including my ninth of the season. I thought that was a decent total, but the most important thing was the result on a fabulous night. The importance of it became clear later when City finished one place below us – if the result had been reversed, it would have been them and not us who were promoted.

But we still needed to win on the final day of the season to be certain of success. And by one of those twists of fate that football so often throws up, the team who were standing in our way were... Watford! Another 39,000 fans turned up on that sunny Saturday. We would have been nervous about slipping up, especially because Watford played above themselves and Stewart Scullion hit the bar for them before Woody opened the scoring from the spot. That relaxed us and Reece rounded off a superb individual display with two goals in the second half to see us home in second place behind Leicester City.

Promotion was the first thing I'd won at club level and it had been hard work over nine months, but we were back in the top-flight after three bloody hard years. I was most pleased for the quality players who had been there for some time; staying at United in that division without asking for moves was a tribute to their loyalty to the club.

Emotion poured out at the final whistle and we struggled to get off the pitch when the fans came on to celebrate with us. Eventually we did and then shared a few minutes together, drinking it all in and congratulating each other before climbing up to the directors' box in the old John Street Stand. It was bedlam.

We each had one long-sleeved shirt and one short and I always wore the short-sleeved version because it made it less easy to be pulled back by an opponent. Unfortunately the long-sleeved one disappeared from the dressing-room while we were outside waving to the crowd. At least my shorts survived and are kept in the museum at Bramall Lane.

That aside, I could still reflect on what a fantastic day it had been to cap a truly fantastic season. We had lost just once at home and only six times on the road and in the final reckoning we trailed Leicester City by three points. But we were top scorers and had the best goal difference, so our success was fully earned. For such an attacking side our defence had still done the job with Flynn coming back during the finale to cement his place. Crucially we now had a balanced midfield with the creativity to service goal-hungry strikers and wingers.

On the downside there had to be casualties and the most notable were Alan Hodgkinson, whose exemplary career came to a close, and Dave Powell, who was forced to quit the game because of injury after the QPR game in March. Fittingly, Alan and Dave both contributed to the success, each playing as first choices until well after the turn of the year. Badger, Woody and I played in all 42 matches and Colquhoun, Dearden and Hemsley just two fewer; and the goals came mainly from Woodward (15), Dearden (14), Tudor and me (nine) and Reece (eight).

The promotion meant that this squad continues to be revered until this day, 50 years on, and I can't tell you how gratifying it is still to hear the Bramall Lane crowd belt out the song they sang back then...

"Oh, we ain't gotta barrel of money... But we've got Woodward and Currie... And with Eddie Colquhoun, promotion is soon... U-NI-TED!"

It is amazing that the fans of today haven't even adapted our names to feature their current favourites, and many of them won't even have watched any of us play! What a tribute to the relationship we had with our supporters and that rightfully extended to John Harris as well. He didn't say much and I don't recall managers in those days hearing their names chanted, but the fans admired how he went about his business.

I questioned earlier his decision to make that transfer swoop, which did seem a bit of a gamble for such a clean-living man. But he was right: and it paid off. The question now was: "How far could he, and we, go?"

A GRAND ENTRANCE

I was 21 years old when that promotion was won and it had taken three years of gradual improvement throughout the team. Maybe if I had switched to midfield sooner, it may have come a bit earlier but, equally so, that team-building period probably helped us to become better equipped to find out if we really could cut it in the top-flight.

There had been no medals from the Football League for finishing second so the lads each received a memento from Sheffield United to mark the achievement. I think some of them still have their black-and-white, inscribed footballs which open up into an alarm clock. If I remember rightly, Sheffield City Council hosted the team and club officials for a civic reception at the Town Hall which was surrounded by jubilant fans as we took to the balcony.

Note to Chris Wilder: John Harris didn't lead everyone, including the supporters, in a raucous sing-song of United chants from up there!

The quiet, studious Harris knew the way we were comfortable playing, but, although he'd start off team meetings, he wasn't a dominant or fluent talker. The players would soon chip in and take over, usually the experienced ones such as Len Badger, Ted Hemsley, Colin Addison and Eddie Colquhoun. But it would always be in a constructive, calm way because of their respect for the manager. We had our defensive duties, but after that we were pretty much off the cuff, executing the patterns and combinations that had evolved naturally through training and playing games.

My new role enabled me to become more effective for the team overall because my goal ratio hadn't been all that great up top and I was able to link up with some quick runners. There wasn't any real apprehension about surviving in the First Division – no fear at all – but we were all of the mind that we needed to stay there. We expected to be a solid outfit and settle around mid-table because of the match-winners we had, plus the fact that Alan Woodward, Badger, Addison, Colquhoun and I had experienced that level before.

Back then, and especially for us, there was none of the modern-day splurge on new players in preparation for the big challenge, but the danger was that realistically we had a squad of only about 12 who could compete consistently. If we were forced to go below that, we were weakened considerably and some who had provided adequate back-up during the promotion-winning campaign would probably struggle to do so at the next level.

Personally I was really pleased we signed Watford's Stewart Scullion, who went on to prove his worth by playing 36 games that season. He was a super little player, rather like Jimmy Johnstone in that he was unbelievable with the ball and opponents just couldn't get it off him if he was in the mood to take the mickey. But he also had vision and had provided me with my first goal for Watford with the cross for the header against Bristol Rovers.

Again there was no advanced warning or speculation about a new player coming in, a bit of a trademark of how Harris went about his business. There was no fuss or bluster, but that was basically it as far as recruitment was concerned that summer, despite Dave Powell retiring because of injury and Addison leaving in pre-season. It would be step-up time for several members of the squad who were new to the First Division.

The season's preparations began with a couple of friendlies in Holland, which was a regular destination about that time, and another in Belgium sandwiched in-between before a 2-2 draw at home to Sheffield Wednesday in which Woodward and I scored. A starting 11 that would complete the season with very few changes, apart from when injuries occurred, took shape with Scullion getting the nod over Reece.

It clicked right from the start and began with a comfortable 3-1 home win against Southampton. They struggled all season, but it gave us confidence. If a crowd of 25,000 was a bit disappointing considering the gates a few months previously during the run-in, the visit of Leeds in midweek a few days later brought the big-time atmosphere back and 40,000 turned up. A Yorkshire derby against a side that went on to finish runners-up to Derby County was not only an enticing prospect, but a more than credible test of how we might judge our prospects for the next nine months.

Second-half goals from John Flynn, his second in successive games, Billy Dearden, his first in the top division, and Colquhoun secured a resounding win that made the rest of the division sit up and take notice. The neutral's sensible view would be to recognise that we had been given a couple of home fixtures to begin with and wait until the away fixtures at Everton and Arsenal had been negotiated before going overboard. Well, that theory was dented when 1-0 wins in both – courtesy of Woodward's winner at Everton and Scullion's at Arsenal – saw us shoot to the top of the division.

It was still early days and we were not arrogant types, but that was a hell of a feeling with another two 'homes' coming up. West Bromwich Albion ended our sequence by holding us 0-0, but we saw off Huddersfield 3-1 in another atmospheric game under lights in midweek. When we beat Forest at the City Ground by the odd goal in five and knocked Fulham out of the League Cup by three clear goals at the Lane, it seemed our swashbuckling style was going to be unstoppable.

Even when Spurs held us to a 2-2 draw, we immediately hit back, winning at Leicester City – with Woodward claiming the only goal direct from a corner-kick! I was really in dreamland a week later when 'my club' Chelsea visited and were sent back down the M1, beaten by a Scullion goal. In that opening 10-game spell there were eight wins and two draws, so we were unbeaten for the first two months. Imagine that happening these days; we would have been inundated with media requests and enjoyed the sort of national attention Leicester received in 2015/16 when they were leading the way.

We were scoring for fun, failing to register only once, and we were doing it by playing in the only way we knew how. It worked because we had so much ability in our team and the bold approach surprised so many teams. Billy Dearden scored 16 league goals – a phenomenal achievement considering that he came to us with virtually no reputation – and on the wing, the ever-reliable Woodward proved how dangerous he was at any level with just one fewer.

I was very happy to reach 10 and 'Scully' got a few as well, particularly in that opening spell. Geoff Salmons, tall and rangy down the left, was such a strong, speedy runner who seemed to float over the turf, and although shooting wasn't his strong point, he terrified defenders and crossed a great ball.

Things were coming off for me. The triangle with Woody and Badge was established and a regular feature of our attacking play down the right flank. And I developed a good understanding with Billy, whose stamina and running belied his slender frame. I knew where he wanted the ball and he made some unbelievable lightning runs into space, scoring goals as if he had been born to play up there in that company.

It wasn't all about flair either because we weren't letting in too many goals in those first few weeks. John Hope set a then-Blades goalkeeping record for going the most games without losing, 22 across two seasons. You have to give John Harris credit for identifying him because he wasn't in the first-team at Newcastle when he was signed.

Perhaps the manager was following the trend about that time of going for goalkeepers of a bigger stature such as Phil Parkes and Joe Corrigan, because he went from Alan Hodgkinson at five foot eight inches to Hope at more than six feet.

People would either like or loathe Hope; Len, Ted and Woody loved him, whereas John Tudor, who was opinionated and entitled to his own theories, didn't really take to him. Either way, I'm sure our defenders liked having a big bloke behind them and had confidence in him. He was a big, brave presence despite the odd blunder – and we all made those.

Len Badger was a brilliant and intelligent, ball-playing full-back who could put the ball on a plate and the ever-consistent Ted Hemsley had made the left-back position his own after converting from a midfielder. Flynn and Eddie Colquhoun formed an effective partnership. Both were good in the air and while Flynn wasn't fast, he made up for it in other ways; Eddie was very quick and a great captain. They complemented each other; John was more a ball-playing defender and Eddie a stopper who was very clever and adept at the nudges with elbows and shoulders.

Our talented side enjoyed each other's company and we were at the top of our game, so much so that after about eight or nine fixtures I was allowing myself to think that a top-six finish and a place in Europe might be in our grasp. After beating Chelsea, we next faced a trip to Old

Trafford. Manchester United were not quite the force they had been, but going there was still the most glamorous fixture on the calendar and George Best, Bobby Charlton, Denis Law and Alex Stepney were all in the side sitting one place below us in second.

It was a massive fixture for both teams; the ground had more than 51,000 inside and an estimated 20,000 locked out, which I can well believe. I know several fans who didn't get in, but who followed the score in TV shops in Glossop on the way back. The routes over the Pennines must have been rammed that day while we were having our usual fillet steak at noon – regarded as the thing to do by most clubs in preparation for a big game back in those days!

There was very little in the game, but the Reds' two second-half goals ended our unbeaten run. We were as sick as parrots and it didn't help that for years after when one of the goals was shown on the opening credits on *Match of the Day*. It's natural to try to analyse, looking for a pass here or a decision there that made the difference, although it is often a harsh judgment because some errors lead to goals while others don't – in other words, it is the luck of the draw on the day.

In this case, maybe if Hopey had stayed in goal instead of trying to send George Best wide, he might not have ended up with virtually an open goal to break the deadlock. But Alan Gowling was then allowed to score the second on the break and it was all over anyway. Despite losing, we were still top and although we were to fall away, we had such a good time and felt unbeatable.

That Old Trafford encounter must have been the first time I had been in opposition to Best, a player I – and anyone in the world – would have loved to have had as a teammate. He could beat anybody. Like Scully, he loved to go past defenders and go back and beat them again – although that didn't always go down well with Bobby Charlton and one or two others.

This may sound a bit left field to some people, given his excessive and high-profile lifestyle, but I really think that, deep down, George would have liked to have led a quiet life off the pitch, like I did. But he was hounded everywhere he went and taken advantage of. There were even coach parties outside his house and consequently people making money from doing it at the expense of his privacy.

That is just not a sane way to live; being followed, fawned over and photographed incessantly and I am not surprised that he rebelled against it. In that situation you can get a liking for drink as a release and in later life I encountered similar demons owing to outside pressures in my personal life.

George and I were rival players, but we did share the same agent, Ken Stanley. I had never thought of having an agent before he approached me in 1972, but when the chance came up, I didn't think twice because of who he was. Don't get the impression that Ken made me rich, though – these were relatively early days for agents and lucrative endorsements. Plus Ken was very much all Besty!

I wish that later on I'd had an agent for wage negotiations as well, but then it was just for commercial aspects and all I got was 500 quid for a picture card with Kellogg's. When I later joined Leeds United, I had Kevin Keegan's agent Harry Swales, who was the England players' man and I got a boot deal – the first player to wear Patrick boots. Again, though, it was pretty much all Keegan and then Ray Wilkins when he came on board. I wasn't pushy enough and having been in that position, with someone representing me, I should have been proactive in urging him to get me more exposure.

After the loss at Manchester United we weren't thinking that the bubble had burst because we had still played well and when we knocked York City out of the League Cup next, it seemed to be business as usual. But the bubble was destined to deflate and we suffered three losses on the bounce, albeit by the odd goal on each occasion. We scored seven times, but alarmingly began shipping goals at the other end. We didn't really know why.

But bad runs are not unusual and we put a stop to it with a goalless draw at Arsenal, again in the League Cup, and followed that up in the league by drawing at home to Liverpool when I managed to score one of my most spectacular goals. It was probably 30 yards out on the angle and I can still see it flying into the net beyond Ray Clemence. I didn't aim for anything but the eight-yards by eight-feet goal, but it found the far corner and I have frequently watched it on video since.

Despite being no Alan Woodward, who was great at long-range shooting, I did enjoy it. There was no-one closing me down and Clemence's goal was there to be shot at. It might have been the hardest shot I ever hit and we should have won that game – the equaliser came from a free-kick which shouldn't have been given. Keegan had the ball on the left-wing and went to go down the line, but I read him and got the ball. I was astonished when the referee gave obstruction and from the free-kick Keegan flicked the ball into the net.

Gil Reece's double saw off West Ham in London before we were to face Arsenal in a cup replay at home. A freak accident then put a spanner in the works. The night before the game I was at home, boiling an egg, when I caught the saucepan on something and spilled boiling water on my foot. The pain was excruciating and when I pulled my sock off, there was an absolutely massive blister all over the instep.

I limped up the road to the telephone box and rang John Harris – I'm amazed I had his number – and he said: "Go home and put ice on it or whatever." It was still very painful when I went to the ground the next day for treatment and I was then sent home to rest. Later I had four pain-killing injections in the instep and during a fitness test pinged a few balls with my right foot. It felt okay despite a strange tingle and the injections were obviously working. I was desperate to play and was deemed fit. We didn't think there would be any long-term effects and, unless injuries involved ligament damage or severe twists, you would try to have a go. As it turned out, I had a good game and we got through to the next round with a 2-0 win.

Although we won at West Ham, knocked Arsenal out of the FA Cup and then beat Coventry in successive games, the next one sparked three months of poor results during the winter period. Just 11 days after winning at Upton Park in the league, we returned for the League Cup fifth round and went down 5-0. For one of the goals John Hope misjudged Clyde Best's shot from virtually the halfway line and took some stick for it, although he had lost the ball in the floodlights. It was just unfortunate; some people remember things such as that, but not the part he played in the long, unbeaten run.

Not surprisingly his confidence was affected and we had some bizarre results; in four games we twice conceded five, but beat Ipswich 7-0 in-between! Len Badger struck from 30 yards against possibly the smallest goalie in the league, Laurie Sivell; Len scoring at all was such a rare event that it probably took the limelight away from Woodward, who hit four! How I failed to score I don't know, but I probably made six of them... Just joking!

There was every chance of goals in our matches which often sent people home happy, win or lose, because of the way we played. But it was odd that, despite putting out a usually unchanged defence, we went so long without conceding many before we followed that with an even longer run when we always let some in. But being hammered at Crystal Palace wasn't the same as losing 5-0 at Arsenal or Liverpool and it was inevitable that it would hit us all confidence-wise.

A couple of December wins halted the slide only temporarily and the customary FA Cup third-round exit didn't help because we went two months before tasting victory again. Halfway through that period Arsenal hit five without reply at Bramall Lane in a fixture that will be remembered by all who saw it as the one in which Alan Ball deliberately sat on the ball during play.

Bally and I were actually good mates and it was just a bit of mickey-taking at my expense at the right time. Although he was an arrogant sort of player, I loved him to bits and to me what he did was quite audacious. He just brought the ball up to me and sat on it. I was gutted at the situation we were in, but it didn't make me lose any respect for him. In fact, I had to laugh because it had never been done before. There were a few of us around at the time with the confidence to do that and have a bit of fun.

I was vilified sometimes for taking the piss on the pitch and Emlyn Hughes and Kevin Keegan didn't like it; as Liverpool players they were very proud, wanted to win every game and didn't take kindly to anyone being a bit cocky with them. But most supporters loved to see players express themselves. Best did it for years, Stan Bowles as well. But on several occasions it resulted in us being on the receiving end of some face-to-face comments on the pitch.

They weren't always nasty but it was obvious that what I had done had been getting to them, even though it had been about getting my teammates going or giving our fans something to cheer about. Emlyn Hughes and I were great mates and roomed together on England duty, but I remember him once sneering at me when Liverpool were putting us under pressure. "Stop taking the piss, TC," he said. I suppose that was better than the likes of Peter Storey and Tommy Smith who in the same situation just used to kick us!

Unusually that season we played a couple of friendlies abroad in early

February, which I can think was possible only because we had already been knocked out of the FA Cup. To start with, we went to troubled Israel and played out a goalless draw with the sound of gun shells going off over our heads. Worrying, to say the least. But while we were there, we also visited Bethlehem, Jerusalem, the Hill of the Rock, Golgotha, where Jesus was crucified, and his tomb.

My itinerary also featured riding a camel and seeing the Wailing Wall. Oh, and we even found time to make the odd visit to a club called Tiffany's! A week later we probably ended up in a less exotic nightspot in Sheffield after Gil Reece's strike wasn't enough to prevent a 2-1 loss to the powerful Ukrainian outfit Dynamo Kiev.

Not long after we had returned to domestic action, there was a dramatic game at home to Manchester City in which the lead exchanged hands more than once. Although I was pleased to score with a powerful header from Woodward's driven corner-kick in the 3-3 draw, the mood was dampened by an injury to Hockey, who sustained a hairline fracture of his leg, but carried on playing. We tended to do that sort of thing in those days...

As a result the team shuffled around and we won only one in our next seven although that was a memorable one for Billy Dearden. He scored a magnificent hat-trick against a West Ham defence containing Bobby Moore, no less, to crown a hugely-creditable first season in the top-flight. We viewed our next game, at Coventry City, as a very winnable one. But two events at Highfield Road left a sour taste in my mouth.

First of all, a snowstorm enveloped the ground during the game and left the referee with little option but to abandon it after 62 minutes. We were leading 2-0 at the time and when the game was replayed six weeks later, Coventry beat us 3-2. I scored twice in that game, but it was no consolation because the points dropped cost us a couple of places in the final table.

Then an incident after the game added insult to injury. A Coventry fan asked me for my autograph as I got on the coach, but after I had obliged, he then tore it up in front of my face. How's that for provocation? I knew that if I reacted, I would have been in big trouble. I just walked away. To tell you the truth, I was in shock as it had never happened to me before. It was really offensive, and like many men my first instinct would have been to thump him. Fortunately, I kept self-control. Whether he deserved that, I'm not too sure.

By this time in 1972 Linda and I had moved from Meersbrook to a better house in a better area of Dronfield, on the fringes of Sheffield. The house cost me a princely sum of £7,000 and my new journey home taught me a costly lesson after we lost 2-0 at Spurs in late March. We arrived back in Sheffield at about 10pm and as I drove home in my Ford Cortina 1600E, I didn't know that rain had made the road a bit greasy.

While I was negotiating the roundabout at Meadowhead, the car's back end spun round. Although I didn't hit anything, it was a warning and, because I was picking Linda up and going back into town for a rare night out, I knew I had better be careful. After a couple of drinks we headed home along Eyre Street at about 1.30am with Linda and a friend in the back seats. Then the rear end of my Cortina – which was then car of the year, too! – went again and this time we went straight into a lamppost.

It was quite an impact and I ended up with cuts and two cracked ribs after my chest had hit the steering wheel. Linda suffered cuts and her friend broke her arm, all because of the impact and the windscreen shattering. It was enough to knock me out for a couple of minutes and, as I was coming round, a bloke came out of a nearby pub to help.

"Flippin 'eck, it's TC!" he said. "Drink that, Tony, it'll help."

He handed me a brandy before the coppers arrived on the scene. They were obviously Blades fans because the first thing they did was to ask me how my legs were before adding: "Sorry, TC. We have to breathalyse you."

The brandy I took after the crash took me over the limit and they told me I had failed. My car was put in a compound for ages and eventually written off, while I received a £25 fine and a year's ban from driving. It was a sickener; my injuries were nothing too serious in the long term, but I really didn't like being in any kind of trouble. It preyed on my mind to think about people knowing about it, especially after drinking and despite being careful.

John Harris, who was strictly teetotal, gave me chapter and verse when he found out and I was out of action for three weeks, which hurt me as much as any of the injuries. I eventually got back home at about 6am and had to tell the unfortunate babysitter, who lived probably 20 miles away at Worksop, that I couldn't take him home and he had to get somebody to pick him up.

Those three weeks seemed to last forever before I could come back and play at Ipswich and there was a further final, painful twist to the story. Rib damage can be painful for ages, as well as making breathing uncomfortable, so imagine the amount of strapping I wore for protection. We kicked off, I immediately had the ball at my feet and a Town player challenged me strongly. I ended up falling on the ball and the pain was absolute murder for a few minutes. And the irony didn't lessen it one little bit.

We stabilised during the run-in and signed off with two wins and ended in a very solid 10th place, comfortably above halfway and just four points behind Arsenal in fifth. It was more than enough to convince both ourselves and our supporters that we had established ourselves at that level at the first time of asking. We were entitled to look forward with optimism, provided that we could strengthen our squad.

Before then came a nice little end-of-season playing trip to Zambia. I invariably enjoyed foreign travel, but this tour got a bit too hot and spicy on and off the pitch. We could only be in the sun for one hour every day, early in the morning, because it was so bloody hot, so well done to whoever had arranged for us to be fitted with burgundy-coloured suits in a heavy wool material for the trip. Unbelievable!

We played a club team first, then the Zambian National XI three times and there were wars on the pitch in addition to the real wars around the region. The flare-ups were so bad that the police and army were on the pitch sometimes and I have a picture of me holding an opponent by the throat with Ted Hemsley in the background.

They were kicking us to bits because they didn't know how to tackle properly and were going straight through us. The last thing we wanted after a good season was a broken leg on a tour – even one that did finish with us winning the Zambian Airways Trophy! There were plenty of plus sides as well, such as meeting the famous politician Kenneth Kaunda and a fantastic tour that included going to the Livingstone Falls, at the bottom of which was a whirlpool reached via a mile-long walk through a jungle.

The falls are the widest in the world, also a mile long, and you could feel the massive spray from a distance which was impressive. But I wasn't so brave walking through the jungle, hearing all sorts of noises from things you couldn't see!

I found our visit to a copper mine really interesting and there was no shortage of things to do in Ndola, Zambia's third-largest city. As players, we enjoyed each other's company and we could let our hair down a bit after the season. But with John Harris, it was like having a teacher on a school trip. He walked the corridors in his pyjamas at night, saying: "Blemming get to bed!"

He would creep around, knowing what the players were like – always up for pranks. I was 21 years old then, had only just started drinking and would do it only when it was officially allowed. I wasn't sneaking out as some of the lads did – and they even had the cheek to nick sheets from my room to tie together and escape out of the window!

8

IF THE CAP FITS...

If Martin Peters was 10 years ahead of his time, then maybe I was 10 years too late. I wouldn't really ever want to disagree with Sir Alf Ramsey, but not playing more for him really put a brake on my international career.

I knew that winning promotion to the top-flight with Sheffield United would have enhanced my chances of receiving a senior England call-up. Playing against top players every week put me in the public eye and crucially attracted media attention that would have alerted the selectors. Even so, despite picking up numerous caps at youth level and several with the under-23s, I didn't allow myself the luxury of thinking that selection would be inevitable.

There were so many household names in the national team, which was one pretty good reason. But Alf Ramsey, who by then knew me well from the under-23s, named me in the side to face Northern Ireland at Wembley on May 23, in the 1972 Home International Championship. That annual tournament comprised England, Scotland, Wales and Northern Ireland and the games were regarded as quite important because there were fewer fixtures on the international calendar. To me they were like FA Cup finals and this debut was the biggest game of my life at the time. I was bang in form, United had just enjoyed a good season and the fans had been chanting "Currie for England" for quite a while.

Just being selected to start was a fantastic feeling and it reflected well on Sheffield United as well. I recall the boys and John Harris congratulating me and one or two, including Len Badger, reminding me that I was the first England international at the club since Mick Jones a few years earlier. I hope it doesn't sound churlish, but with so many more matches now sometimes caps are easier to come by. I say that only to emphasise how special it was for me. But I was still pretty scared during the lead-up and preparation.

I was well used to being with younger lads in the under-23s, but having to go and meet people such as Alan Ball, Bobby Moore, Martin Peters, Allan Clarke and so on was nerve-wracking. I needn't have worried really because I had played against them at club level and was made to feel welcome. Moore had been captain for so long he probably took responsibility for that and was charming. What a lovely bloke.

I had nine days off after our end-of-season tour to Zambia and the on-field wars we encountered before the Northern Ireland game. It was a midweek fixture and we met up two or three days earlier at the Hendon Hall Hotel – one mile from where I'd lived as a boy! It was almost a home from home in that we trained, I think, on a muddy pitch at Oakhill School with a little hut to change in – a far cry from today. If the pitch had been any muddier, we would have used the pitch at Hendon FC, another important part of my childhood or occasionally at Roehampton.

We only trained one morning until about 12.30pm so, after a shower and coach back to the hotel for a meal, there was very little to do but knock about in the hotel and our rooms. Alf wasn't one for arranging much, apart from the odd trip to the London Palladium, so it could get boring. But the location was so convenient for me that in later years I was allowed out to visit my mum for a couple of hours, which made a welcome change.

Once we went to the West Park Lodge Hotel where a fantastic chef prepared wonderful smoked salmon and prawns and also scampi to die for with chips. Even the tartare sauce he made was unbelievable and, even to this day, if I could choose a final meal, it would be his!

Alf announced the team the day before the game, although he had already spoken to us individually to confirm that I was playing. At Wembley. That's when the butterflies started, but not around actually playing. It was more the occasion and the stadium. I had been in the crowd at Wembley as a kid, watching Hendon win the Amateur Cup, but had never played there and I can't put into words how it feels to be so close to fulfilling a childhood dream.

Representing your country at one of the most famous stadiums on the planet – on the turf where England had won the World Cup just six years previously. And the winning manager was still in charge.

I actually thoroughly enjoyed the lead-up to the game, including the drive to Wembley. Alan Ball used to get all hyper and patriotic on the coach, reacting with and having a laugh with opposition fans through the window, even though they couldn't hear what he was saying! The pitch really was lovely, like a carpet, and the best I had played on up to then. Bert and Jim were there and although Mum wasn't – she never saw me play a professional match until many years later in my QPR days.

I know that may sound strange but there was a good reason. She had watched me at school football matches when Bert could get, but later she developed ulcerated legs after a fall. The condition made her reluctant to go out and the longer it went on, the less she did. It was a shame, but understandable, so having her at Wembley was a double bonus really and I felt immensely proud just walking out.

But the game was a massive disappointment. We lost 1-0 to a goal in the 33rd minute from Terry Neill and I don't have much memory of the match, apart from walking off when I was subbed for Martin Peters just before the hour mark. Northern Ireland did a job on us or we were off our game – probably a combination of both – and I couldn't impose myself because of it. *England v Northern Ireland: Shilton; Todd, Hughes, Storey, Lloyd, Hunter, Summerbee, Bell, MacDonald, Marsh, Currie (Peters, 58).*

Afterwards I understandably had negative thoughts about how my debut had gone, but I eventually realised that Alf liked me as a player and had probably protected me by taking me off. A long time later he did something that gave me a massive boost. He wrote an article saying I should have had many more caps and that I could have gone on to be captain in different circumstances. And he had said that even without being aware of what I'd been going through in my personal life. It was just my luck that he got moved on far too soon for me to benefit further.

It was a little more than a year until I won my next cap, in a 2-1 friendly win in Russia, but I went on to earn five in all in 1973, including a three-game tour of Poland, the USSR and Italy. The first, in Poland, was a World Cup qualifier and the result was to have massive repercussions for the team and the English international game in general.

Alan Ball was dismissed during a 2-0 loss, a game in which I was an unused sub – but I was to play in the infamous return four months later. England hadn't expected to lose and to do so because of two Bobby Moore errors made the result even more unlikely.

Four days later, with Ball suspended, I was in the team in the USSR and had a great game, spraying the ball about in the 2-1 friendly success. Martin Chivers and an own goal put us two up before the Russians scored a consolation. I had already been to Kiev, but I did enjoy that second trip to that part of the world, visiting Red Square and other sights including Lenin's tomb, where I got a nice photograph with Mick Channon and Malcolm 'Supermac' Macdonald.

At the time, when the political Cold War was at its height, Russia had such an air of mystery and even menace to us all back in our country. The ever-visible security did feel a bit oppressive and even in June it seemed dark and dingy with high ceilings adding to the atmosphere. I'm pretty sure we used to take most of our own food away with us, but it was on that tour that I tasted my first gazpacho, a soup served cold. I liked my soup almost burning the back of my throat and to me it was horrible, with bits of red cabbage in it. Admittedly we weren't very sophisticated then!

We moved on to Turin to take on Italy, who boasted Romeo Benetti in their ranks. He was a defender who was well-known to be as hard as nails and his methods were underhand, to say the least. Basically, he was virtually a dirty, hard as nails thug. And he was detailed to man-mark yours truly. He was intentional in his approach, tackling me from behind, while I really just wanted to play. But I gave almost as good as I got and to be fair I was given decent protection from the referee.

But we went down 2-0 in a game when Bobby Moore overtook Bobby Charlton as England's most capped player. The Press kindly marked the occasion by handing him a commemorative clock. Imagine his embarrassment when Bobby dropped the gift during his acceptance speech and smashed it!

After the tour and the summer break were over, thoughts were turning towards the return with Poland that would decide which team would qualify for the World Cup finals the following year. A friendly with Austria at Wembley had been arranged as a warm-up for us and I was in the side that hammered them 7-0. They hardly had a kick. All my England goals were gems, starting with one that night; when the ball came in from the right, I controlled it on my chest, swivelled and volleyed a dipper into the far corner. It was a goal that gave me great personal satisfaction and a result to take us into the crucial qualifier in good spirits.

There was now no question that I was established in the England set-up, to the extent that I would have been disappointed if I hadn't been picked. The team was more or less settled, with Colin Bell, Martin Peters and me in midfield for the big occasion. Alf was a big advocate of Martin, labelling him "10 years ahead of his time" – which I have to admit seemed a bit over the top to me.

Martin was known as "the Ghost" because he had a rare ability to float about, not being involved much in the play, and then pop up in the penalty area to score. No doubt that he was an educated player, but he wasn't a tackler or a dribbler or a long passer. A bit later along came Trevor Brooking. He wasn't the greatest header or tackler and he lacked a bit of pace, but he was a great player. No-one could argue that Martin wasn't a calm finisher who got a lot of goals and caps. But in my view Trevor was the better of the two. Just my opinion ...

Colin Bell was an altogether different midfield player. His nickname – Nijinsky, after the thoroughbred racehorse – was appropriate because he had a fantastic engine which enabled him to get up and down the pitch. There were few to match his rugged tackling and ability to win the ball for others, but he was more than that. He did a bit of everything; he was quick enough, could glide over mud and also get into the box. Colin was a good finisher, great to play with and we became great mates. The pair of us and Allan Clarke were in a card school as only a bit of fun, even if a fiver at a time was a decent bet in those days.

There was also a lot riding on the Poland game, the last one in the qualifying group. It was us or them for the finals in Germany in 1974 and despite losing in Poland, we had been easily the better side. It had been widely regarded as a shock result and we were still favourites to qualify by winning well enough at home. Lightning wasn't expected to strike twice.

There was no hangover from the first leg as far as we were concerned and we were all confident on the night. Although the goal we would have liked to set us up didn't come along early, there was still the feeling at the break that it was only a matter of time. We were creating chance after chance and their eccentric goalkeeper, Jan Tomaszewski, surely couldn't continue to be alternately brilliant and downright fortunate for another 45 minutes.

But as time went on, everyone in the ground began to get a bit nervous. The place almost submerged with gloom when Poland scored on the break; Norman Hunter missed a tackle on the halfway line before

Domarski sent a low shot skidding under Peter Shilton. I had some stick as well after losing a ball on their byline in a move I would usually be successful at 999 times out of 1,000, so it had been a comedy of errors with uncharacteristic mistakes by a succession of us. We had battered them all the way through and now we faced a team that really had their tails up, with the Wembley crowd baying us on almost hysterically.

Clarke did score a penalty for a push on Peters which possibly wasn't merited, but given our dominance it shouldn't have mattered. Chances were scorned and Tomaszewski, often portrayed as a clown, certainly wasn't on that night. He was downright lucky or somehow got in the way of everything that was on target. But he didn't hold everything and one save in particular had to be down to good fortune when Clarke turned and hit the ball from eight yards past a clutter of players. The goalkeeper couldn't have seen it, so he dived blind. The ball hit his hand and went round the post. We couldn't believe it.

I had a lot of shots, but they were too straight and close to the goalkeeper and nothing went right for us on the night. It was like the Charge of the Light Brigade all the way through, but another freak result went against us and our World Cup hopes were shattered. When I watched the game back again years later on video, with Polish commentary, I was surprised to notice that they had a few breakaways themselves. They might have had another one or two themselves as well, largely because we were so much on top. But I think I ran about too much instead of playing my usual game; the match was so crucial I felt I had to, even though I was probably the best passer in English football at the time.

England not making the World Cup finals in that era, only eight years after winning it, was unthinkable and it was then my worst experience in the game, along with Sheffield United's relegation a couple of seasons later. The despair we felt on the pitch was felt very sharply because we had given our all and that wasn't eased at all when Alf and Don Howe tried to console us with sympathetic words and arms round our shoulders. The downbeat mood for us and the nation went on for weeks and, although I knew I had a chance for the 1978 tournament, that wasn't the case for some who would be too old by then.

At least the Press were kind. Nobody hammered us because nobody had a bad overall game although they did have a pop at Brian Clough for calling Tomaszewski a clown before the match. That backfired big time, as the goalkeeper spectacularly proved. Alf had endured some criticism following the 1970 World Cup for subbing Bobby Charlton while in a winning position and then losing, and doubts about him emerged again after the Poland game.

One month later we were back at Wembley as an 86th-minute goal by Fabio Capello – remember him? – consigned us to a 1-0 friendly defeat to Italy. They had some great players, such as Franco Causio, Roberto Bettega, Dino Zoff, Luigi Riva and especially Gianni Rivera. He was one of the greatest and most elegant footballers and I swapped shirts with him after the game. It was my best game for England up to that point and we had paralysed them in my opinion, so losing was again hard to take. Zoff had been brilliant in goal and Italy got a couple of breaks here and there. Again we just couldn't stick the ball in the net.

It is a genuine bugbear with me that Sir Alf was shunted aside within a few short months of this fixture. He didn't deserve such an inauspicious departure and for me it was the biggest mistake the FA could have made. And I know that without a doubt other players thought so as well.

Why hadn't we qualified? We had a lot of bad luck during the campaign, but weren't short of talented players; Martin Chivers, Clarke and Mick Channon, for example, were great names and consistent goalscorers, household names who were still scoring goals elsewhere. Perhaps the reluctance of the media to criticise us was in part because few experts or pundits could put their finger on why we had failed. There seemed to be nothing blindingly obvious.

We were easy on the eye and certainly not outplayed, so were there other subtle factors at play? An interesting school of thought worth considering suggests how we in England had for too long been complacent about our place in the world order of football; we invented the game, made the rules, have a great domestic system and so on: therefore, no-one could teach us anything new. Our lack of international success in tournaments seems to support the theory that we are not as good as we think we are, or at least slow to adjust to new ideas and developments.

Have we followed them instead of leading? Do we favour the 'tried and tested' methods instead of having the curiosity to see how they could be bettered? Typical British qualities of courage, togetherness and bravery are commendable and will always play their part in a physical sport, but shouldn't they play a supporting role to skills, tactical awareness and better preparation? Even in 1974 the continentals had a style and sophistication we didn't and from what I saw when watching their training camps, it stemmed from there. It was so different – they often trained with footballs, while we would stick mainly with running endless doggies or playing forwards-versus-defence.

They were on diets that befitted proper sportsmen and comparatively few smoked or drank, so our perceived fitness advantage was often nullified when we played the top teams. On the pitch they were adaptable, adept at getting the officials on their side and liked a dive, a gouge or a spit; frequently in sly ways that incensed our traditional view of how the game should be played.

You pay your money and you make your choice as far as what makes a good game of football and I am not underplaying just how many brilliant footballers have emerged from outside our shores. In the intervening years the new ideas have prevailed and our game has also now become continental in numerous ways, especially in the Premier League. We were used to a manager, trainer and a physio and not much else; a far cry from the entourages of staff and specialists common now in the top couple of divisions.

Kit, boots, training and medical facilities, sports science and so on have undoubtedly been influenced from abroad and pitches have evolved to give the best surfaces for football and the tuned athletes who use them. But overall, for my taste, I'm not sure it has all been better for the game. In the Premier League in particular, players can't tackle any more so games are dotted with free-kicks because players can't be touched without the whistle being blown. There seem to be more penalties and the spectacle seems to have changed so much.

I hope these comments aren't received as the inevitable ramblings of an ex-player, bitter about not benefitting from all the positive features of being a modern player today. It is so tempting to be nostalgic and maintain that everything was better in my day and I suspect most of us end up being that way. It is just an opinion. England can still grind most teams down. The only trouble is that they are still likely to face the same stumbling-blocks in Germany, Spain, France and Italy when they do reach the last four!

***

Sir Alf Ramsey was already a legend in the game by the time I had my first dealings with him at youth and under-23 international level. He made an impression on me from that moment on and I still hold him in the highest regard. It was no different when I progressed to the seniors; he was a quiet man who definitely had an aura of quiet authority and greatness. Yes, his record spoke for itself, but just as importantly he still retained the respect of virtually every player he selected: even the experienced ones who had been around him long enough to perhaps take him for granted.

There were plenty of those around when I broke through and it was noticeable how much they liked and trusted Alf. Respect must go a long way for a manager, especially dealing with top players, and I think part of why he attracted it was down to the way he dealt with us – with respect. You knew you were talking to a gentleman. He hardly ever swore and you could count on him to approach every situation in just the right way.

It would have been a mistake for anyone to mistake his placid, calm manner for weakness, though, because he wouldn't suffer fools gladly. Members of the media sometimes found that to their cost because he would never slag the players off to them. Basically he didn't want to speak and that wasn't a great basis for a good relationship anyway. If he didn't like a question or thought it was unnecessary or too probing, he would often be pointed or curt in his response. Or pause to think first about a measured answer, which invariably left the poor questioner feeling distinctly uncomfortable.

For example, he would know there were lots of big drinkers in those days – lads including Bally, Clarkey, Moore and me – and he knew how to deal with them, so a difficult journalist wasn't going to faze him. Alf had won the World Cup, after all – not necessarily with the best players either, although there were some great ones – and he had a quiet authority that you wouldn't want to risk challenging.

I used to join in drinking with the boys a bit after the Wembley games because we were usually staying over before parting ways, but I was by no means in the big league. When I got older and needed a drink for comfort, I was invariably on my own at home.

Players were quite comfortable with calling him Alf, as he was, and we appreciated him talking to us individually off the pitch as well as in a group on the training pitch. Most of us had not really had that kind of approach before. And I am assuming that it was one he employed at Ipswich when he took them from nowhere to league champions in next to no time before taking over as England manager.

This was a different environment from club football. Alf did it all usually and it was a privilege to be part of his squad; a great, but slightly funny feeling. We all ate together in the mornings before training and hardly ever did extra in the afternoons. I had been selected by the great Sir Alf Ramsey for England and couldn't help but feel special wearing that tracksuit.

It was as if everything was a lovely haze of fulfilled ambition and dreams coming true. The fact that we were probably on a muddy training pitch somewhere in Barnet didn't diminish the upbeat experience. There was nothing grand about it, right down to the shed we changed in!

He was tactically very aware and his motivational work excellent. Alf was shrewd, but not a tub-thumper because he wanted his players to have a clear idea of what he wanted when they went out. He regularly achieved that during his one-to-one chats. In my case he would tell me to play as I did at club level. It was reassuring because it meant I wasn't given anything else to worry about when it came to my own game; he valued my normal way of playing and wanted me to incorporate it into his national team. *Wow.*

As an individual Alf was naturally quiet and private, in a similar mould to John Harris at Sheffield United. Although that might not have been a typical-manager type back then, his players loved him. Just as the Leeds United players under Don Revie had a *thing* for their manager and his work at Elland Road, the England players would not have a word said against Ramsey.

What was his genius? I won't even try to suggest I know the answer to that, but I do know one thing. In my early days with England youth and under-23s I wasn't the greatest at defending, but that was a period when I was played mainly as a striker. It was a deficiency in my game that needed improvement, especially when I dropped back into midfield, and I firmly believe Alf did that by developing my awareness of it.

The Italy defeat was in November 1973 and there wasn't another international until early March 1974, which proved to be Sir Alf's last as England manager. The team drew a friendly 0-0 in Lisbon, but I was absent after undergoing a cartilage operation. It meant the end of my time with the great man, who had lost just 17 of his 113 matches as England manager.

I was devastated and felt sorry for him because the team hadn't disintegrated. We had just fallen a bit short when our luck was out in games we had controlled. In my eyes he was still the best man for the job and a good group of players never lost respect for him. He'd given me 13 under-23 caps and the captaincy and then made me a regular at senior level. So I was proud that I had earned his approval.

Alf was out of a job and I knew that I had a job on my hands. All the players felt they had to start afresh and impress whoever came in, but Joe Mercer knew he had only seven games as the caretaker boss until the new manager – either Brian Clough or Don Revie – took over. So Joe decided he would do things his own way – with his own players. There's nothing wrong with that, but I was unselectable anyway because of the injury. Mercer was popular because he liked an attacking style with players such as Frank Worthington, Keith Weller and Martin Dobson, who hadn't had a sniff under Alf, and I'm pretty sure I would have been in his squad if I had been fit. But as it turned out, I missed all of Joe's caretaker reign.

My lateral cartilage operation had been towards the end of the campaign and maybe the staff and I didn't work as hard as we should on building up muscle again. The result was that it split and surgeons had to go round the back of the joint as well. It still wasn't right during pre-season when I was even using my kitbag with some boots in it as makeshift weight for exercising the leg.

At Bramall Lane Tony Field thought it would be a good idea to try to wind me up about what might have looked like a trivial exercise. That did annoy me because I was desperate to get back to playing. Len Badger, our captain and my good mate, was aware of it and gave Field a real verbal broadside to enlighten him. The injury delayed my Blades return and I wasn't chosen for my next international appearance, under Don Revie, for almost two years.

9

DECISIONS – AND CONSEQUENCES

When we kicke● off the 1972-73 season, I suspect few supporters or players fully un●erstoo● the future ramifications of Unite●'s huge ●ecision. Wishing to be progressive, the club ousted cricket from Bramall Lane in order to build the South Stand, making the ground a four-sided football stadium. We were happily playing or watching, oblivious of how the far-reaching consequences would inevitably pan out...

There was an extra dimension to our pre-season matches because Sheffield United had been invited to participate in the Watney Cup, a domestic tournament held in south-west England. It meant that there was more of a competitive edge to the games with something to win at the end of it. We all just enjoyed playing matches and our league status made us firm favourites to lift the trophy against lower-level opposition. Fans seemed to like the idea and there were very decent attendances for all our games with more than 14,000 watching us overcome Notts County 3-0 in our opener.

Having scored a couple in that fixture, I was well up for the second against Peterborough United, but this time my contribution was very different. Presumably in an attempt to put me off my game, they kicked me to death right from the outset, and I don't just mean going over the top in tackles – they even came in at thigh height. I do have a bit of a temper and can handle myself, so the level of the attention I was getting eventually sparked retaliation when a player tried to go past me down the line. I lunged to make sure I did a good job of fouling him after only 20 minutes and was given my first ever red card.

By now I was used to a degree of rough treatment from the opposition, but this was something else and I chose to show that I wouldn't stand for it. No doubt it played into Peterborough's hands, but we were still good enough to win 4-0 with the 10 men remaining and I was still eligible for the final against Bristol Rovers three days later. It was extremely hot and we should have won, but we just couldn't find the net that day and it ended goalless with penalties set to decide the winner.

The shoot-out was a lengthy one and although Alan Woodward, Keith Eddy, myself, Billy Dearden, Eddie Colquhoun and Stewart Scullion all scored, our safer options had run out and Ted Hemsley stepped up next. His effort was more like a backpass and the goalkeeper more or less threw his cap on it. In fact, if he'd left it, the ball probably wouldn't have reached the line! We lost 7-6 on penalties, missed out on a major trophy (!) and although poor old Ted didn't get stick from us on the day, he's had enough to make up for it ever since. Don't forget to ask him about it...

Keith Eddy's penalty was literally his first kick for us after coming on as a substitute. I was really pleased when he signed after knowing him at Watford where he was without doubt one of the best players. I suppose Harris would have had a word with me about him and I would have praised his talents to the hilt.

Keith was fantastic in a back-four and although he was very comfortable in midfield as well, I believe he was brought in to play at the back eventually. I'm not joking when I say I likened him to Bobby Moore, who for me kept him out of the England team. He had so much in his arsenal – an almost flawless reader of the game, a great leader and passer, excellent vision, decent in the air. He wasn't slow, but he wasn't quick either and his reading of the game gave him a yard start. Like me, it was a yard we both bloody needed!

The young Scot Tom McAllister was a highly-promising goalkeeper who had come in at the end of the previous campaign – ahead of Hope – and went on to be ever-present that season. Despite summer recruitment being limited to Keith, expectations were high and seemed justified for the first couple of months when results, after a couple of early defeats, were promising. Then the impact of injuries to Scullion, Salmons and Eddy started to bite. Our goalscoring output – barring Dearden and Woodward – was down and I managed only one league goal.

Harris dipped into the market for a shake-up and put together an exchange deal with Cardiff City when Gil Reece and Dave Powell went back to Wales and burly striker Alan Warboys came the other way. Alan should have been the foil to Billy Deaden up top, but injuries restricted him from having a clear run at it and he failed to score in eight appearances. We really struggled in the autumn, missing some quality players all at the same time and not having the same quality replacements. No disrespect whatsoever to the squad players who always gave their all, but it was becoming apparent that we were unable to compete in the transfer market.

Inconsistency dogged us, but the arrival of Scottish striker Jim Bone in February was a real tonic – even though we lost Trevor Hockey, whose form had dipped, to Norwich City in return. Jim was a real character – a favourite with the boys – and fitted in straightaway on and off the pitch. Granted, he didn't have the greatest skill set in the world, but he was a proven goalscorer at Norwich and had a strong will to win.

Surprisingly that's not always a given quality, even in the professional game. He was tenacious in the box, brave as a lion and we didn't lose many when he and Billy were paired up. Jim – who moved to Dronfield with a few of us – liked a drink and didn't mind buying a round either.

When Trevor Hockey was left out, he didn't get back in to displace Eddy in midfield and never played for us again. It shocked our supporters because he was a fans' favourite and they still talk to me about him even today. It's easy to forget just how short a time he was with the club, such is the impression he made and the connection he had with our crowd.

He played as if he would fight to the end for them. Keith Eddy was a very different animal and very much his own man; educated, much more mature than most of us and good at darts, too. Especially in The Castle at Bradway with Badger, Colin Franks and me over half a shandy.

The reconstructed side lost just two of the final league fixtures to finish 14th and two of the games were significant for me personally. I picked up my second red card, but first in the league, when we lost 2-1 at Everton in March. I already had a yellow for a tackle that was nothing more than a 50/50 challenge really. When their winger John Connelly, I think it was, ran down his line, I thought I could just slide the ball out for a throw-in.

But he just got a toe to the ball first, dinked it over my foot and down he went. Another yellow came out, followed by the red, and I had to walk right across the pitch amid a chorus of boos from all over the stadium. I was livid because I shouldn't have been booked for the first one and the cards were within a few minutes of each other. They would be only fouls in today's game, when they are given for nothing really, but they shouldn't have been back then.

I was more pleased to be part of the United team that faced Manchester United, in what was Bobby Charlton's final match at Old Trafford. For some reason I was captain that day, so the whole occasion was a huge honour and a very emotional occasion for Bobby. I wished him all the best at the coin toss and got on with the game, which I remember very little of apart from Dearden and Eddy scoring as we won 2-1 to spoil Bobby's fairytale goodbye.

Bobby was difficult to play against because he had great control and could spray the ball about with both feet and I saw that at first hand by playing against him on many occasions. He was definitely one of my own heroes, after Greaves.

But he was never the one detailed to mark me. That was Nobby Stiles, a sort of mini-Peter Storey destroyer who could employ kicking, scratching and fouling tactics designed to put someone off his game and initiate retaliation. Nobby was like Hockey, Billy Bremner and one or two others, who were needlers. They would run through a brick wall for their teams and always spring back up if they went down. Their job was to chase an opponent all over the pitch because they were terrific man-markers. Invariably, if they did a good job on me and Woody, they would nullify us. I knew when they were coming but didn't have the speed to get away, so I had to get a pass off.

About that time there was an issue with one or two barmy fans throwing darts at games and I remember one being thrown at Old Trafford when we were there. Unbelievably scary. If we got a corner, I was more than a bit nervous and took it as quickly as possible, avoiding staying still as much as I could!

Three days after that Everton fixture came a special occasion – a hugely-deserved testimonial for Len Badger, for so long a great and dear pal of mine. The opposition were our rivals Sheffield Wednesday and to help to drum up support for it, Len bought an old banger, painted it pink with flowers on and drove it about the city. It worked because 23,000-

plus turned up – well on a par with our Division One average – to witness ex-Owl David Ford get our goal in a 1-1 draw.

Len, then not quite 27 years old, was young to be having a testimonial, but he had already done his 10 years or so and those were his best years. He had captained the club and came very close to winning an England cap at senior level. It would have been well-merited. As a ball-playing full-back who could read the game very well, he had a footballing brain rare for a defender in those days and his advice on the pitch was always first-class.

That didn't prevent Woody often winding him up by encouraging him to go on the overlap, but then not giving him the ball. "I've run f*****g 94 yards on the overlap," Len would fume, "and you never gave me the bloody ball...!"

The lads still laugh our heads off at that memory. But Len, Alan and I had a telepathy about our link-ups that genuinely were not practised; Len would feed me and Woody's timing of runs to lose his marker was fantastic, so I could use the space in behind with long passes with a bit of backspin on them. In my book the ball can't be intercepted if it is in the air, whereas a low threaded pass can be.

I was loving playing in this team in the top division and had thrown off any inhibitions I might have had off the pitch. Yes, I had always been very confident while playing football, but I had developed a personality and an image without really trying – and the United fans loved it. During the promotion season I had grown my hair and wore my shirt outside my shorts, not for affectation, but because to me it felt better with the stripes right down, almost covering the shorts. I was comfortable with it. I didn't like wearing shinpads either, but started to, especially when they became thinner, because of all the naughty stuff being dished out. I tried wearing the shirt outside my shorts for one game and thought: "This will do for me."

Those shirts were lovely, a sort of slimline fit. I didn't have a six-pack – not many of us did in those days! – but it suited me fine. I had a big build and a good physique. I certainly didn't have any fat on me and wearing the shirt as I did wasn't anything to do with making me look slimmer. I didn't risk it with England, though. I had huge respect for Sir Alf so didn't try to do it. In any event it wouldn't have looked the same; the shirts were fuller and didn't hang as nicely as United's.

As for my hair, I never liked going for a haircut so I just let it grow and ended up with what I got. I wasn't following fashion, so maybe I actually started one! Eventually I knew I had something of an image because I was often pictured in magazines such as *Shoot!* and *Football Monthly*, mainly because the England squad, including me, were frequently included.

A feature of my playing style was the ability and strength to hold off opponents by shielding them from getting a foot to the ball by using my arms, elbows and backside. You had to, especially in midfield, but the use of the 'Currie Arse,' as someone once christened it, wasn't coached. My thighs were massive, I had very strong arms and I could punch a ball almost from one side of a football pitch to the other.

Strangely I was crap at press-ups, but I often put that good punch to good use on that punchbag thing at the fairgrounds. I transformed from a relatively-slight lad at 11 to being a solid, big lad who weighed 12 stone, three pounds at 15 years old, adding three more pounds at Watford and filling out to my best playing weight of 12 stone, 11 pounds at United. It enabled me to perfect a very effective hand-off, which did seem to go unnoticed or ignored by officials. Waving to the crowd – even blowing kisses – was just a natural reaction, again because I was so confident on the pitch.

Like most footballers I was a bit of a sporting all-rounder and could have a decent go at anything with a ball. I was quite good at tennis, okay at table-tennis and had the stamina for long-ish distance running. *Superteams* was a popular programme a few years later and in 1982 I took part in a footballers-versus-athletes-versus-rugby players sporting challenge alongside Glenn Hoddle, Garth Crooks, Micky Hazzard, Mark Falco, Gary Brook, John Pratt and Petar Borota. But the only event we won was basketball, a game I hated. And in the televised *Superstars* series I was probably last in the swimming!

Cricket, above all, became a real love for me and at Sheffield United we had a few players who also were keen to play friendlies. One regular match was against Retford CC – where I was a social member – and who occasionally featured Test player Derek Randall. The Hall family were heavily involved in running the Retford Club for about 100 years and I am still close friends with them to this day.

We had Badger opening and Alan Hodgkinson and John Flynn played a bit. Ted Hemsley was also a professional cricketer, of course, playing for Worcestershire for 20 years, and Gil Reece used to join in, although his bowling attempts usually bounced twice before reaching the other end. Well, he was Welsh! In the late 1990s the players and staff resurrected the interest and began to have the odd friendly. I can recall Curtis Woodhouse being a very decent quick bowler.

My biggest assets in football were the ability to see something, an available teammate or a space, and be able to hit the ball there. My peripheral vision made me feel that I could see, as well as hear, what was happening elsewhere on the pitch and I was very lucky to have it. Once upon a time I would find it frustrating to see players being signed or picked who didn't have that gift, until I realised that my own good fortune didn't give me the right to be critical.

Indeed it gave me the platform to do my thing and I loved the crowd, who loved me in return. They could hear a lot of what went on during matches, including me incessantly shouting: "Just give me the f****** ball! It don't matter if I have somebody on me." I always wanted to win and was a bad loser, so if I didn't get enough of the ball to affect the result, I was a bit of a sulker as well.

At the end of that second season in the First Division we finished 14th, but – completely unexpectedly – I had been given something to think about. Almost straight after that Manchester United fixture at the end of April, I started getting telephone calls sounding me out about a possible move there.

The basis of what they were saying was that they wanted me to replace Bobby Charlton and in doing so I would secure my financial future. It was the summer of 1973, I was 23 years old and I have to admit that I was honoured – who wouldn't have been? Half of me thought it would be a great move, but me being me off the field, I just wasn't confident enough to deal with all that it would entail.

I was basically afraid of change and worried about the fact I might be walking into a Manchester United dressing-room as one of them. It wasn't that I lacked ambition: it was just my personality. It wasn't as if I was unhappy at the Lane, either. I adored it there, loved the blokes I played with and we were doing all right.

I had no doubt that I could compete and handle the football side but my response, as soon as they came on the phone, was to get rid of them as soon as possible. I'm sure my nervousness about the situation must have been pretty evident. The Reds had long been the club everyone looked up to and it was still an exciting prospect, but Bobby was going and George Best and Denis Law had already gone so they were a team undergoing a transition. Linda had been suffering from depression since 1971 and wouldn't have been excited about the prospect, so there was no pressure from there. But I didn't tell anybody, apart from her, because the calls would have been interpreted as 'tapping up.'

What I had not known was that Manchester United had already sounded out Sheffield United about whether or not they would be prepared to sell me. They made probably 10 calls in a couple of weeks, never mentioning figures and just talking in general about finance and the move on a simple level. It didn't do my state of mind any good. The insecure introvert off the field that I was probably made me different from other players who would just have jumped at the chance. The Reds were relegated a season later.

It's inevitable that I have looked back since and wondered what would have happened if I had made the move and it is very fanciful to assume that I would have won the trophies, caps and medals that did elude me. But there was my family's future and happiness to consider. Linda had produced Sharon – named after Sharon Tate, who by then had not been tragically lost – in 1969 and two years later came Ryan, who owes his name to actor Ryan O'Neal.

There was a reasonable chance that a move there would have affected me negatively and that would in turn have affected them for the worse, too. I wasn't chasing the money. But I was in the final year of my United contract and went in to see Harris about a new one.

I should have felt pretty much justified about doing so, knowing how much some of my England mates were on at their clubs. But for me, such a meeting was really hard. I was so uncomfortable and virtually shaking at the prospect of asking for my wage to be raised to £200 per week. Negotiating, asking for improved terms, generally playing hardball – with anybody – just wasn't in my locker at all and I never asked for more money in any of my moves.

I didn't get very far because United surprised me by deciding that I would sign a six-year contract, plus a one-year option. That would potentially take me to 30 years of age – virtually signing my life to United – and chairman Dick Wragg made promises about bringing in players of the calibre of Francis Lee and Mike Summerbee. It was an attempt to convince me that staying would be a good option because the team would be strengthened. It sounded encouraging enough to me.

The additional offer of a verbal agreement that if we went down, I would be allowed to leave seemed a bit hollow, though. I was confident that we wouldn't be relegated. And if we did, they would have had to cash in on me anyway. In effect United had come up with the offer of security rather than bigger money so, because the phone calls had now stopped, I went ahead and signed a seven-year deal.

This was just a year after my previous agreement so in two years I had advanced from £60 per week to £240. It was down to my form, winning England caps and possibly a whiff of interest from Manchester United. Or from anybody else for all that I knew. It seemed a decent outcome, but one year on Wragg sold Geoff Salmons, who was a big player for us, and didn't bring in any big names. Perhaps Dick had only mentioned Summerbee so that he and Hemsley wouldn't be able to kick lumps out of each other any more!

The manager did bring in yet another recruit from Watford, 22-year-old midfielder Colin Franks, although initially he wasn't able to maintain a place in the side. Despite a losing start which we soon put right, I was thinking that now we were established and with big players presumably on the way, we might finish in the top six. We certainly had the desire.

The problem was it might also have been the bottom six if we continued to lack that top-team mentality to make winning games the priority rather than continuing to play our own way. Harris didn't attempt to change that and, to be fair, I didn't even think about it. I just wanted to play, win and worry about my wife.

As a team we were relatively unsophisticated – tactically – compared with others, refusing to sit on slender leads or worry about the opposition. For example, if we played Chelsea, we would put a man on Alan Hudson, but didn't do that against Arsenal with Alan Ball because he was regarded as a five-yard player and not perceived as equally dangerous. But Huddy would go past you anyway.

Generally we didn't make special plans or modify our game, although we did have football thinkers such as Ted, Len, Colin Addison in his time and Keith Eddy, who could change things and push people about when they felt it necessary. After the losing start against Burnley and Wolves, we won at Chelsea – Woody and me getting the goals – and were then at home to Arsenal on a Tuesday night. It was about 18 months since Bally sat on the ball during their 5-0 win and although we had beaten them since, there was a lingering grudge in the air from some fans for what they saw as a humiliation.

We always felt we could win at home and the match couldn't have gone any better for us – we were four up in 17 minutes. We added a fifth before, late in the match at the away end, just outside their penalty area, I repaid the compliment and sat on the ball... in front of Alan Ball. It was more appropriate than in recent wins against them because we were five goals clear, and it was nice to do it for our fans as much as anything else.

Bally was great. He appreciated it, smiling and saying he'd have one for me next time. He was a lovely bloke and at Highbury – only one week later, during their 1-0 victory – he kept his word, putting his foot on the ball and doing up his laces right in front of me!

Our season began to falter when two players sustained fractures in home fixtures within one month of each other; Keith Eddy hurt his collarbone against Norwich and Tom McAllister damaged his leg against Manchester City. John Connaughton replaced Tom, but Keith had become very influential and was a bigger loss because of it. We did seem to have a spate of injuries, especially cartilages, within a six-to-nine-month period and an average set of December results led to United ending their search for a younger, tracksuit manager.

John Harris moved upstairs again, a switch away from the frontline which might have suited him because I felt he had just about had enough. The appointment of the man who replaced him caught me by surprise. He had given me my start in league football at Watford, but also had upset me occasionally. Ken Furphy had done well at Watford and later at Blackburn Rovers, building his reputation within the game.

It was five years now since he had sold me and I was well-established, doing my bit as an integral part of the team. But despite what I was achieving, with both club and country, I was concerned that the way I played, being a bit arrogant on the ball and blowing kisses to the crowd, wouldn't be his cup of tea.

I might have been a big favourite with the lads and the fans, but the potential for friction was eating at me enough to seek the advice of Len Badger. I usually turned to Badge if I had a problem and he advised me to seek Furphy out to talk things over and bury the hatchet, so Linda and I went to his house one Sunday afternoon. Ken and I had known each other since I was 16 years old and it went okay, but I wasn't confident that things would change as far as his attitude towards me was concerned. The meeting turned out to be largely a waste of time.

On the field I just got on with it as I always did, enjoying playing and being able to put any other misgivings out of my mind for the 90 minutes. Any new manager coming in would try to gee the players up and that was no different with Ken. I was up for that, but we lost at Ipswich in the FA Cup third round and won only six more matches that season, so there was no immediate improvement.

Training with Cec Coldwell had largely been forwards-versus-defence, but the manager was very much his own man and wanted to do things differently. Furphy was still in his early forties, very confident and wanted to do well, so he did most of the coaching himself. That wasn't typical of many managers then. In fairness he inherited a situation with very little available in terms of transfer funds, which must have been difficult for him. The big money incomings I was led to expect were never, I suspect, going to materialise, so incomers were at a relatively-modest level in terms of fees; Terry Garbutt and Tony Field from Blackburn were his former players, plus goalkeeper Jim Brown from Chesterfield. Both those clubs were in lower divisions than we were and although I appreciate well enough that there can be value for money in that approach, we weren't investing to the level we needed.

I had played up-front with Terry at Watford. He was an honest professional, essentially a workhorse, but a nice finisher and good in the air. He wasn't a bad buy to have in the squad, but the new lads were never going to be enough to get us higher. Jim wasn't the tallest, but he was agile, brave and a fantastic shot-stopper who went on to represent Scotland. Field could be quite tricky sometimes, but he wasn't consistent enough and if I'm being honest, he was a horrible little shit who wound our players up.

I experienced it when I was getting fit after my cartilage operation, suggesting I was lazy. Badge had a real go, telling him to leave me alone, and in my view, Tony wasn't a nice or likeable person. Maybe, like most managers, Furphy wanted players around him he was comfortable with and often went for the tried and tested.

I suppose he would say that he added what he could to deepen the squad with experience and he still had a settled back-four. But even though it wasn't all his fault, it was a policy that would lead to stagnation. With money so tight, Scullion and Bone had been moved on for quite small fees, which didn't go anywhere near offsetting what was shelled out for Furphy's three new signings. Worse was to come when Geoff Salmons had to be sacrificed later in the summer before the new campaign. A season that began with hope and ambition ended with the team finishing one place higher than 12 months previously, and under a new manager.

Sammy had been fantastic for us and then did a great job for Stoke, but his departure affected me – I really rated him and he got on well with everybody. Geoff was a big part of our team because of what he could give you with his speed and stamina and I can liken him only to Paul Madeley for the way he was up and down the pitch for the whole game. Nobody could keep pace with his long strides and he'd get between seven and 10 good crosses in every game – even though I always wanted more!

The changes in personnel during the previous couple of years didn't really affect the camaraderie that existed among those of us who had been around for a while. Although Woody and Eddie Colquhoun were not the going out in a group type, Badger, Franks, Keith Eddy and I would go out for a drink and play darts and on most Monday nights, if we didn't have a Tuesday night game, some of us headed into town and to the Penny Farthing nightclub.

We were virtually idols to some of the punters, but we were pals with them as well, so they behaved themselves instead of wanting to fight or stitch us up. I do feel a bit sorry for today's stars who earn millions, but are so restricted in what they can do and where they go. We weren't playing Jack the Lad and our wives and girlfriends would come with us to the Penny Farthing on Saturdays after games. That's how close-knit we were.

10

FALLING JUST SHORT

When the 1974/75 season began, I wasn't in the best frame of mind about our prospects. Ken Furphy was now established after half a season in charge, but I still had reservations about our relationship and we hadn't done great during pre-season matches in Poland and in the Texaco Cup games. But two other issues were more pressing to me; further lack of investment and an injury.

After finishing 13th, there was little justification for increased expectations. We'd made just one signing, David Bradford, and it was another low-key one from the manager's previous club, Blackburn Rovers. At £10,000 David was regarded as a utility player on the Billy Dearden scale of investment and a far cry from the big signings I had been promised. But that wasn't David's fault and he became a great friend, a lovely bloke who enjoyed a laugh. And he could play.

For me he wasn't just a utility player: he was better than that. He was a busy little midfielder and despite not being a regular, he was capable of putting in a performance. It was obvious he had a lot of respect for my ability – in fact, he seemed almost in awe sometimes – but it worked when he played in the engine room alongside Keith Eddy and me. Eventually at the end of the season he even slotted in very effectively at left-back when Ted Hemsley was out. It was a creditable effort, considering that he had no previous experience in that position.

The injury had been sustained the previous March during a 1-0 win at Manchester City. My cartilage was damaged, but for some reason I carried on and then played the following two games before having surgery to remove it. I must have been an idiot. I was now trying to get fit properly and build the thigh muscle up again with exercises, using a bag with weights in.

It was taking a long time and I probably should have done more on it during the summer because, when pre-season came, I still hadn't regained the muscle. I was playing and giving 100 per cent as usual, even with maybe 50 per cent fitness.

Two draws and a defeat wasn't a great start, but five straight wins, including one in the League Cup, got us back on track. Inconsistency was to be our bugbear across the winter months, but it was a characteristic of the whole division that year. Teams were beating each other with no real pattern emerging, exemplified by Derby going on to become champions with only 53 points. That was a low total compared with a normal season and our cause was definitely made harder by Billy Dearden being restricted to just 31 starts and eight goals.

Although that was up on the previous season, it proved just how much injuries were now affecting him. Before that he had been a real talisman for us, consistent in his appearances and goals. No-one could ever accuse Billy of shirking because he so often played through pain when he should not have even been on the pitch. It's easy to make a case that his absence was probably key, because so many matches were tight affairs that we might have edged if he had been playing and match-fit.

And realistically that was also the case for me as well that season, with six goals in 29 appearances. Playing through pain is very much a personal issue and I am convinced some players get themselves out of the firing line because of that. I am talking about making the most of injuries or illness because they are not totally confident, sometimes even when they are fully fit. Perhaps it occurs even more today with the big wages top players are on. We were on appearance money, so not playing hit us in the pocket.

However, we did have 10 players who played more than 30 league games each so there was at least some consistency in our teamsheets. The ever-reliable Alan Woodward top-scored with 12 goals, while Tony Field was also an ever-present and contributed 11, the best of which was a wonder goal he will always be remembered for against Ipswich.

He actually picked the ball up in the centre=circle and went on a mazy run, beating opponent after opponent to score a fabulous goal in front of the Kop. His ball control generally wasn't always that good, but obviously he made a decent contribution overall.

You could hardly claim that the FA Cup was a highlight, but we actually won a game this time! Billy and I scored the goals against Bristol City, but we then reverted to type and lost 4-1 away to Aston Villa. I never enjoyed much success there with United, but Villa were a division below us – albeit doing well – and the game was only a week after we had beaten Spurs 3-1. The cup defeat was at the end of January and we then bizarrely managed to gather some momentum in the league, losing only twice more by the time the season was all over. We lost only once in March and began to think we might be in with a chance of finishing high enough to qualify for a place in Europe. Imagine that!

One of the wins in that month was against West Ham United. I got two of the goals in our 3-2 victory and I am often asked if my second was my greatest ever. Well, it's up there and I'll diplomatically leave others to judge – and plenty did because the fixture was one of those featured on *Match of the Day* that evening.

The first was virtually a tap-in after the ball had hit a post and rolled along the goal-line, while the second began in our own half. A headed clearance from our defence went towards the scaffolding that held up the TV gantry at the side of the pitch. I made a block tackle on the sideline and when the ball didn't go out of play, exchanged passes with Woody who continued up the wing.

With nobody really reacting to me, I just really ambled upfield with the ball until I got close to the penalty area. Kevin Lock was in my way; he was a good, experienced player and kept backing off, which defenders often did against me because they didn't want to commit and get beaten. I was now on the edge of their box and shaped to shoot. Lock covered it, so I checked back and switched the ball on to my other foot. The same thing happened again as I looked to find space for the shot and I was waiting for Lock to buy a dummy and give me the space I was looking for. It became a game of cat and mouse with him; nothing and no-one else seemed to be involved as the game stood still.

Lock bought the dummy and the opening was there, so I shot with my left foot. It wasn't scuffed, but it wasn't the best contact either and that did for Mervyn Day in the Hammers goal, who was probably wrong-footed as the ball rolled pretty slowly past him and into the net. I didn't go in for the elaborate, pre-planned sort of celebrations they do today, or even try a Mick Channon windmill action. I just stood there, blowing kisses to the crowd and waiting for everyone to jump on me.

At that moment, BBC commentator John Motson was shouting into his microphone. "A quality goal from a quality player," he said and that iconic phrase has followed us both around ever since. I still hear it being quoted today and many fans regard it as my best-ever goal. I don't mind. I'm just glad people remember them and I'm happy to let them have their say.

I scored about 80 times in my career and probably should have had a lot more goals, but I wasn't selfish enough. My first instinct usually was to look for passes. That hadn't been the case when I had got that one from distance against Ray Clemence and Liverpool, nor was it a few weeks after that West Ham game when we hammered Leicester 4-0.

We were already two up when I cut in and hit a left-footer which skipped across the turf like a rocket, giving Mark Wallington no chance. I remember a goal earlier in my United career that gave me special pleasure, at Stamford Bridge while the new stand was being built. It was a lovely goal, scored against Peter Bonetti to boot, and was typical because so many of my goals were from long-range – including three for England.

We see numerous goals these days which are skilfully bent into the net, but times and conditions have changed. New skills – and footballs – have evolved that enable controlled swerve, which we never thought about doing because the ball was so much heavier and difficult to bend out of the mud. The standing foot has to be stable for a start and, for a big part of the season, that could be a problem.

I concentrated on hitting the whole target, leaving some margin for error which meant that if I was too accurate, the ball would go straight down the goalkeeper's throat. But I doubt Woody did the same because he hit the woodwork so often – he was a natural goalscorer and had the ability to aim for wherever he wanted.

In my early days I scored my share, but gradually got so much pleasure from sliding the ball 10 yards to make a chance for others or hitting 60 or 70-yard balls pretty accurately. When that worked, I was hardly likely then to get in the box to score anyway and I was never encouraged to create fewer and score more. So the balance was about right, I guess.

For me Jimmy Greaves was the greatest goalscorer ever, a Lionel Messi-type if you like, because he never seemed to shoot from range, even though he had a great left foot. Jimmy was a great dribbler, too, but was at his deadliest when he was sniffing around the box for half-chances.

If the West Ham goal was a career-defining moment from a purely footballing point of view, an incident eight games later made even bigger headlines. And I'm talking about on a world level. It did occur on the pitch, but the ball wasn't even in play at the time when Leicester City came to Bramall Lane. We were destined to win 4-0, an extremely important victory for us, but the result has been largely forgotten. The incident definitely hasn't.

Alan Birchenall was big, blond and charismatic and had enjoyed a successful start to his career with United before being sold for £100,000 almost 10 years earlier. As United's other star forward, Mick Jones, had also gone for the same fee at about the same time, the Blades fans were disgruntled about it, to say the least. But the moves had happened before I joined the club and my dealings with Alan had been very limited; just a few games in opposition. That was to change and in this fixture I got to know him well. Very well.

The game was nothing out of the ordinary until he and I competed fairly for the ball which went out of play at the away end. The challenge saw us both fall head over heels at the same time and we ended up sitting side by side. No animosity. Everything was just fine. Then Alan, with a big smile on his face, looked at me and said: "Give us a kiss, TC." Just like that, completely spontaneously, for a bit of fun. So I did, and a photographer captured it perfectly; two young, fair-haired, heterosexual footballers sharing an intimate moment.

It was, of course, completely innocent, but when the picture appeared in the papers, news of the 'moment' took off and in modern parlance it went 'global.' Perhaps it was a good job that social media hadn't been invented or we might have been tempted to pack football in and forge new careers!

I don't know how much the picture was sold for, but it was in magazines in Germany and, according to Birchy, won sports photograph of the year. I'm not sure if it was the first published snap of a kiss on the lips by two blokes, but Alan has a massive reproduction of it at Leicester City where he now works. I didn't begin to worry until our sneaky kiss started to appear in German porn magazines!

Since then it has been a constant source of amusement. It's always brought up at events where either of us appear and, based on how many people have told me they saw it live in the years since, about 350,000 people must have been at the match! We've done the kiss for charity as well, on Leicester's pitch and in a hotel, and all for good causes. I once drove to Junction 28 on the M1 to meet a photographer who was doing a picture of me for a feature on the kiss, but all the proceeds went to Birchy's charities and not mine. And *he* got a bloody MBE for charity fundraising!

Seriously, Birchy is a big mate now and we stay in touch even though we wouldn't appear to have any connection in terms of personalities. We've done question-and-answer sessions together and get on well even though I'm quiet and he's an extrovert. I try to get a word in occasionally, but he's so outgoing – and he's flippin' good at it, too.

***

With four games to go we were on the fringes of the group vying for a tilt at Europe, so wins were essential. Everton were one and were above us in the table, so a visit to Goodison Park was not for the faint-hearted, especially when they had taken a 2-0 lead. But we showed our spirit and Keith Eddy and Billy Dearden brought us level.

Now it was all to play for, but having equalised, our tails were up and we were going for it with more menace than they were. Then Len Badger hit a long ball down the right for Tony Field to bring down and put into the box. But it wasn't just a hopeful cross because I – with my phenomenal speed and workrate! – had gone past defenders and was in space. Just enough space to let the ball come across my body before I larruped it into the net from about 12 yards out for the winner. It was a big game for both teams and when you win it that way, you just don't forget it.

After drawing at Chelsea and hammering West Ham, it was all down to the finale at St. Andrew's to decide our fate. We went into it knowing that we had a chance of qualifying for Europe, for the first time in the club's history, but we drew 0-0 in a real anti-climax. I don't remember much about the game and worse still, I apparently cost us by missing a sitter. Or so Badger always told me anyway.

As it happened, it wouldn't have mattered because a win wouldn't have been enough because of other results. But I do recall feeling the worst I had ever felt on a coach after a game; we knew we had to win and hadn't. I recall Furphy saying some things that would have contributed to my mood although he would undoubtedly have been disappointed as well.

Ken often picked out something I had done which he reckoned had contributed to a loss. At St. Andrew's it was about a long throw to our near post. I knew that if I tried to head it the ball would have skimmed off my head and been a problem, like a flick on. So I ducked my head and put my heel up behind me to try and get the ball away from the danger zone. I think it went for a corner, but he thought I had tried to be too clever and showing off, which definitely had not been the case.

The following day I could have been celebrating qualifying for Europe, but instead I was making only my fifth reserve appearance for the Blades at home to West Brom. It was the reserves' final game of the season as well and they needed to win by two clear goals to avoid having to apply for re-election, so Mick Speight, Tony Field and I all volunteered to play. We won 3-0, Field scored two penalties and at least I was playing football again and not mulling over the 90 minutes from the day before.

We finished sixth in the top-flight, above some very big clubs including Leeds, who were reigning champions, Spurs, Arsenal and Manchester City, so it was a good season, especially considering I was so angry at the beginning. It was the club's highest finish for 14 years and quite rightly Furphy, who had a big ego, would have loved it because he did about three times more coaching than Harris.

The reason we clashed was because he wanted a "bit more" out of me, whatever *that* was, but I must have been doing okay for the team to do as well as it did. If I am being honest, I think he probably got more out of us that season than Harris would have been able to achieve at that stage of his life. Furphy tightened the team up and put more defensive structure across the team. He might not have been the most popular, but there were no grudges when we went on the pitch; we all wanted to win and do well.

He had taken the captaincy off me and given it to Keith Eddy which, after my original hurt about the decision, wasn't a problem. Keith was very capable, highly-respected and was probably a better skipper than I was. I didn't order people about, preferring to just demand the ball to my feet all the time. My theory was that I could do more with it than anybody else in the team.

All skilful players have to have a certain amount of arrogance to want the ball continually and mine was really just self-confidence on the pitch.

I simply loved playing and training, as anyone who has played with me would confirm, and some players just need to play every week, such as 30-goal-a-season strikers.

We were not a one-man team by any means, but in midfield you are always in the thick of it and I attracted more clog and attention because of my ability and influence. Some teams put a man-marker on me which would make my job harder, so it could have been a bit off the mark occasionally for a critic to say: "Oh, Currie didn't fancy it today." In reality it might have been more a case of my marker doing his job well on the day.

I know I was a languid-looking player and that could give the impression that I wasn't up for it, but I wasn't fat or work-shy. I was well-built and stocky; not a sprinter, but I had loads of stamina. When I look at old film clips, I wasn't the most elegant mover, but I suppose I got away with it because of my ability. Hitting 60 or 70-yard passes was difficult and sometimes I'd admire them; you couldn't chase them up and down the field as well all the time because it was hard work on those pitches.

Calling me lazy was an easy label that some latched on to, but I would strongly argue against that. My favourite response is to cite an England game against Switzerland in 1975, the only cap I won under Don Revie. During his pre-match Press conference he said about me: "He's got to work." So that's what I went out and did. I was running about all over, chasing passes and hardly had a kick. So why pick a team with players who had specific characteristics and skill sets and then not use them?

United's system of play suited me and I enjoyed playing 4-4-2 or 4-3-3, so much so that if I'd become a manager, I think I would have played 4-3-3. But the third player would invariably have to be someone like Geoff Salmons, who could get back to defend as well. The game is different these days and teams can play 4-5-1 or 3-5-2 because of the quality of the pitches – but it works only if they use players with the football intelligence and mentality to do it.

11

DON'T CALL ME DON

My international career under Sir Alf Ramsey had really taken root during 1973 when a run of starting berths ha• me feeling justifie• in hoping that I was being more and more regarded as a regular. It was a period in which I was approaching my prime, pretty highly-regar•e• across the country in the top-flight and very happy. At least with my career ...

I didn't know that what followed would be a couple of seasons of wildly contrasting fortunes at club level, closely accompanied by a change of the guard at England level that affected me in a big way. When the two years were up, I would be facing a change of club and the possible end to my international career.

It began in March 1974, with the dispensing of Alf Ramsey whose respect I had earned, and meant that all the squad were starting again to impress a new man. It was no-one's fault that the cartilage operation ruled me out of the chance to stay in the side while another permanent manager was installed. But when one was, I barely had a look-in.

My final cap under Sir Alf had been against Italy in March 1973. He was only there for one more international, which I missed because of injury, and then he was dispensed with. Joe Mercer enjoyed seven matches, basically in the close season, as caretaker boss, all of which I missed while still recovering. Stand-in bosses were not uncommon, especially if a target was already in charge somewhere else and couldn't be obtained in a hurry.

Joe's appointment was greeted with a fair amount of bonhomie across the country. Football followers loved him, as they did Terry Venables years later, for the expansive game he wanted his teams to play, largely due to what he did at Manchester City with Malcolm Allison. Although I didn't really know either, I wished I'd had the chance to play for them because it sounded a lot of fun. That said, although Frank Worthington, Keith Weller and Stan Bowles were given a go, players such as the elegant Martin Dobson were given quite a few more caps and weren't exactly flair players.

During the Mercer period the Press were very sure that the FA were torn between Brian Clough and Revie to be offered the job on a permanent basis. With Bill Shankly winding down his career at Liverpool, those two were probably regarded as the best club managers in the country and quite rightly boasted admirers right across the board.

I think the FA went for Revie because they were more scared of Clough and his reputation for straight talking. Don was canny enough to give a 'good' interview, whereas the impudent and irreverent Clough would just have been Clough! Unfortunately for me, months earlier, I had done an interview with someone who was asking me who would be the best candidate and I had gone head over heels for Clough. I don't know if Don had seen and remembered that interview, which might explain what was to come. Subsequent events lead me to think that he was a man who held grudges. After all, he was to leave a lot of good players out.

I still had an open mind about what my prospects would be like when I fully recovered and was available for selection. The following season, Don's first in charge, Sheffield United had a great campaign in the top-flight and I was playing well, but England team selection didn't come my way. In all honesty I think I could reluctantly accept that I just wasn't his type of player. It happens and the fact that I only ever encountered that when he managed England shouldn't be enough for me to feel as strongly as I do. There were other England candidates, mostly a handful of forwards and midfielders known collectively as 'the mavericks,' who shared the opinion that they didn't get a fair crack of the whip.

Players such as Charlie George or Alan Hudson, who had the skill and courage to try different things to create or score, regularly thrilled the fans but weren't considered worth the risk by Revie and considering the ability they had, and the popularity they enjoyed, their international careers amounted to very little.

Not being picked is part of the game and getting the hump about it doesn't go down well, especially if it comes from individuals who want to entertain and are used to public adulation. Fans don't want the boat rocked by players who could destabilise their clubs. But it's different at international level, because there are fewer fixtures in which to work a way back into the team and you can be out in the cold for a long time. Granted, selfishness – or at least personal pride – does come into it as well. But in Don Revie's reign there was enough media and supporter support for the mavericks to be more involved, to suggest that we had a point. But Don was not for budging.

You could say that is fair enough, that he had a job to do and that he stuck to his principles. What frustrated us more than anything was the way he dealt with us and, as things turned out, his record in charge didn't seem to reflect the wealth of talent he had available to him. During his England tenure there was a raft of players who regularly got fans off their seats with excitement and who might have turned tight international fixtures by a piece of brilliance. But they were allowed only the briefest look-ins for their country.

There were call-ups to the squad, but when it came to trusting them in the team... I don't think so. It was in my honest opinion a decision that robbed the English public of watching a team they would have enjoyed representing them and who might have caused problems to the best of oppositions. All international players are 'good' players, but winning games often boils down to individuals producing something extra special. Players such as Alan Hudson, Peter Osgood, Rodney Marsh, Frank Worthington, Stan Bowles. But Revie appeared to believe that workmanlike, organised performances were what was needed to beat the world's best.

What I still find intriguing is that although his fabulous Leeds United team had those characteristics in spades, its success was also a tribute to the ability and personality of the players. That team was functional, ruthless and efficient, but it would be doing them a disservice if they were the only words you think of when you consider Billy Bremner, Johnny Giles, Eddie Gray, Allan Clarke, Peter Lorimer, Mick Jones and so on. Brilliant players with skill in abundance.

Unquestionably Don Revie has to be given credit for putting that bunch of players together. He created an unbreakable bond and I am left in little doubt when I speak to the lads who played under him that he was, to them, a great manager they would always revere. I can't argue with that and wouldn't wish to diminish his Leeds legacy. But I wasn't part of it and can judge it only on my own experience, which could never be described as memorable or even one of progression. His man-management certainly didn't appear suited to that stage.

Revie's success with Leeds undoubtedly weighed heavily in the FA's thinking when they decided that he was the man to reproduce what he had achieved there. He at least had experience of European club football and his Leeds team had acquitted themselves very well in that company. At that stage, still at Sheffield United, I had realistic hopes that I would be given the opportunity to reclaim the place I had established under Alf. But I couldn't have been more wrong.

Despite being regularly named in Revie's squads, it wasn't until his ninth fixture that I was selected, against Switzerland in September 1975 – the only time in his 29 internationals in charge that I was capped. Even being transferred to his beloved Leeds nearly a year later didn't convince him of my credentials. Leeds were a physically hard side, but also one of the best teams in the world. They could really play. I was envious of their success and had played against them many times, so Revie must have been well aware of what sort of midfielder I was. A season later Sheffield United had a dismal dive towards relegation and I probably wasn't playing that well so it was becoming clear that he didn't fancy me one bit. An episode when I was on the bench against Portugal at Lisbon's Stadium of Light in November confirmed my fears that the manager had an issue with me.

During the first half I began feeling unwell. It got progressively worse, so quickly that at half-time I went to the toilet and threw up. Don must have thought I had been on the piss and although I went back on the bench, not surprisingly I didn't get on. The fact was that I had an appendix problem. We stayed overnight and the England backroom team refused to let me be operated on over there. They gave me an injection in my backside and we flew home the next day with me lying over three seats and air hostesses looking after me by the dozen. It may sound great, but it really wasn't.

Back in a hotel in London I had another injection in the same place and was put straight into Revie's car for him to take me back to Sheffield. It was a bumpy ride all the way up and I was in agony, screaming for treatment. The appendix must have been close to bursting by the time he dropped me off at the old Royal Hospital in Sheffield, where I was eventually operated on. I always wondered if Don had believed me, even after the problem was diagnosed and my appendix was removed!

On another occasion I went to the toilet at the team hotel before we were to board the coach for a game. It took just a little bit longer than I thought, but when I got outside the coach had gone, on Don's instructions; apparently to teach me a lesson. The hotel told me that it was waiting round the corner, just far enough for me to panic a bit and get the message. All right, it's a relatively minor discretion and punctuality is important, but I didn't have a bad reputation and to me it was another blot on my CV.

So it was something of a surprise to finally be picked for the starting 11 against Switzerland in September 1975. I don't know what prompted it. Maybe it was something to do with media and fan pressure after the Blades' high-placed finish a few months before. Whether the clamour was justified or not, Don didn't seem the type to bow to it.

During his interviews leading up to the game I hated hearing Revie talking about me needing to show him that I could work hard. Of course I had to go through the motions of agreeing with him during my own interviews when asked about it, but it seemed unnecessary pressure and expectation on someone whose career had been built on being creative and bringing other players into the game.

The predictable outcome was that I ran my knackers off, but never had a kick in the 2-1 friendly win in Basel. Friendlies never really are friendly, especially if you are trying to win a place in the team and, as was usually the case, Revie never said anything to me after the game. I didn't think I'd had a good one and that was confirmed by the fact that he continued putting me in his squads, but nothing beyond that. That piece I did with the journalist Michael Morgan, in which I had championed Clough as the next England manager, was an honest opinion shared by many. But might it have cost me a few caps?

The situation became a really frustrating one and I remember a qualifier in the Czech Republic when I watched the game from the stands, not even on the bench. It was foggy, I wasn't playing and we had to stay over an extra day because of the weather. I was frightened of flying, just wanted to get home and it was still foggy when we did fly back. My international break seemed as bleak as the weather and it showed me where I was in the pecking-order.

Revie never spoke to me about the situation and I wouldn't have raised it to clarify a situation I really couldn't understand. My club role was to run the game and bring others into it and I really regretted running around for him during that one international instead of playing my game. Maybe if I had, I would have made an impression and improved my prospects even under this manager. I couldn't believe he wouldn't at least give me and players such as Alan Hudson a little run with the freedom to replicate our club form. It still shocks me that he didn't want any of us players who could keep the ball; that was what was needed and he had that at Leeds.

Once, at somewhere like Bisham Abbey during a squad training session, he got six of us in a crescent shape in front of him for a word. There was Frank Worthington, Rodney Marsh, Charlie George, Stan Bowles, Alan Hudson and me and he came out with words to the effect of: "None of you figure in my plans." That was hard to hear – we were regarded as the biggest talents in the country!

It must have been quite early in his reign because it still came as a bit of a shock and when we talked about it afterwards, we were pretty hostile in our thoughts towards him. It's a wonder that no-one from such a gifted group of individuals thought it worthwhile confronting Revie about what was going on. He seemed determined to look for a more functional midfielder in the mould of Brian Talbot, Martin Dobson or Trevor Cherry, who was admittedly a great defender. But they weren't really creative and although Talbot was a box-to-box player, he wasn't as effective as someone such as Hudson.

Don did like Gerry Francis, a fantastic player with great vision and passing ability, and made him captain. Gerry was injury-prone because of a bad back, but deserved to be in the squad and probably as captain. Revie surely had to pick somebody with creative ability who could really play and balance the team. Instead he often turned to Dobbo, who liked to play one-twos but wasn't my cup of tea, to do what we needed at that level. Let me make it clear; my criticism is definitely not of the players – more of the manager's refusal to trust a few others.

He had assembled some of the best players in the country when he was at Leeds United, but I don't know how much he had to do with them becoming as good as they were. I don't recall him doing much tactically with England, although there really was so little time then to do much other than set-plays. Most of the time it seemed to be all meetings and dossiers and he wasn't popular with many of the players; the fact that he eventually quit England didn't endear him any further.

There was this funny paradox going on with me – I always looked forward to being called up, but there was also anxiety about meeting up again. I didn't have enemies, apart from one or two of the lads who might have thought I was a bit arrogant on the field. Most recognised that wasn't the real me: it was merely self-confidence. I just wasn't like that off the pitch. In club games Emlyn Hughes was always calling me names and trying to wind me up, but that was maybe just the Liverpool way to get at teams. It was often: "Stop TC and you win the game" sort of stuff and most of us did it at times. I was okay with that; it was par for the course and wasn't really personal.

I think Revie lost it when he switched from club to international football and failed to adapt. Introducing what he was used to with Leeds – carpet bowls and bingo in our downtime, with the incessant dossiers to read – I didn't personally like. I'd want to be in my room watching telly in those days. He never seemed to have a settled team, which is not always a manager's fault, but it is a big handicap on the national stage when games don't come thick and fast.

Picking the wrong players and failing to get the best out of everyone was his responsibility, though. Alan Hudson was hugely talented and it was a crime he won only two caps in successive matches, both in 1975. After starring in a 2-0 win over West Germany, he was retained for a 5-0 thrashing of Cyprus – and was never picked again!

Revie didn't manage to qualify for the big tournaments in his three years in charge and there was no discernible progress made during his appointment. Those years were wasted by a man who probably couldn't handle the task. That can happen, but it doesn't excuse the way he went about it – maybe unwittingly preventing the development of what I believe might have been a hell of an England national team. We were set back for years and some careers never blossomed at that level because of his intransigence, which at times seemed to border on selfishness and arrogance.

One evening a few years ago during a question-and-answer session, I was asked about Don and my own experiences with him. It must have come over as a slagging session – especially to Revie's son Duncan, who happened to be sitting in the front row. Naturally he wasn't happy, but I felt I had to tell the truth as I saw it and I know the other 'mavericks' who were glad to see him leave the job felt the same.

It was ironic that the Press, like the public, seemed to love that little group of misfits, mainly because we talked to journalists such as Jeff Powell and Steve Curry whom we could trust and who had sympathy with us. We understood that in those days teams couldn't play two of us in midfield together, but things have changed since then. Barcelona are, I concede, an extreme example, but they incorporated Andrés Iniesta, Xavi, Lionel Messi, Neymar and others into their style of play without restricting themselves to just one of them in the team at once. And they didn't tackle!

When I think back to how things went wrong for Revie, I remember the very beginning just after his appointment when about 80 or so players were invited to a Manchester hotel, so he could formally introduce himself to those most likely to be picked in future squads. I was sitting next to Emlyn Hughes in the front row, the both of us interested in what he was going to say and really wanting to hear things that would excite us about playing for him. "Any questions, lads?" the new manager asked. Emlyn started to ask one.

"Well, Don..." he began. Emlyn didn't get any further before he was shut down.

"Don't call me Don," Revie replied. "It's boss or Mr. Revie to you."

Emlyn was the current captain of England! He, like the rest of us, used to call Sir Alf Ramsey – a World Cup winner, a knight of the realm, England's most successful manager – Alf. If such an intensely private and focused individual as Alf could accept that level of familiarity, did Revie's rejection of it suggest arrogance? Or possibly self-doubt that he could work with these players without needing to remind them just who was in charge? Things were certainly going to be different under him.

I have frequently wondered how my own career would have gone if Don had not taken the England job and remained at Leeds in 1974. It seems extremely likely that had he been there two years later, he wouldn't have pursued me to join him at Elland Road. I would probably have gone to another club and someone else would have been England boss... and my international career might have been very different. Apologies for the overused cliché but, as Jimmy Greaves famously said: "It's a funny old game."

12

A SHATTERING DECLINE

Since that sixth-place high point I have often won•ere• about why Sheffiel•
United did so well and, even more intriguingly, why it all went so badly wrong
just a few months later. We did exceed expectations – and maybe that blinded
the club as to what needed doing?

At the time I had been a bit taken aback by Ted Hemsley and Len Badger's view that in some ways we had just got lucky and finished higher than we should. But they are not daft and I eventually saw the wisdom in their reasoning. It had been a really open division; we were basically a mid-table team, and no more than that. Numerous teams had inconsistent results, including us, but we had a great spirit. It was a team effort with a few highlights to get us up there.

Our squad was small and shallow and another couple of quality players might have made the difference. But it didn't help that the board didn't feel they could invest on the scale required, because of the commitment to paying for the South Stand at Bramall Lane. It was too simplistic to say that the board lacked ambition. They just weren't financially equipped to buy the players we needed to make us real contenders. I don't see shame in that. It's just the way it was.

My feeling at the time was that this may be as good as it gets. The team was ageing and although that didn't seem to be a problem when we were out there playing, subsequent feeling among us suggests that may have been the case. A large nucleus of the team had been together for four or five years and some of the lads brought in during that time hadn't made the team any better. Naively I was still hoping that we would buy upgrades, that clever planning was taking place to oversee a gradual turnover of players to maintain a good average age and make steady improvement. But then again I am as good with the benefit of hindsight as anyone else.

Talking of strategic planning, was it a good idea to follow the season immediately with six games in a two-week period on the other side of the world? We went to New Caledonia, finishing on June 7, and then started pre-season friendlies in Tunisia on July 20. Without wanting to sound churlish, after being shown the world and having some great experiences doing it, 18 flights in 21 days wasn't great rest and preparation for a fresh start. The financial benefit to the club must have been very influential in the decision. I understand to a point that books had to be balanced, but I'm also convinced that the tours took a lot out of us.

I regarded end-of-season trips after long, hard campaigns as jolly-ups, but on this occasion we had one game in Kuwait, three in New Zealand and two in New Caledonia, just off New Zealand. There were loads of flights, hours of sitting in airport lounges – and I didn't even like flying. But Len, Tom McAlister and I did get a bit of unscheduled time off when the three of us were chucked out of Kuwait the day after we arrived because we had stamped passports from going to Israel the year before. Why that didn't apply to several other of the lads was a mystery to us, but we were actually deported to Bombay as a result and missed the game in Kuwait.

The whole thing was eventually sorted out diplomatically and the rest of the lads joined us three days later. But the three of us had already enjoyed a three-day break in a fantastic hotel, the Taj Mahal – regarded as one of the best in the world. It is known as the Gateway of India and has a big monument with an arch which is regularly seen in films. As a result there were sightseers outside constantly as well as numerous beggars.

We were actually very fortunate to stay there because back then there couldn't have been many suitable hotels for cosseted Westerners. Seeing the squalor was a sobering experience and we hardly went out of the Taj. In fairness we rarely had to. It had five restaurants and we were basically in paradise! I'll never forget the night we went to the hotel's nightclub. There were just the three of us in it, repeatedly asking to listen to *Smoke on the Water* by Deep Purple.

All that is not to say that we would have wanted to miss the Kuwait fixture although we were told afterwards that the lads didn't sweat over there – the sun is so hot that perspiration dries up before it even comes out. Alan Woodward and Billy Dearden were the piss-takers who took the mickey out of us when we all met up again, but that soon stopped when they learned where we had stayed. They were quite envious, especially considering they had been in a 'no-alcohol' country in Kuwait!

That was a long trip for anybody at the best of times and for more than 40 years I have been saying that it had a knock-on effect a few months later. But football was taking off and young developing nations were bringing in big-name clubs from England to promote the game in their homeland. Len told me that before I came, United would go to Ecuador in South America and such places in the 1960s and that it had to be done for financial reasons. If you were fortunate enough to gain international recognition, there were extra demands during the summer months and whether they were with the under-23s or the full squad, you needed a rest.

Before the 1975/76 season started, we spent a week playing four games in a week in Tunisia, France, Belgium and Holland and then three more back home in the Anglo-Scottish Cup. A week later on August 16 we started against Derby County, the champions, and a crowd of 31,000 were the first to witness a game at the Lane after the new stand was opened for the first time. The new-look Bramall Lane was now a complete, four-sided football stadium and Keith Eddy's penalty helped us to a 1-1 draw.

We had played for a few years with the new stand under construction and although it was a bit weird, we were used to it and used to believe some teams weren't in the right mind when they came to Bramall Lane. It was a distraction; it affected the atmosphere and it was less like a football ground for them. Still I was looking forward to the stand actually being built, even though the dressing-rooms hadn't been constructed yet and we continued using the old ones in the opposite John Street Stand. On this first day of the new one in use – a lovely, warm afternoon – it was only a basic structure for the supporters with seats and toilets at that stage. Nostalgia aside, I have to admit that having a 'four-sider' was great for me as a performer. I was closer to the fans and could hear the shouts and cheers when we did something special.

Suspension kept me out of the first two fixtures and Furphy, right on cue, blamed me for our poor start, even after John Flynn had dislocated his shoulder at Arsenal in the second. We were never to get close to a recovery. I came back and we lost 5-1 at Manchester United, 3-0 at Everton and then 2-0 at home to Leeds during a shocking run.

Furphy had brought in Chris Guthrie from Southend for almost £100,000 in the summer, a move to bring height and physicality to our attack and either to replace or play alongside Dearden. Chris was a big target man who was great in the air, had a tremendous shot on him and really should perhaps have been on free-kicks. He wasn't particularly mobile or quick, but was another great lad who was perhaps a bit out of his depth in the top-flight.

Billy again hardly played through injury and his ever-increasing absences made him a big miss for Chris, who did at least get a hat-trick of headers in a 4-2 League Cup win at Halifax Town and our first in a 2-1 home victory over Burnley on September 23. That was our first league success and by February 14, we still hadn't won another one. I think we had only six points by Christmas and were on a desperate run that we couldn't get out of. I was really down – we had done so well the season before, but the factors I mentioned earlier had such an effect that there was only ever going to be one outcome.

The board must have been as shell-shocked as Furphy at our demise and, fearing that the team would be relegated if they did nothing about it, they sacked him after a loss at Birmingham in early October when Len was sent off. Early in the season he had brought in Cliff Calvert, who was no Badger – who could be? – and most of the experienced lads weren't sad to see Furphy go. I had more reason than most to be relieved, but I was mostly bothered about how we were performing. I just wanted the club to survive, but we were well adrift.

After handing temporary control to club stalwarts Cec Coldwell and Alan Hodgkinson, the board appointed the former Notts County boss Jimmy Sirrel at Christmas. He surely would have thought we were down and set about changing the team. Almost all the lads who had been there and done well for so long were phased out because of injury, age or whatever, especially the back-four.

Sirrel had been successful at County and I didn't mind him at all. Personally I liked his training methods, which consisted largely of a training match every day with not much on a Friday. I always thought those matches got us playing, embedding a structure and being competitive, but I know some of the others didn't believe in that.

Furphy can't have shown signs of being able to arrest the slide and getting beaten every week must have affected those whose confidence was fragile. There seemed to be an inevitability that the slide would continue without a change in manager, players or method. We basically needed a miracle. We felt we were virtually down at Christmas.

Sirrel sensed that as well, but he wasn't a miracle-worker and wasn't really under pressure because he inherited the slide. It's not unheard of these days for teams to improve dramatically and turn round long, bad runs to survive, but we never looked like coming across a miracle.

Jimmy did rub some senior players up the wrong way on occasions. He would come to me, a 26-year-old England international who had been popular with the fans for years, and all he talked about was what a thoroughbred Don Masson, the QPR and Scotland midfielder, was. It was Masson this and Masson that and I really have no idea why he thought that would get more out of me.

Masson, who had played for Sirrel at Notts County, was decent but... someone I should try to emulate? Really? Jimmy never got a consistent run of selection or results, didn't seem to bring players on in his short time in charge and didn't improve our position. Whether lack of money or his tactics were responsible for that, I don't know. To be honest, that season is too painful a memory for me.

He recruited defender Paul Garner and Scottish legend Jimmy Johnstone halfway through the season. 'Jinky' was a likeable lad and one of the greatest footballers you could wish to see, but he liked a drink and was coming to the end of his career. Unsurprisingly he played only a handful of games and it begs the question of whether his signing was just a gamble on him proving to be the inspiration for a massively-unlikely climb up the table.

I was initially quite pleased at the prospect of him joining us, even though it meant that Woody had to change position. On reflection it wasn't a great scenario for the unfortunate Guthrie, who was trying to establish himself, although he did manage nine goals, just one less than Woodward.

Garner had a great left peg and the heart of a lion, and played at left-back for the rest of the season. He was a very decent player and was able to make the spot his own, with the additional advantage of Ted Hemsley not seeing eye to eye with Sirrel. Senior players don't want to be replaced and have pride in wanting to keep going, but a transition had to be made in the situation we were in.

Sirrel also blooded youngsters such as Keith Edwards, Simon Stainrod and Tony Kenworthy. They all went on to have fantastic careers, so I don't blame him for trying that route. He had to do something. Almost from nowhere in April we won four games in five and although it did nothing in terms of avoiding the drop, it at least gave the young ones belief that they could make progress in the game. It left us with 22 points, six fewer than Burnley and eight below Wolves.

That relegation remains my biggest disappointment in football for a number of reasons. The campaign had begun with optimism after a successful season the year before and the new stand had given the ground a new dimension. It had to be done, but I'm certain that the burden of paying for it cost us dearly on the pitch. The club I loved had lost its First Division status and this felt worse than my first relegation with United; I had played only a handful of games then, but at least I had done well and one more point would have saved us.

This time there had been nothing about the season that had been enjoyable. It had been nine months of misery. And the realisation that this group of players were finished as a group was crippling. I was only 26, at a club I was besotted with, but this was the end of an era with good mates and great players soon to be parting.

Eddie Colquhoun and Woody stayed, but Ted and Len had got to the stage where they knew that the manager wasn't going to pick them and the only option was to leave and go where they could contribute. Ted was going to concentrate on his cricket with Worcestershire before Billy Bremner at Doncaster came in for him, while Len switched just down the road to Chesterfield.

I can't say I had noticed any decline in our top players, but then again I was on the pitch and maybe that is a more difficult place to assess it from. We had some lads who fell short and in general we just didn't have the ability and drive on the pitch that we used to. Our ball retention had deteriorated and I accept that everyone's personal performances suffered, including my own. We couldn't control games any more.

We had always given each other bollockings during matches, about not picking up or being out of position, and we still did that. But the whole season was just so frustrating. It never started for us and we had nothing to hang on to. Furphy couldn't stop the slump, blaming everyone but himself, and having been subbed early on at West Ham United, I had even more reason to have issues with him. Then Sirrel replaced him and although I quite liked his style, the other lads didn't respond to him. It wasn't a happy situation to inspire us to any improvement or even a few wins to change the atmosphere.

The top-flight adventure was over, but fans to this day still chew the fat over what might have been if the club had possessed the nerve – as well as the financial clout – to have been bolder. It's easy to say when it's someone else who has to dig into their pockets or gamble with the future, of course. But what isn't in doubt is that we'd had some terrific players in those years and we would have been an attractive option for a few more. Who wouldn't have wanted to come and play with the likes of Woody and me?

The England players I played with always claimed that they could beat us or get hammered by us because of our style. We were well-respected, not least because of our matchwinners, such as Billy Dearden for a start. Eddie Colquhoun was a real stalwart, bloody great in the air, deceptively speedy and he could read the game. If he had been a bit better on the ball, he would have been right up there.

Then there was Len who was good on the ball and formed part of the triangle down the right that was so successful. I could see teams thinking they should get right on Woody because he wasn't so keen on a tackle, so they'd give him one early or do the same to TC straightaway so that he didn't have time on the ball. That was sensible thinking by the opposition, but Len was good enough to hold on to the ball if a pass wasn't on and instead come inside and play. He always gave you a chance.

Our speed up-front was like no other team in the league; Salmons, Dearden, Reece, Scullion and Ford were like lightning. That made it easier for me to use the channels or space behind the back-four because there was always somebody available. Missing anyone out is harsh because everyone contributed and we were a team in every way. Talented players and pals I will love forever.

13

WE'RE MOVING, DEAR...

Whenever a team drops out of the Football League, I try to imagine how utterly despondent their players and fans must feel. It must seem that their whole world has fallen apart, that they have failed and there is no way back. I sympathise with that because – and I appreciate that the circumstances are not so horren- ,ous – that's the way I felt when Sheffiel, Unite, were relegate, from the top- flight. What now?

As conversations go, it was pretty innocuous.

"Oi, TC?"

"Yeah?"

"When you get back to the ground, go and see John Harris."

"Why?"

"Dunno. But you'd better go, 'cos he asked me to tell you."

"Oh, right. Thanks."

And to be absolutely honest I had absolutely no idea what it would all be about. But it was Jimmy Sirrell who had spoken to me, during our post-season tour in Gibraltar, so I was pretty sure that it wasn't a hoax, as I would have suspected if it had been one of the lads. And the meeting turned out to be a significant turning-point in my life.

Since relegation was confirmed so early, we'd all had a lot of time to think about the consequences. And although most of them could be pre- dicted, my mind couldn't find the clarity to address them and face up to what would happen.

I didn't want to. The thought of perhaps leaving and seeing my friend- ship group break up scared me. Should I request a move? Being a born worrier like mum dictated that I wouldn't do that and I wasn't looking forward to making any decision, particularly because there hadn't been any inkling about anyone wanting to buy me. Maybe that was because we had lost so many matches and I hadn't been at my best either?

On the other hand I was in the England squad and wanted to stay in the top-flight, play big games and maintain my profile to be considered for selection. I desperately didn't want to leave, but felt I had to and in the end I made my mind up without being influenced by anyone else. I didn't even talk to Ted and Len.

Off the pitch my wife had never really settled in Sheffield and I thought overall that a change would be best. I put in three transfer requests, one after the other, as each one was turned down. No doubt the club were pleased to see that reported in the Press because it indicated to the fans that they had made attempts to keep me.

It was fair enough – I was their player and in the end I accepted it and gave up asking, relieved that I didn't have to make a decision, and went with the squad to Gibraltar for a mini-tournament in late May, against Lincoln and Wolves. We had a good time for a week, even taking part in a plant fight on a traffic island with Sam Ellis and his Lincoln team-mates. They were staying at a different hotel and one night, when we were all pissed, we bumped into them and pulled plants out to throw at each other. I admit it was very naughty and not the sort of thing I would normally do, but high spirits and drink had definitely taken over. My shame is still buried inside me!

I remember Sirrel doing his backstroke out to sea and some of the lads hoping he didn't come back and it was on that trip that he later told me to go to see John Harris. I did as I was told and John simply told me to get in his car. We set off, without him ever telling me why or where we were going. There was no conversation about what was to happen and I was certainly too damn scared to ask. Believe me, it dawned on me only when I saw the Elland Road ground come into view.

Harris pulled into the car-park. "Go and talk to Jimmy Armfield," he said.

Armfield was the Leeds United manager and when I returned to the car a short time afterwards, John asked: "What have you done, son?"

"I've signed," I told him. John's head dropped forward on to the steering wheel in disappointment. He obviously didn't want me to go.

Jimmy, the former Blackpool and England defender, was a real gentleman and made it clear to me during that first meeting that he was a fan of mine. There were just the two of us in his office and he showered me with compliments as he set about seducing me into joining Leeds United. It's fair to say he wouldn't have needed to work hard, largely because I didn't have an agent and I wasn't any good at all at speaking up for myself. Instead I listened as he outlined how he saw taking Leeds forward and how I would contribute.

"This is a great club and Don Howe and I want to restore it to its recent place at the top of the pile," he said. "We know there are one or two changes to be made to the team and you are first choice to replace Giles. We still have great players here, but with Jack Charlton and Giles both long gone, we have a big job to do in reshaping the team. You are a key part of how we want to do that."

Jimmy was no bullshitter: he knew what was needed and I instantly felt that he was an honourable, fair and genuinely pleasant man who faced a big challenge. How big was soon to be seen because Billy Bremner left after we had played together just four times – so he had been on his way out – and Allan Clarke was gone just a year later. But Paul Madeley, Paul Reaney and David Harvey were still there with Peter Lorimer. Peter really was a great player – very talented, with much more than just the hard shot that he was famed for – and much better than I had appreciated previously.

There was a lot of talent in the squad, which was very tempting to me, and I did remember the chairman Manny Cussins talking on radio long before I joined, saying he wanted me at Leeds. The only stumbling-blocks I could see were all off the pitch: leaving my mates, moving further away from London and the effect it would have on Sheffield United supporters. In their eyes Leeds were still big rivals and they had never forgiven the club for selling their then-hero Mick Jones to them 10 years previously. It would hurt them massively.

I was on the spot, with my mind racing and unable to handle it all in a detached and professional way. Priorities and emotions all over the place. I didn't want to leave Sheffield, I was worried about what people might think and I didn't want to be badly thought of for leaving. That office, alone with someone I had only just met, feeling nervous and under pressure to make a decision, was the last place I wanted to be. But I was there. Gullible. Fretting about going for it, fretting about not going for it.

Bizarrely as it seems these days, I wouldn't have even thought about asking for time to talk it over with my wife, even though I wasn't a dominant type who made all the decisions at home. Feeling intimidated by not knowing what to do when not on a football pitch had become a problem for me, in stark contrast to how I felt whenever the first whistle went, wherever I was.

I signed for £240 a week, the same as I was on at Bramall Lane. Memory suggests I had told Jimmy what I was on and he offered the same, saying that they had a wage structure and no-one was on more. But I should obviously have used the opportunity – as an international player – to bargain for another £50 or so, maybe as much as £300. That just wasn't in me and although my signing-on fee during the length of the deal was £13,500, Gordon McQueen and Joe Jordan later negotiated deals worth £500 a week. They then quickly buggered off to Manchester United.

I was naive and stupid not to try to hold out for more, but I was 26 years old and just wanted to play football. I already knew Clarke, Reaney, Madeley and Trevor Cherry from the England set-up, so that was a big plus in helping me to decide. After all, this was the mighty Leeds United, who had played in the European Cup final a year earlier, and it felt enough for me to get the thing signed and still be a top-flight player with a top club. At least it meant an end to the uncertainty in my mind, but I was left wishing I had been a quarter as self-assured off the field as I was on it.

After I'd returned to the car and told John Harris my decision, the drive back was filled with more silence than chat. The clubs must have already agreed a fee in advance of £245,000, plus tax, but I gauged from John's reaction that he disagreed with the club's decision – or at least hoped I would turn the move down. He had been caring towards me during the years without ever saying much and he had the dignity to wish me luck – which I really appreciated amid the turmoil I was feeling inside. Relegation and debts related to the new stand would be weighing heavily on the board's mind at that point and presumably selling me must have seemed a good idea in the circumstances.

Fortunately, when I got back home Linda and I talked and agreed that the transfer wasn't an issue, other than it taking us another 30 or 40 miles further away from London. That was in part due to us wanting to live in the Wetherby area, north-east of the city, and we settled on Collingham, where lots of Leeds players had houses. It is a nice village and we were able to upgrade our house, although for the first two months we continued living in Dronfield after enrolling the kids at a school in Wetherby.

It wasn't ideal because it meant me taking them from Sheffield to Wetherby in the morning before I stopped off at Allan Clarke's for a bit of breakfast and travelling in with him to training. Clarkey was very opinionated, but we were mates and I still love him to bits. He was a senior professional I looked up to and I admired what he had achieved in the game. After training I would wait at Allan's until I could pick the kids up again for the journey back until the new house was sorted.

The travelling became a bind for me, adding two hours to my day, and it took its toll on me a bit. It was a relief when we finally settled in and I had a more conventional routine like everyone else.

I used the break between leaving Sheffield United and starting at Leeds wisely. Even though I knew I would have no England commitments in that period, I wanted to be fit for a new start and arranged a month on Sid Bennett's building site at Barrowhill, Chesterfield. The summer of 1976 was a scorcher so I got my shirt off, worked hard and got a tan for my efforts. That was about all because I didn't bother about any wages; I just wanted to get fit, which I wouldn't have done so well if I had not been transferred.

Linda and I became great friends with Sid and his wife, Wyn, as we all lived in Dronfield. He had his building company at nearby Sheepbridge and I reckoned it would be great to get in good nick by helping him out there. It was no picnic though – I didn't want it to be – and working from eight in the morning until six at night represented a solid day's graft, largely made up of wheelbarrowing, lifting lintels, hod carrying and other general labouring duties.

Sid and Wyn would go out on Saturday nights with Linda and I on Saturday nights and in fact, Linda did Friday nights as well. I wouldn't go out on the night before a game, but I would stay up late until she came home because we were having our troubles, even then. I was insecure and I suppose a little possessive as well. I felt I wasn't getting any affection, despite her not settling up north and me making a big effort to get her back to London for regular visits.

When pre-season began I was ready to take in a new club, different players and a new training ground. Apart from the cross-country, training was brilliant and I did well following my fitness boost on site, which really paid off. I was the lightest I'd been for a while, developed a bit more muscle – we didn't do weights back then, as they do now – and I was surprised that I was leaving people such as Bremner behind in training.

Some of the lads were spewing up – in those days you had a month off for the summer doing sod all and nobody minded. It was a level playing-field in that regard so if you kept in trim, you were a step ahead although I was always a hard trainer and fit. We always had five-a-side, which we didn't have at Sheffield United – and the infamous yellow jersey was awarded every day to the worst trainer.

Don Howe, such a positive man and a great coach, was great for me and the methods and training were a bit more upmarket than I had been used to. Don had extensive knowledge and used savvy methods and different techniques to put ideas across in a way players could relate to. I became more aware of things during games and I put that down to Don's influence, although there was a big motivational element to it as well. We also had physio Les Cocker, who was on Alf Ramsey's England staff, and had plenty of bases covered.

The players welcomed me and I was 100 per cent confident in playing among them, no matter how big their reputations. Like most clubs they had their little cliques, but they all loved their successful former manager, Mr. Revie, which was entirely down to what they had achieved together. They wouldn't have a word said against the man they regarded almost as a king, a father to them, and a god that no-one else was going to replace. That is only human nature, I suppose, but it was always going to work against any new manager coming in until the whole thing had worked out of the system. It seems very plausible to look back to Brian Clough's 44-day tenure and assume that there were forces on both sides that ensured it wasn't going to be a happy marriage.

Working relationships in football can sometimes be extremely obvious or subtle, and not always predictable. There are clashing egos and personality traits; coaches who need power, players who need a friendly ear. The good guy-bad guy alliance on the coaching staff is one of the oldest and most common – or at least it was anyway – and there was some of that balance between Armfield and Howe.

Don was a hard guy, tough, outspoken and definitely in charge when he was leading anything, while Jimmy was the nice guy, softly spoken with a much more genteel approach. It was friendly, very clever and it worked. Had Leeds not sold McQueen and Jordan and kept Jimmy and Don together, I really feel we could have won the title a year later.

My first game for Leeds was at Borussia Dortmund in pre-season. That sounds great, but it didn't start well as far as the players were concerned because we were given an 11pm curfew. The Gray brothers, Frank and Eddie, Bremner, Terry Yorath, Clarke and 'Lash' Lorimer would have all been out, but Billy and I stayed out longest in a bar until about 3am. My excuse is that I was easily led!

We came steaming out of the club and discovered we had lost the bit of paper with our hotel name on it. We got on a tram and, while I was virtually holding Billy up, I made up my mind we were going the wrong way, so we staggered off and caught one going the other way. By this time, at about 5am, I saw a baker's shop just opening and because I was dying for something to eat, I dragged us both off the tram again. I left Billy outside and went in; when I came out, he was slumped in the baker's van! When I managed to get him back on his feet and asked someone for the hotel address, it turned out to be only yards from the bar we had been in anyway.

The next morning Jimmy Armfield had us in and fined us – a mild bollocking – and we apologised. I hated being confronted that way. Jimmy always made sure that everybody had to be awake at 9am and on the coaches, especially if we had been out the night before. We weren't allowed to doze off so he made sure the drinkers had to suffer a bit! Incidentally I had a great debut in a terrific stadium and we won...

It helped enormously that I hit it off early with all the players there, particularly with Peter Lorimer, Eddie Gray, Billy Bremner and mainly Clarkey, who I was probably closest to. Then as the years went by, I got on well with Arthur Graham, Paul Hart, Ray Hankin and Brian Flynn who all became good mates and who appreciated my play. Even those who arrived later in my spell – Byron Stevenson, David McNiven and Peter Hampton – I loved to bits. And don't forget that they were bloody good players as well.

That didn't make me wish I had left the Blades earlier, though, because I had such an affection for everyone back in Sheffield. But I had left a declining team for one with a great level of all-round ability, even if some of the players were ageing a bit. They had been through it all, won things, been bridesmaids as well on occasions, but these boys still oozed confidence and were used to being up there with Liverpool every year for about a decade.

I was looking forward to it, definitely, not least because playing in a better team makes you a better player. It gets more out of you and improves your appreciation of the nuances of the game, which undoubtedly made me better as well. A player can't make a team but it works the other way round is my motto.

When a player has a season as Sheffield United did in 1975/76, it is going to get to you physically and mentally, even to the best, and it must have done to me despite my self-confidence. Now I had drawn a line under it, done the hard bit in moving on and could get my teeth into winning things where I was most comfortable – on the pitch.

Mum and her brother, my Uncle Bert, on holiday in the late 1960s, somewhere on the south coast. The whole family would have gone, although Mum didn't always manage to get along. Below: Happy days lining up for the all-conquering Whitefield School football team, with two of my favourite people. I am in the middle of the 2nd row next to good pal, Bob Turpie (second right) and the PE teacher we loved, Les Hill on the same row (extreme left). This was 1965 and yet another Tradesmen Shield and League double!

Watford's new boy lifts the gloom

CURRIE IS TOO HOT FOR ROVERS

Not at their best — yet Hornets win

Watford 4 .... **Bristol Rovers 0**

Currie (2), Scullion, Garbett

Attendance 7,500

IRONIC though it may seem, Watford never lived up to the promise of recent weeks against Bristol Rovers on Saturday—yet they won by four clear goals!

At times—notably before they opened the scoring—Watford were a ragged bunch. They could not strike any sort of rhythm against a Rovers side who played as badly as they are ever likely to this season.

What was needed was a flash of genius to inspire them—to put some purpose into their energetic, yet ineffective, play.

And on that score, Watford were fortunate enough to have a player as promising as 17-year-old Tony Currie in the side.

Currie, making his League debut in the senior side, swung the game Watford's way with two goals.

Extrovert

But the goals were not ordinary affairs. In keeping with young Currie's extrovert style of play, they were goals to be remembered although Rovers will put them down to slack marking and poor covering.

Without a doubt, this was Currie's match.

defender and right on to the end of Garbett's boot which promptly dispatched it into the roof of the net.

Watford. — Sinter, Welbourne (2), Garvey (5), Eady (6), Williams (3), Hale (4), Walley (10), Scullion (7), Currie (8), Garbett (9), Owen (11). Substitute: Irvin (did not play). **Bristol Rovers.** — Briggs; Hilliard, Parsons, Williams, Taylor, Munro, Jarman, Ronaldson, Biggs, Jones, W., Jones, R. Substitute: Stone (did not play). Referee: W. Castle (Sedgley).

IT'S A GOAL

Tony Currie carefully takes the ball round Briggs before slidin in the second goal. In the background is Stuart Scullion.

Sheffield Newspapers

THE STAR, SHEFFIELD, Tuesday, February 27, 1968   11

CURRIE STARS IN GREAT BLADES WIN

By Peter Howard

LOOKING back over the years since Sheffield United returned to the First Division, some of their most memorable matches have been against Spurs—and so it was last night when the Blades were once again in battling mood and climbed the table with an exhilarating 3-2 triumph.

A night to remember. Chiefly because of the fantastic debut impact of 18-year-old Tony Currie, who marked his first senior match as he did his first outing with the reserves . . . with a goal.

Half an hour had gone and the sides were level when Carlin sent Munks galloping away down the right.

A perfect centre — and there was the blond head of Currie, leaping high above Beal to head down past the frustrated Jennings.

If he hadn't done anything else, the goal-starved Lane crowd would have taken him to their hearts for this alone . . . but the youngster did so much more.

STUPID MIX-UP

He worked hard, shot hard, showed excellent control and distribution and only flagged a little in the dying stages. Which was to be expected.

All round, this was a heartening show, even if there were certain failings which frightened the 27,000 fans for a while.

Like the stupid mix-up which led to Greaves opening the scoring. Hoping Jimmy Greaves will miss from that range is like asking a sniper to miss a house side from lsx yards.

Like the shortage of cover when Chivers was left on his

VERDICT

own to take a shot at goal with 10 minutes remaining. And what a shot!

Fortunately, he has scored four times against the Blades in three matches this term, England's costliest player has not been on the winning side once.

NO REPETITION

Most heartening for the fans was the bombardment of the Spurs goal in the last few minutes. There was no repetition of the Blackpool match panic this time, and Jennings made great saves from Badger and Woodward.

Addison shot wide from two chances he would normally accept, but he led the line well and laid on the equaliser by Barry Wagstaff with a great run and astute pass for the wing half.

Reece scored the third with a fine shot, deservedly punishing the so-costly side with a so-stupid negative approach, and Carlin and Addison played no small part in the general effectiveness of Currie.

A grand, exciting performance by United, and having now notched their first League win of the year, this sort of enthusiasm, coupled with an increase in skill, should see them climbing still further.

● Picture Back Page

I had a good record for scoring on my debuts early on in my career, managing it for both Watford and Sheffield United as covered here by the *Watford Observer* and the *Sheffield Star*. I had already scored a diving header before a second for the Hornets (top) who included other eventual Blades Keith Eddy, Stewart Scullion and Terry Garbutt. My first United goal was also a header, against Spurs. My hero, Jimmy Greaves, was in the Spurs side that day. He scored, of course!

Colorsport

Above: I think this was at West Ham but I am sure of two things: I am wearing my favourite-ever Sheffield United away kit, I am with the greatest player I ever played with. Alan Woodward made and scored goals in equal measure, so I knew the best thing to do was to get out of his way! Below: Scoring past Liverpool's Ray Clemence with a bullet from 30 yards at Bramall Lane. We drew 1-1 and I was disappointed that I was incorrectly adjudged to have fouled Kevin Keegan ... and he scored from the resulting free-kick

Sheffield Newspapers

Sheffield Newspaper

Celebrating promotion in 1971 with the Blades lads. Clockwise from Eddie Colquhoun, front left and reading the newspaper: David Ford, John Flynn, John Hope, Geoff Salmons, me, Colin Addison, Len Badger, Alan Woodward, Ted Hemsley and, I think, Trevor Hockey. Below: Mowing the small lawn at home near Sheffield with my pride and joy Toyota Celica in the background. I wasn't really comfortable doing this type of publicity shot - and I certainly didn't normally wear those clothes to cut the grass!

Sheffield Newspapers

Above: When I signed this seven year contract in 1973 it seemed I had committed my career to Sheffield United. Chairman Dick Wragg and manager John Harris, both pictured, would have thought so but three years later I joined Leeds and continued top flight battles with players such as Glenn Hoddle, who I rated so highly. Here we are at White Hart Lane, left. Below: With Norman Hunter, Mick Jones and Trevor Cherry at a Leeds old boys charity golf day, probably at the Moor Allerton course. Golf is a popular pastime for players and Trevor in particular was pretty decent

There were frustrations about my England career but I can't deny that I am immensely proud of playing at that level between 1975-1979. It fulfilled one of my two childhood ambitions. Above: In action against Brazil in 1977 - their manager praised me after the game for playing them at their own game. I'm tussling with Zico who went on to become one of the best ever to pull on a Brazil shirt. Right: I love memorabilia and here's me with my cap from 1973-74 against Italy. Below: How many can you name from this England squad? Standing, from left to right: Les Cocker, Trevor Brooking, Dave Watson, Emlyn Hughes, me, Paul Madeley, Norman Hunter, Colin Bell, Ray Clemence, Phil Parkes, Martin Chivers, Peter Storey, Bobby Moore, Martin Peters, Harold Shepherdson. Front: Kevin Keegan, Kevin Hector, Colin Todd, David Nish, Peter Shilton, Allan Clarke, Mike Channon, Ray McFarland

Colorsport

Colorsport

George Herringshaw

Left: Leading out QPR for the FA Cup final replay was a huge honour. Peter Hucker is behind me and Spurs boss Keith Burkinshaw alongside. Right: Not at Loftus Road but playing on another plastic pitch

Sheffield Newspapers

Torquay United was my final Football League club, and here I am against Chesterfield at Plainmoor in 1984

TONY CURRIE TESTIMONIAL

50p SOUVENIR PROGRAMME

Miss Sheffield United, Samantha Sears, will draw out a lucky programme number at half-time for a £400 video recorder kindly donated by Finlux U.K. Ltd.

T.C.'s UNITED ALL STARS
(THE 1971/72 PROMOTION SQUAD)
V
DENNIS WATERMAN SHOWBIZ XI
SUNDAY 5th OCTOBER 1986. Kick-off 4.00 p.m.

MATCH SPONSOR

GILDERS
Talk to Gilders - we're worth listening to!

Audi VW

SHEFFIELD UNITED

My Blades testimonial was arranged principally by businessman Howard Stephenson, who greeted me as I ran out - you can tell I was surprised by the size of the crowd. My 'All Stars' played a Dennis Waterman XI

My testimonal side, with a couple of spcecial guests, lining up alongside Miss Sheffield United Samantha Sears before kick-off in front of well over 20,000 fans at Bramall Lane. One of the greatest days of my life

Football brought me into the company of some colourful and larger than life characters. I didn't know George Best well - above, pictured together at a speaker dinner at Aston Hall - but darts champion Eric Bristow, the 'Crafty Cockney', and the often-underrated Frank Worthington became proper friends

Billy Sharp

Taking on the Football in the Community role was a huge awakening and challenge for me - I don't think I even knew what an office was before I started it! Getting to grips with it was a real achievement, although I'm not claiming credit for Billy Sharp's success! He is pictured bottom right at one of our soccer schools, along with defender Kevin Gage (inset)

Above: Walking to the stage through the crowd after being introduced at the *This is your Life* event at Bramall Lane. It was such a memorable evening and former international athlete David Bedford, below, was one guest who went down a storm. He told a few stories from our school days, usually at my own expense!

Above: Frank Barlow, Bill Dearden, David Ford, Ted Hemsley, me, Len Badger and Geoff Salmons on stage on my big night. They are a bit shy on the microphone but Ted always comes to the rescue!

Right: Sheffield actor Sean Bean and I were both in the film *When Saturday Comes* and he never wastes an opportunity to let people know that the Blades are his team.

Above: Pictured with my nephew Darren in front of the stand named after me at Bramall Lane, which I officially unveiled just before United's friendly against Inter Milan (top right). Right: Chris Gascoigne, *Coronation Street*'s Peter Barlow, rushed over the Pennines to attend *This is your Life*

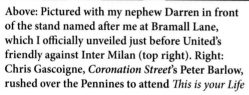

Alan Birchenall and I re-enact our kiss many years after we should have lost our German porn stars reputation!

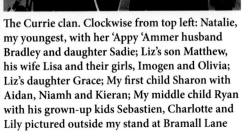

The Currie clan. Clockwise from top left: Natalie, my youngest, with her 'Appy 'Ammer husband Bradley and daughter Sadie; Liz's son Matthew, his wife Lisa and their girls, Imogen and Olivia; Liz's daughter Grace; My first child Sharon with Aidan, Niamh and Kieran; My middle child Ryan with his grown-up kids Sebastien, Charlotte and Lily pictured outside my stand at Bramall Lane

Liz is usually by my side and never misses home games. This was taken in my very own Tony Currie Suite

Above: My beautiful, placid German Shepherd dog, Hendon, came to work with me every day and that rugby ball was his favourite. I miss him terribly and keep the ball for sentimental reasons. Right: Out of respect for all the wonderful Sheffield United players over the years, I have to rate my award for being the greatest ever as my top achievement

14

I AM LEEDS

This was my second move and the fact that they were eight years apart illustrates how much I ha• enjoye• my time in Sheffiel•. I may have been ol•er this time and had grown up in many ways, but this was an important switch for a number of reasons. It needed to work...

Whatever my insecurities and inhibitions off the pitch, they always disappeared when I had a football match to play – wherever and whoever it was against. And that also served me well when I played *with* players of the highest quality. Many good players have found it initially difficult to adapt to a fresh set of circumstances when joining a new club or stepping up to international level; the expectations of teammates and supporters can overwhelm your best intentions.

I recognised that some factors had to be taken in my stride, but nerves just didn't affect me when it came to football. I never worried about facing the crowd in a new environment and was looking forward to playing with so many internationals. Why should I be nervous? I was 26 years old, ultra-confident, very fit and felt well-equipped to cope with the challenges to come. The boys welcomed me, which was a positive help, but I had played with and against most of them and they knew that successfully replacing Johnny Giles was vital for the team. Johnny and I weren't identikit players by any means, but a link player in the engine-room with Bremner was essential for continuity and creativity.

It was still a fantastic squad of good footballers whose ambition remained high. Their appearance in a European final just the year before continued to fuel expectations, and it seemed as if an ageing squad was the only potential weakness to stop us making further progress.

Our opening day opposition at Elland Road were newly-promoted West Bromwich Albion who, thanks to one of those fickle fingers of fate that sport so often throws up, were player-managed by Giles, who had joined them a year earlier. It was an intriguing fixture for the 40,000 there and my reception from the home fans chanting my name was something I won't ever forget. Mind you, there were a lot of Blades fans there, at least according to what many of them have told me during the years! Either way it was a fantastic welcome and got me going from the off, which helped me to play my normal game.

No doubt I would have wanted to show I could run around a bit as well because that 'lazy' label that I hated was always on my back. I was always supporting the ball whenever I played and that meant covering a lot of ground. I wanted a goal and I didn't want an injury, but both wishes went unheeded; I didn't score and was on the receiving end of an over-the-top tackle from Alastair Robertson whose stud left a bullet hole-type dent in my leg.

It required stitches, but I was back on the field in 10 minutes and trying like mad to get a goal because I had scored on all my previous debuts. It didn't happen, but I had a great game, apart from the debut blank and not having the chance to give Robertson one back! We'd been without Jordan and McQueen and had to fight back from behind to get a 2-2 draw so that was a struggle, but I enjoyed the occasion.

Standing on the halfway line before kick-off, waving to both sides of Elland Road as the supporters belted out *Marching on Together,* the Leeds' fans song, was spine-tingling to me. I'd seen it done so many times when I had been in the opposition and wondered what it felt like as a Leeds player. No other English team did that. I have to say it was brilliant to be part of and it created such an atmosphere and bond with the fans.

Before my time there the legendary Leeds team had tags on their socks and tracksuits with their names printed on the back, while the players were so confident they ran out along the touchline, juggling footballs with their feet. Leeds, under Revie, introduced these new looks and skills for the crowd and I'm convinced they helped to build the aura around the team. In fact, I still have my tracksuit with my name on the back. It really did feel great wearing it, as had the continental-style numbered shorts we'd had at Sheffield United.

Looking at who played that day I think our midfield would have consisted of Cherry, Lorimer, Eddie Gray and me, so it was a surprise that we only drew. In fact, we won only once and drew three of our first eight league fixtures. One of those losses was at Coventry, where at least I got my first goal for the club as we went down 4-2. Although I followed with a better one a few days later, a hard, low volley inside the far post at Stoke, they knocked us out of the League Cup and the fact I found the back of the net only once in the league all season illustrates how poor my strike-rate for Leeds would turn out to be.

Another personal disappointment was the loss of Bremner, who I looked forward to playing with so much. We had lost two and drawn one of the four matches he played and whether or not that helped to signal his departure, I don't know, but I didn't have any inkling about the move until it happened. I didn't know whether Billy's legs were going either. But whatever the reason, it was sad. It was the end of an outstanding top-flight career for a man regarded as a Leeds legend.

I had been out of the international picture for three years and hoped that playing with Billy would increase my prospects of getting selected again. He had been such an influence on the team; he and Giles were gritty, tough opponents. They were little terriers who gave you hardly any time on the ball and having played together for so long, had a great understanding of their roles and each other. That pairing was a big part of why Leeds were such a good footballing side, hardly ever losing possession.

After Billy had left I played several games alongside Trevor Cherry, who was more defensively-minded. Like Madeley, he kept himself wonderfully fit, but could definitely play. He was very effective as a man-marker and a real winner with that determined frame of mind instilled into the team by Don Revie. Everyone remembers the big names and it would be easy to forget that we had so many other very good players who were not even regulars, such as Carl Harris, David McNiven, Gwyn Thomas and the versatile Byron Stevenson.

What a footballer Byron was. He had a lot of ability and could ping the ball with both feet, but was never a regular. He would have been an automatic pick for most other teams, as would Terry Yorath. He was not the best technically, but could more than hold his own as a man-marker. Both were so reliable for us when they came in to do a job.

At last, after beating West Ham in early autumn, we found some form and consistency to recover from such a poor start. An impressive run included setting off on a long tilt at the FA Cup. It began with a 5-2 home romp over Norwich and goals from Jordan and Clarke edged us through by the odd goal at Birmingham City in round four. Next up was an Elland Road fixture with Manchester City, who had already beaten us there in the league. They were in the running for the title and a big test was in store when the day came round.

By now Linda and I had moved into our lovely house in Collingham and although it thankfully ended my daily commute, the move hadn't made her feel more comfortable. Our home and area had improved, but in her mind it didn't compensate for being an extra hour from London. She didn't get out or mix much and her visits back down south only increased.

I wished we had stayed in our Dronfield house because it would have been more convenient for her and the kids wouldn't have been uprooted from school. It wasn't a healthy domestic situation for either of us and it's fair to say that neither of us blamed the other. We both felt our share of guilt. But we were a family and didn't want it to break up, so we got on with it.

Maybe an FA Cup final appearance for me and an extra trip to London for her would ease some tension. When Cherry of all people squeezed us past City, who went on to finish as league runners-up, the odds against us getting to Wembley shortened. And they dropped again after Eddie Gray scored the only goal at Wolves in the sixth round. For someone used to habitual early exits in the competition with Sheffield United, getting to the semi-final was exciting stuff and I couldn't help but wonder if my turn had come at last. We had improved, we were in much better shape and I'd had several months of working with these incredible players week in and week out.

I was a massive Alan Woodward fan, but Peter Lorimer impressed me greatly because I hadn't realised what skills he had. Top players, the pair of them. Eddie Gray had beautiful skills and despite carrying an injury just kept going all season. I loved Clarkey as a striker. He was quick and great to play with, but could handle himself despite that willowy frame of his. He was as hard as nails and could be a dirty bugger.

Centre-halves feared him because he would niggle them in a very clever way, biding his time, getting his free-kicks and then his revenge equally cleverly. He was too canny to have stand-ups and fights straight-away and he wasn't called 'Sniffer' for nothing.

Leeds had been a top side along with Liverpool for 10 years and no other team got anywhere near them. The best players see things coming and ride challenges because if they don't, they get hurt, and Giles and Bremner could handle themselves – if one didn't get you, the other did. They would be sent off within five minutes these days! Leeds knew when and how to leave a foot in here and there, but they were great passers of the ball and real footballers as well as having the physical side of the game.

Norman Hunter was Norman, simple as that; a fantastic player who was hard as nails and unable to play any differently. Everybody feared him because he would stick his boot in, but he also had a lovely left peg and was confident in the air. Fantastic. The trouble was that there were so many at the same stage of their careers in terms of age, showing signs of getting to the end. Armfield was learning that things would have to change very soon and must have known he had a very big job on his hands.

Our form leading up to the semi-final had stuttered, although we had won the week before and decamped to Hillsborough for the game as fa-vourites. Clarke got on the scoresheet, but I felt we were nowhere near good enough on the day, especially with the players we had, because we lost 2-1 to Manchester United. We didn't threaten very much, but I give the opposition credit for that as well.

Gordon Hill, Lou Macari, Steve Coppell and Sammy McIlroy were four formidable terriers – those little blighters again! – in midfield, who were virtually non-stop all afternoon. My ambition to reach an FA Cup final had to be put on hold for another year, but the journey had helped to rescue our season and we'd played in front of some massive crowds; 47,000 against Manchester City, 50,000 against Wolves and 60,000 in the semi-final back in Sheffield.

It was a step in the right direction, but our league form tailed off again and a 10th-place finish meant we had fallen short of all expectations. We fizzled out, possibly because we saved ourselves for the semi-final, but there was no excuse during a full campaign and the statistics told a true story. We were a full 15 points off top spot. And it was still two points for a win as well back then.

Losing as many as we won was a real shock, but not surprising because our goal tally was well down. It seems fair to attribute some of it to age, departures, injuries and not having a settled side, and we paid for it. But it's also true that a high percentage of the lads took part in virtually the whole season and the others who filled in when required, such as Peter Hampton as well, were all very capable.

We lacked big individual scorers because Jordan and David McNiven, our two top scorers, claimed only 10 and seven goals respectively. It really reflected the change that was inevitable as the members of that great old team gradually moved on. In much more recent years Manchester United, for example, had a similar issue. Even they couldn't lose four top players such as Ryan Giggs, Paul Scholes, Rio Ferdinand and Nemanja Vidić without transition and a patient settling-in period for their replacements.

Fortunately there was an acceptance of that from the Leeds supporters because, despite the modest placing, there was no clamour for change from the terraces that I was aware of. Fans seemed to understand that the old team had to be disbanded and that Jimmy and Don were a good pairing. My own relationship with them had been brilliant, as it was with coach Jimmy McAnearney, who I had played with in Watford reserves. It had taken no time at all for me to be accepted by the crowd and, without wanting to be immodest, I knew that I had become a favourite – their reaction made it obvious.

It helped me to enjoy a solid season and I was honoured to be given, I think, 20 of the 22 player-of-the-year trophies from various branches of the Leeds Supporters' Club from all over the country. I'd played 35 games and received a lot of cut glass – which I'd asked for – and a lovely silver platter. Leeds was a fantastic club to be with and I was glad to have made the move. The Brian Clough business was over as well and a few of the greats were still around. Yes, it still needed improvement. But it was the start of a new era.

15

UNFINISHED BUSINESS

*The motivation for joining Leeds was predominantly down to giving myself the best chance of fulfilling my footballing ambitions. An FA Cup semi-final ha•
been a good step towards doing it and I was now reassured that it would happen
at Ellan• Roa• un•er Armfiel•.*

I can't deny that Don Revie wasn't my favourite person and I know that won't go down well with Leeds fans who had good reason to revere him, as his players did. He built a fabulous team and inspired loyalty and respect on and off the field to such an extent that, more than 50 years on, he is still the Elland Road benchmark for managers.

The Leeds side he put together took English top-flight football by the scruff of the neck and no team looked forward to playing them because they had a bit of everything, not least the camaraderie that made them fearsome opponents. They could provoke, both through the brilliance of their football and their combative approach, and they always stuck together when the battle was at its fiercest on the pitch.

To his lasting credit, the component parts of Revie's team dovetailed perfectly, a squad of differently talented and charismatic individuals put into a framework that allowed every one of them to flourish. I would have loved to play in that Leeds team from a few years before, but Don would have rated Giles more than he did me. The fact was that we were different players. Johnny was busy and I was languid, which would often deceive people and affect their opinions. I can see that. But what first set me against Revie was when he told me, during a training session when he was England manager, that I wasn't in his plans.

Why was I in the squad then? It negatively affected my England career along with a handful of others of similar styles. In my opinion it robbed the nation of seeing a more entertaining and successful national side. But I hadn't given up on playing for England. All through the 1970s I believe I developed into a more mature player and now, at 27, I was perhaps becoming more professional, which I hoped would boost my chances of playing again for my country. I was also a father again when, in September 1977 Linda gave birth to our daughter, Natalie – named after my favourite actress, Natalie Wood. The theme of our kids being born in Yorkshire continued.

At Leeds we had more of a footballing team than at Sheffield United, where we played to utilise the speed merchants up-front. Now I'd be going to Paul Reaney and Eddie Gray, spraying the ball to our wingers and so on, instead of to Len Badger at United, who could ping an accurate ball himself. Things were generally more organised at Leeds than at Bramall Lane, where the lads really used to organise themselves. I had hated Leeds when I was at Sheffield United because they were high-achieving Yorkshire rivals, but now I naturally had a different perspective and wanted to help to repeat their success.

The signing of the always-dangerous Arthur Graham was of great significance because he could be a mercurial performer. Arthur, who eventually moved to Manchester United, was a fabulous winger who could use both feet and was very quick, although not as speedy as Carl Harris. Carl was the fastest thing I've ever seen on two legs, but he didn't quite know how to harness his impressive talents to become an even better version of himself.

Armfield was recruiting well and when Welsh international Brian Flynn also arrived, it proved to be a shrewd signing. I enjoyed our partnership. He was great, a little 'ratter' like Trevor Hockey, but with more skill, and we linked well together. Ray Hankin had been a key signing for Armfield the season before, but the repercussions of a knee-ligament injury sustained with Burnley had curtailed his debut season after just four games. It was a big blow in limiting the scoring output which was admirably proved the following season; he had rehabilitated and never looked back, claiming 20 goals in his 33 league appearances.

He may not have been the most mobile or skilful, but Ray was a great target man and header of the ball. For a big man he had something special and could find the net – in short, he was a right handful for the opposition. I rated him so highly that I recall being in a pub with him once in Linton, telling him pretty forcefully that he might play for England if he applied himself. But like so many gifted players ever since football began, he had his problems and liked a drink or two. It wasn't over the top, but, I suppose, just a bit too much to make that next big step.

We would pop out for a drink together, going to the Alpine pub just up the road on the A1 on a Wednesday night, and sometimes to the Windmill at Linton, near Wetherby, at Sunday lunchtimes. That was a really exclusive area and you could hardly move because it was so packed, but Linda's depression might have contributed to the feeling that I sometimes just needed a couple of hours with a mate.

An opening-day defeat was put behind us and we recovered well, dipped and picked up again in November with Flynn's arrival. It left us heading towards the new year in the mix, if not threatening hard, although a third-round FA Cup loss to Manchester City was a setback.

Another came when Gordon McQueen and Joe Jordan upped sticks and, after playing for us in a defeat Newcastle on January 2, signed for Manchester United. It sickened me, for the same reason I was upset when Sheffield United sold Geoff Salmons to their divisional rivals when he wasn't injured or ageing. The pair were both Scottish internationals and very influential for us. It was a massive double blow to the team and we didn't bring in an adequate replacement for Gordon until we paid Blackpool £300,000 for Paul Hart in March.

I don't know if Jimmy had ever been given adequate funds to perform the overhaul he was required to do, or perhaps when that season started, he was convinced that we would be okay because he still had Jordan and McQueen. It's a point of discussion as to whether Revie had neglected recruitment for the future, preferring to play the same lads every year. When you had that quality, you could understand the temptation to keep them. But other teams gradually and more seamlessly changed their squad.

If there was anything else that affected our season as fundamentally as player departures, it would be Don Howe being lured back to coach at Arsenal before Christmas 1977. He was a tough disciplinarian, but a motivator and great coach and I really enjoyed what he brought to us all. You need a bit of that on matchday and Jimmy didn't mind that from his assistant – who wasn't afraid to tell you if you needed to up your game or do something else.

Howe was passionate and specific in his coaching, demanding: "I want this then, then that from you." I found it easy to comprehend. I always did respect the title of managers and coaches – apart from once, which I'll touch on later – and Don's departure hit Jimmy hard. He was a lovely bloke and talented manager, but needed someone such as Don to handle players better in certain situations.

We improved our league position by four points and one place, finishing ninth and way behind the champions Nottingham Forest, who were by far and away the best team that year. But we had won more than we had lost, scored more goals and enjoyed another cup run, this time the Football League version. After knocking out Rochdale 3-0 away, Colchester United 4-0, Bolton away 3-1 and Everton 4-1 at home, we faced Forest in a two-legged semi-final. It was a shame we had to meet at that stage because it would have been a good final and ironically we got a win and a draw against them in the league games. Forest triumphed in both semis, though, beating us 3-1 at Elland Road and 4-2 at the City Ground.

It was the third time in three years that Leeds had reached a domestic or European semi-final, but our attendances had started to decline and Jimmy had started getting a bit of stick. I was playing the best football of my life, voted player-of-the-year at Leeds and was back in the England squad. But being realistic, we had made virtually no progress under Jimmy during the last two seasons when he was under pressure, mainly because of the long period of success that preceded him.

He had to make the top three at least and I thought he went about it the right way, but he was never the same after Don had left. That was the beginning of the end really for Jimmy and when that happened, it upset me. Letting Don go was a very big mistake. But despite all the change in the air, I still never regretted the decision to join Leeds.

***

I believe that we managed to manufacture quite a reasonably successful season in 1978-89 because it was against all the odds from day one. During its course only the Grays, Madeley, Harvey and Lorimer of the real 'legends' made any appearances, with the latter managing only three.
The changing of the guard was nearing completion and that included managers. There were three of them in the chair by October. What

hadn't changed was the lack of activity in the transfer market; big players with big names weren't arriving to stimulate the fans and invigorate the team, which, I think, made a fifth-place finish even more remarkable.

Armfield had run out of time and there was no air of surprise about his sacking. He had been handed a hell of a task and went about it with dignity and no little intelligence, but fell short of performing a miracle. I am glad he went on to become such a respected and successful figure in the media, rounding off a fabulous career in football. He deserved it all.

There was no new man in place for the first few weeks of the season so Maurice Lindley was in caretaker charge, having once teamed up with Revie as assistant manager and chief scout. He was to stay at the club for about 20 years in various roles, including three more stints as temporary boss. Maurice had seen success and great players at Leeds and was well-respected in the game. He loved a laugh and a joke so the players didn't exactly fear him, but he had enough football experience to get by. I think he was managing director at some point and was a lovely bloke who loved a great player.

Naturally everyone was waiting for and speculating about who was to come in long-term. It had to be a big name, surely? This was an opportunity to restore a huge football club with a recent history of success and a large fanbase to the pinnacle of the English game. I don't think many were disappointed when, out of the blue, 'Jock' Stein was unveiled.

He was a blue chip, bona fide god of the Scottish scene, having made Celtic serial domestic winners and then seeing them crowned European champions. Although his time at Celtic had drawn to a slightly disappointing close, no-one thought Stein's career was over. His reputation ensured that it was still seen as a massive coup. But so had the appointment of Brian Clough when Revie left ...

When Stein arrived, it was soon apparent that he was very aware of my career and rated me highly. Considering what he had already achieved, his complimentary words were encouraging and I liked the idea of Jock taking us forward. It was reasonable to believe this was the start of something big and getting on well with him only added to my excitement.

Optimism was high and the country was expectant about how Stein would take to the English game. He was another who would speak to players individually in addition to the whole team and there was definitely something about him, as there seems to be with all great managers.

His arrival coincided with me scoring twice in our first three games and I went on to total seven for the season, a much more respectable figure this time. The first, in the opening fixture at Arsenal, was particularly satisfying; they were old rivals of mine and the strike into the far top corner from way out on the right was a spectacular way to start. Stein's results were a tad disappointing, but it was still early days and the lads were still getting to grips with his demands.

And then he left... after just 44 days. Again. Just as Clough had done.

The lure of the Scottish international squad was too strong for Stein to resist, but he had to resign in order to leave because Leeds' chairman Manny Cussins had refused to just let him go. We never found out if he could repeat his success over the border. And the nagging possibility that he had somehow manufactured the whole scenario was whispered in some circles.

Had he used the Leeds job as a stepping-stone to the national team? Had he known all along that he was going to get the opportunity to take over from Ally MacLeod? The lads didn't really work long enough with him to know how he operated and we were without a manager again.

Our results continued to be mixed and it couldn't have been an easy situation for striker John Hawley, who had come in from Hull City in the summer. He will have wanted to make an impression at a higher level and was still trying to settle in during a bit of an unstable period. In the circumstances finishing top scorer with 16 league goals was a creditable effort, comfortably outscoring Hankin. The fact he had allegedly cost only about £80,000 showed it had been an astute signing by Armfield, but also revealed that investment was again on the conservative end of the scale.

Eventually, to some surprise, Jimmy Adamson, formerly of Burnley and Sunderland, was appointed and on the face of it, fifth place and another semi-final berth was a respectable achievement. It was about the time of his arrival when I had a bittersweet return to Bramall Lane to face Sheffield United for the first time since I had left. It was a League Cup fixture I was desperate to play in and only just made, having been out for a month with injury. My old team were struggling in Division Two, currently the Championship, which gave me no pleasure at all, considering the strong feelings I retained for the city, the club and the fans.

Maybe I was naïve, but I was looking forward to being given at least a muted welcome. So I was a bit taken aback when the United Kop decided against that, opting instead to chant: "You fat bastard!" at me. It was their way of telling me that they still hadn't forgiven me for leaving – and joining, of all teams, Leeds.

At least I hope it was – and not a reference to the condition I was in. I had never been as fit in all my life! It didn't help their mood either when I scored and we went on to complete a pretty routine 4-1 win. Of course, I know enough about football to understand the fan mentality about such things … They wouldn't have shouted it if they didn't care.

In November I scored one of the most admired and talked-about goals of my career. It's a fact of football life that long-distance drives or spectacular goals in general attract the most attention and probably live longer in the memory. Because of where I mostly operated on the pitch a good percentage of my goals came from distance, as did this one in a four-goal drubbing of Southampton at Elland Road.

We were already two up in the second half when I tried a forward pass which was slightly under-hit and headed away. I nicked possession back a few yards outside the area and, as I shuffled forward, a defender kept his body between me and a clear sight of goal. So I shifted the ball slightly to my right and before he could get across and completely shut the space down, I curled the ball with the inside of my right foot from about 20 yards out. Terry Gennoe, the Saints' goalkeeper, probably had his initial view blocked and although he did everything he could to reach it, the ball was perfectly placed, just inside his left-hand post.

Even if I say so myself, I knew what I'd done – that it was special enough to warrant just standing there, blowing a kiss and taking the congratulations. I'm often asked about my mentality regarding long-range shooting and have discussed it earlier, but this one was a premeditated swerver and I don't remember scoring that way ever again.

By this third season with Leeds I had regained my England place and seen my profile raised enough to have George Best's agent, Harry Swales, representing me. Again, though, I wasn't the most important client so he didn't take care of my wage contracts; just off-the-field stuff such as boots and the Kellogg's picture cards. I wasn't maximising my potential for that type of income and although it would be very different today, it wasn't just because these were early days for lucrative endorsements. I just didn't have it in me to ruffle a few feathers and pursue it. I was probably more concerned with fulfilling the twin aims of playing in European competition at club level and playing in a cup final at Wembley. And we were in the running for both.

Four wins and two draws in a six-game spell at the business end of the season put us well in contention, so it was unfortunate that we faced the top two in our final games, both at home. Although we lost them, 2-1 against Forest and 3-0 to Liverpool, we had enough points to claim that spot in Europe that I cherished so much. We had exactly the same won/drawn/lost statistics as we had the previous season, yet finished higher. That was a bit strange, but Liverpool ran away with the title really and only Forest could be considered also to be at that level. Leeds had dominated the league for years and now these two were sharing it in an annual two-horse race.

Liverpool undoubtedly had great players, plus Bill Shankly, but Clough's team just intrigued me because they were so different. John Robertson smoked like a trooper, but was in my view – with his weird shuffle and great crossing ability – one of the greatest wingers ever. They had talented 'up and downers' in midfield, a solid defence with Kenny Burns and Larry Lloyd and goals were not hard to come by with Peter Withe, Trevor Francis and Tony Woodcock up top.

They were a really entertaining outfit and Francis was a phenomenal player who was like lightning and a good finisher. While he didn't have the physique to play a physical role, he could play effectively off a big man and was much better doing that rather than being put out on the right, as he often was with England. Brian Clough was unconventional in his methods and in his dealings with the media and football people, but he knew how to pick players and get the best out of them. He did it with Derby and then that Forest team, in no small part because of his man-management skills.

A lot of managers and their assistants employed the good cop-bad cop type of partnership, which usually served its purpose in getting through to a broad span of players with different personalities. I understood that and always respected the people taking on those roles…. with just one exception.

I found Dave Merrington, Adamson's assistant at Leeds, to be a horrible and aggressive bloke and I thoroughly disliked him. He threw the cups about in the dressing-room at half-time once, but that wasn't as nasty as it got. On another occasion we were having a team meeting in the changing-room at Elland Road and I made a gesture behind Merrington's back. Syd Farrimond, one of the staff, saw it and snitched on me. That was fair enough: I was caught, but it was only a mild gesture that didn't merit the fall-out that followed.

When the meeting was over, I changed, went out of the dressing-room door and there was Merrington waiting. He got me against the wall. "If you ever do that again," he bellowed at me, telling me what he would do. I wasn't a troublemaker or a bad dressing-room influence. His response was way over the top and said more about him than me.

Although our FA Cup run was ended by West Brom in a replay at the fourth-round stage, three months earlier we had overcome them in a marathon League Cup contest in round two. Paul Hart got the winner after two goalless draws and that win at Sheffield United got us a step further. The next round, this time at QPR, was successfully negotiated 2-0 and then at home in round five we had our shooting boots on as Luton Town were trounced 4-1. Trevor Cherry, both Grays and I netted during a comfortable passage to our third semi-final in successive years.

We had already beaten Southampton by four goals without reply in the league so we were quietly, but justifiably, confident that we could at least establish a healthy lead before the return. It seemed as if that would be the case when Ray Hankin and I had put us two ahead with only minutes remaining. But Steve Williams, hardly a prolific midfielder, stunned us with a brace to send us to The Dell six days later all square.

As if that wasn't bad enough, the simmering difficulties in my home life were now to play a more direct part in my football career. Linda's isolation problems had continued all the time we had been at Leeds and we were still going down to London virtually every week, sometimes only stopping overnight. It affected our daily life as a result and it wasn't great. Our three kids, two of whom were only about nine or ten, were at the stage when changing schools would be an important decision and I can't help but wonder if my old-fashioned view, that she should stay at home and look after the children, had been wrong from the start.

She had nothing else to focus on and no workplace in which to make new friends. And the repercussions of it all were to affect my football even more after I left Leeds. Linda reached a crisis point, decided that enough was enough and upped and left for London with the kids in tow. It reminded me of the time at Sheffield when I had sped to the station to talk her out of fleeing back to the capital which she missed so much.

Because of the upset I didn't go down with the team as normal for the second leg and at the time I was already taking a mild form of valium; it helped me to sleep and also improved my mood a bit during the day. Eventually I did take the train to Southampton to meet up with the boys for a decision to be made about whether I should be considered to take part.

Jimmy Adamson knew the state I was in – worried that Linda's move might be permanent – but elected to play me. I had an absolute stinker as we went out 1-0 and failed to reach a cup final yet again. It had been the wrong decision to play me because I really wasn't in the right frame of mind, but I don't necessarily blame Jimmy. Maybe these days he would be assisted by individuals with more relevant expertise about how I was being affected.

Linda and the kids had stayed with her mother during the game. When I went back there later, we discussed things and went back to Leeds as a family. It wasn't a split, but I accepted that the only way to alter the situation and realistically improve our marriage was to return to London. In the summer I asked for a move. Linda hadn't wanted to move out of the capital from the start and for a long time I had felt under pressure to return.

It had created pressure in our relationship, a gradual build-up of certain things that would ensure it would not survive. If I had wanted it to end, I could have just initiated a split, but I didn't want to lose her or my kids. I wanted it to survive for all the right reasons, but in the end I think I said: "Right then, let's go back to London" – even though I was having the time of my life on the pitch at Leeds.

There is no doubt in my mind that I had played the best football of my life at Leeds, largely because I was more mature and playing with some really top players. We could keep the ball better for longer, which really helps a player of my type. The more I had the ball the more I could do. I was selected in the best XI of the division – chosen by players of the teams in the top-flight – every year I was at Elland Road. It was a great accolade, spoiled only slightly by those three losing semi-finals and latterly not getting past the England squad stage often enough.

When I had told Adamson that I needed a move to London, he was visibly disappointed. "They are going to hang me," he said. I assumed he meant the board and supporters, but to be fair to Jimmy he understood my reasoning. When I apologised for putting him in that position, he went to his drinks cabinet and quietly said: "I'm having a large whisky. Do you want one?"

"Go on then," I said. It was a civilised way for both of us to deal with a situation that neither of us really wanted.

Leeds' squad, including myself, were due to go to Holland for some of pre-season and a game at PSV Eindhoven threw a spanner in the works of any transfer I was anticipating. I went into a sliding tackle, missed the ball and caught my opponent's ankle, which was planted on the ground. Honestly it was like tackling a wall and as a result I damaged all the capsule of my ankle joint. You can imagine my worry at what that might mean.

Geoff Ladley, Leeds' physio and one of the most qualified in the country, was brilliant. He strapped me up and out I went again. The strapping actually went round my boot, but I was still in so much pain and when the game was over, it was a matter of icing it like mad.

Incredibly – or stupidly more like – I went out with the group that night, despite my foot being turned at a silly angle and Ray Hankin helping me to hobble along. It was a really stupid thing to do because I should have rested the joint. In those days no-one would have realised how serious an injury it was.

I don't have any bitterness about how the injury was dealt with at the time. It was abroad and more difficult to do what would have been done in more normal circumstances back in England, but it was severe and I should have had an X-ray at least.

If today's medical methods had been available back then, I'm sure it wouldn't have caused such a problem for so long. My career might have progressed differently. But my toes almost touched my shin and God knows how the Achilles survived. And what I did didn't help either. I was having problems with my wife, I knew I was going home to go through with a transfer and going out for a drink would have been many people's solution at the time.

Secretly I was hoping that Spurs or Chelsea would come in for me –

and I heard later that Arsenal were interested – but Leeds wouldn't sell me to another First Division rival. It reminds me how I could have gone to Anderlecht, like Duncan McKenzie did from Leeds, at another point in my career, although I can't remember which club I was with at the time.

Now, though, I just wanted to get it over with and QPR were an emerging club with good ambition. They had recruited highly-rated players such as Steve Wicks, David McCreery, Chris Woods and Mickey Walsh, so were intent on building a promotion-winning team. It wasn't to happen overnight, though.

Tommy Docherty was in charge and had tried to sign me when he was at Manchester United, where he used to shout at me if they stuffed us because I had turned him down! Now he had finally got his man and I was looking forward to playing under him.

When the deal had been done, we had nowhere to live to begin with and stayed in a hotel, just down the road from my mum, for 10 days before renting a flat for a year. Then it was to Radlett, close to Boreham Wood. I was relieved, of sorts, to keep the family all together, but gutted to have sacrificed playing European football with Leeds. Linda wasn't bothered who I was playing for or where it was – as long as it was back in London.

16

INTERNATIONAL DEPARTURES

By April 1978 I had won seven full international caps ... but none for two-and-a-half years. During those 'lost years' I hadn't given up hope of adding to them, although I would be lying if I said I was confident my career at that level would resume. One national manager had shown complete faith in me and the next wasn't having me at any price. It would depend on who would come in next...

My club form was as good as it had ever been and the irony of it being for Leeds United, the club Don Revie had taken to the top of English football, wasn't stopping their fans from taking to me. I was totally immersed in the way things were done there, very much wanting to help restore Leeds to their previous heights in the top-flight and in Europe.

My issue with Revie didn't affect my relationship with the players who had played for him either – we all seemed to accept that it shouldn't change how we got on. He had left well before I arrived and had nothing to do with me being at Elland Road. I can assume only that he would not have signed me if he had still been in charge there when I became available down the M1 at Sheffield United.

Not surprisingly I was one of several England players left fuming at the manner in which Don walked out of the England job. Writing in the *Daily Mail* on July 12, 1977, Jeff Powell shocked the football world – including the FA – by revealing that Revie was going to quit because the hassle and criticism that went with the role had become too much for him, his wife and family to bear.

That being the case, my own disillusionment with Revie doesn't prevent me from sympathising with his predicament. It can't have been much fun enduring the amount of scrutiny he was subjected to. But it was surely a mistake to announce his departure in the Press first because it would have been possible to do it properly and leave with more dignity and understanding.

Tipping off a national newspaper and benefitting from the story before telling his employers only increased the level of hostility towards him. When it emerged that he had allegedly secretly agreed a deal to manage the UAE while still England manager, he effectively made himself *persona non grata* in English football. That exit, followed by his death just 12 years later from motor neurone disease, was a sad way to go after his exploits with Leeds. No personal dislike can mask that.

When the FA sat to choose their next international boss, they turned again to a man who had made his reputation at club level and again with one team in particular. This one, though, was a completely different animal. Revie had built an uncompromising outfit designed to win trophies first and entertain second, notwithstanding the fact that his team had great ability. On the other hand Ron Greenwood was a diplomatic and well-liked football thinker who was in love with the skills and patterns of the game as he saw them.

All managers want to win, but some, such as Ron, have to do it with style or for them it is hardly worth winning. He was a West Ham United man and it is to some extent incredible that this ideal seems to have epitomised that club for so long, decades after the revered and well-known players and managers have departed. It looked a promising appointment for my ambitions and I was happy with it because he had the Hammers playing some lovely, flowing football. I expected West Ham's Trevor Brooking to be first on the teamsheet and although back then you didn't pick two creative midfielders in the same team, I did feel I was in with more of a chance again.

All managers have their favourites at whatever level and Trevor was well-positioned with Ron and I maintain that he was good enough to have won more than 47 caps. At 28 I was still young enough to have a good international career and things can change quickly when a new man comes in. They did ... I won 10 caps in a year!

It was quite a turnaround although initially neither Trevor nor I were selected. Trevor got in for Ron's third match while I first appeared for him in the friendly against the Brazilians in April 1978. They were in transition themselves, but it was wonderful to walk out against players such as Zico and Rivellino. The former was just establishing himself in the side, while the latter was at the other end of his career. But I got the headlines in a 1-1 draw.

The Press said that I had played Brazil at their own game, dribbling and going round them with ease. It was so nice to read and probably why I went on to win so many more caps in such a short space of time. Although it wasn't the Brazilians' strongest team, they knocked the ball about very well and took a 10th-minute lead. Their control and vision were obvious and not every English player has those attributes, but I genuinely felt I could hold my own in that company. I wanted to pit my skills against theirs and wasn't nervous, even though I did wonder beforehand if we would even get a kick!

Kevin Keegan's goal levelled the score and I was just grateful to have played against such a magnificent football nation – and at Wembley, where I ended up playing 12 times. After all, many players have represented England and not had the chance to play at our own national stadium for their country. And my form there was pretty consistent.

I reckon that apart from my first international against Northern Ireland and that game against Switzerland under Revie, I would have got decent marks for my performances. I must have been rated only about two out of 10 against the Swiss, but I feel better about that when I recall Jimmy Adamson at Leeds telling me that great players don't drop below eight out of 10 very often – and that I was in that bracket.

One month later in a home international clash with Wales at Ninian Park, Brooking started with me on the bench. I came on for Trevor Cherry and scored with virtually my first kick, a first-time, left-footed shot following a one-two. The ball absolutely flew in from outside the box and left goalkeeper Dai Davies tangled up in the goal netting, setting us up for a 3-1 win. Then a single goal from Phil Neal enabled us to squeak past Northern Ireland at Wembley again. Four of my 17 caps came against those lads in green!

I can't recall whether injury or anything else intervened, but at this stage Ron seemed to be playing either Trevor or me, irrespective of performances. The next fixture against Scotland was a difficult one for me and I played poorly despite Steve Coppell's strike securing us another single-goal win. The surface at Hampden was the bobbliest I ever played on, and that is saying something for those days. Looking back now, it reminds me of the farce we had in England when the team played on the Wembley pitch just after it had been used for the Horse of the Year show. Not a great idea!

The Hampden game may have been awful, but I did take something from it that I had always wanted to experience. I had played there before and scored for England under-23s, but this time the famous old ground had 88,000 inside – which gave the home crowd ample chance to let us know how they felt about us. No-one abuses us like the Scots!

At an earlier fixture between us at Wembley I was left out, owing to injury, I think, but I stood in the crowd watching with my uncle Bert. I got us tickets and must have paid for them because we were in the Scottish end. Fortunately I wasn't recognised because we were behind the goal surrounded by thousands of Jocks. Rest assured, I kept my head down!

Of course, indifferent pitches were a regular occurrence for us all – especially towards the end of the season – and they didn't stop me from enjoying the home international series, which were played annually in that period. I loved them, partly as I wanted to play all year round. My attitude was: "Sod sitting back and having a rest!" These were opportunities to gain more caps against familiar players, many of whom I played against every week in the league. Some of them were good friends.

It wasn't always easy to play the English game because of the tighter marking in midfield; space could be hard to find, whereas foreign teams usually backed off and gave you time on the ball. Admittedly that would normally suit me, but I could rarely play long balls against foreign teams when their defences left less space in behind. That hadn't happened earlier in my career; during my second international against Russia I got great reviews because I was hitting long, straight balls with backspin, 40 or 50 yards to strikers in the channels.

The Russians had employed a less sophisticated system that enabled me to do that and they preferred to play the game hard, fast and direct. The Brazilians were sneakier in terms of fouling and the Italians cynical, whereas the home internationals were frantic without necessarily being dirty. The Scots would field players such as Dalglish and Macari and I always remember the Welsh having Leeds players including Terry Yorath and Brian Flynn.

I always looked forward to those fixtures, as did the fans, so it was sad to see them phased out. And why? I don't really know, but the game was developing and I can see the arguments stacking up for abandoning them; knackered players, poor end-of-season pitches and not playing enough fixtures against foreign opposition. Maybe it was a pointer to how football was going in favour of international club football. For me I shall always recall the fans' fervour and Alan Ball loving winding the Scots up on the coach to our clashes.

Ron Greenwood's reign was a breath of fresh air after the chaos that had gone before. The group was smaller and there were fewer changes from game to game as he tried to formulate a way of playing. He just seemed to pick the right squad and kept the basis of it while gradually introducing others in a measured, progressive way. And crucially he told us to play our normal game.

There were similarities to Sir Alf. Both were gentlemen, thoughtful, measured and calm in their approach. They talked to us both as individuals and as a group, which earned our respect. Ron was a nice man, a good manager who talked well and I liked him, irrespective of whether he selected me or not. It was almost inevitable that he would want to replicate the West Ham style of football, with early balls in for our forwards to attack whilst opposing defenders were made to turn backwards. The Hammers were brilliant at that and so were England under Alf.

It was a great way of playing and Sheffield United had used it extensively when Geoff Salmons and Alan Woodward were running riot on the wings. It suited me down to the ground. My fears about playing second fiddle to Brooking weren't exactly played out as I feared either, at least throughout Ron's first year in post. Both of us were given opportunities and there didn't appear to be favouritism as I clocked up plenty of game time, although we were rarely on the pitch at the same time.

In fact, during the next fixture against Hungary at Wembley, I came off the bench to replace Brian Greenhoff and Trevor created a goal for me. Out on the left he laid the ball into my path and I hit it with my instep as it came across to contribute to the 4-1 win. I had tried the same kind of shot against both Poland and Italy in 1973, but sadly neither found the net in two games that really mattered.

It was becoming apparent that Ron would usually go to Trevor for European Championship qualifiers, so I missed the next two games but was restored for the 1-0 Wembley friendly win against Czechoslovakia.

Three months later Northern Ireland visited for another qualifier, and this time the manager selected us both as starters. It might have given Ron food for thought as we duly won 4-0 with Keegan, Bob Latchford (two) and Dave Watson on the scoresheet.

I retained the shirt when the two teams met yet again in the return qualifier in May 1979. It was an extremely troubled time politically because of the Irish situation and there was some anxiety in the camp when we flew in. There was definitely a strange sort of tension as we were escorted through checkpoints and so on by armed guards in a country so close to us.

These days players might be given the option to withdraw, as happened more recently with the England cricket team when Eoin Morgan declined a tour to Bangladesh for security reasons. Although I liked Windsor Park and there were no signs of any trouble as we were well chaperoned, it was just as scary as going through Checkpoint Charlie and the Berlin Wall when on tour there with United. Anyway, I was in midfield with Terry McDermott and Ray Wilkins as we got through safely enough by a couple of goals to nil.

Within four days we were back in action against Wales in the Home Internationals, a game that ended goalless – which probably is the reason I have no meaningful recollection of it. Maybe it was a bit of a letdown after the importance of the qualifiers we had just won, or perhaps fatigue played its part. Either way, I was selected and Trevor was benched, but the roles were reversed for the next two fixtures against Scotland (won 3-1) and then in Bulgaria (won 3-0) when the squad clinched qualification for the 1980 Euros.

June 10, 1979, Rasunda Stadium, Stockholm. *Friendly International.* Sweden 0 England 0

My 17th cap over a seven-year span. After that it was over with England. But I didn't know at the time that it was coming and neither did I know that my circumstances back home were about to change dramatically. It wasn't my best game and it was summed up when I went to cross the ball which hit a divot – it was almost a fresh air effort – and went out for a goal kick. Terry McDermott and I were both substituted, so we were both pissed off and went to the bar after having a shower while the game was still in progress. Ron probably understood our frustration, left us well alone and didn't reprimand us.

Neither the manager nor I were to know that I would soon be leaving Leeds, or that I was going to be pretty badly crocked before my next transfer was even completed. It is inevitable and tempting for me to speculate whether I would have won more caps if I had stayed fit and, perhaps crucially, remained in the top-flight. To his credit Ron picked me in a couple of his squads even when I was still on crutches with my next club a few months later. It was nice to feel that he wanted me around, even in that condition, but the call never came again.

No call, no message, although I get annoyed when today's players get upset by things like that. In my case I was convinced that the injury finished my international career, so that was that. No use in dwelling on it not being sugar-coated.

Not achieving all your ambitions in football is nothing to be ashamed of. But not doing as much as you can in pursuit of them is more damaging, particularly if you look back and consider what might have been if only you had tried harder. There are so many factors that a player cannot control so I am immensely proud to have played 17 times for my country. Although it might have been more in other circumstances, I have to acknowledge that under other managers it may have been fewer anyway. Most players have their bad luck stories and as far as England caps are concerned, my deepest sympathies lie with those whose beguiling talents were recognised even less than my own.

Yes, 17 is a decent enough number but it is almost beyond belief that the era of the 'mavericks' was to reward them so meagerly when other nations were producing – and regularly playing – their own flair players. Just think, for example, of Alan Hudson (two caps), Frank Worthington (eight), Stan Bowles (five), Rodney Marsh (nine), Charlie George (one) and Peter Osgood (four), all of whom could have had influential England careers. And I'm sure you might be able to think of others worthy of suggestion. Ultimately selection comes down to one person's value of someone else's ability, attitude and usefulness within a system so, basically, it's being in the right place at the right time.

I sometimes wonder if other players cling to the physical reminders of their time with England as I have. Photos, videos and so on of our own England years are relatively rare so I'm glad I was always one for saving the stuff I was given as mementos, including ties, tie pins, menus and call-up messages etc.

International tours were a good source for me to snaffle stuff some players weren't bothered about keeping. I always asked politely even though I couldn't easily understand their casual attitude to giving away something I thought was an honour to receive. Newspaper cuttings form a considerable part of my collection, along with match programmes from every game during my career. Each item tells a part of the story of my life as a player and if I lose anything, or lend it and don't get it back, I am honestly absolutely gutted.

I have parted company – usually reluctantly! – with a few shirts but a cap I gave for display in the Sheffield United boardroom in the 1980s sadly went missing. On another occasion I needed a gift for Joe Elliott, Blades fan and lead singer of Def Leppard, and as no-one knew what to give a millionaire, he was presented with one of my England U21 caps. At least he appreciates it.

The only cap that Don Revie gave me, against Switzerland, was auctioned off for £500 at my testimonial dinner. I was less distressed at giving that one away as you might imagine – it just didn't mean as much to me as the others. Another one, from my last against Sweden, was sold for £2,500 – twice – and ultimately given back to me by the first buyer. He knew I never really wanted to be parted from it and felt sorry for me; a great gesture I really appreciated.

Those mementos are genuinely significant to me and were sold at the time only because I needed the money. Working part-time as I was then and having to eat into our savings wasn't very nice and I had to raise cash from somewhere, however painful it was. England caps normally fetch around £1,000 now but it really depends on the buyer, the market and whose cap it is. For example, if Bobby Moore's World Cup winning cap came up, it would be almost priceless.

The culture of exchanging shirts, mainly after international games, always appealed to me for obvious reasons, so when the final whistle went I was on a mission to get hold of the best one I could. It invariably meant trying to get to the opposition's star player before anyone else did and I built up quite a collection that includes shirts from Austria, Brazil, Russia and Italy.

It was a well-known and popular custom. Most players wanted foreign international shirts as mementos, especially if it was one that belonged to a great player or their immediate opponent. Mine included Leeds' teammates, Brian Flynn and Terry Yorath, plus the fabulous Italian Gianni Rivera. It was just what we did. Rivera was dubbed Italy's "Golden Boy" and as a result, his shirt is one I prize highly. To have a piece of kit from such a famous player you have done battle with at the highest level of the game is such a personal and direct reminder that it brings memories flooding back. I wonder if he still has mine!

I wasn't so lucky after playing against Brazil because I ended up with one from a player who was less well-known, when I had actually wanted to try for Zico's. Later, at a signing event, I had a word with Carlos Alberto and told him that I didn't know the player who I had swapped with. He revealed that if the number on the back had been one usually worn by the great names of Brazilian football it would have been worth a fortune over there. Unfortunately, it had been worn by somebody else on that day! These days it resides in Sheffield United's Hall of Fame and has subsequently been signed by Pele.

Getting the shirt you wanted was easier if you already knew a player and pre-arranged it, which is why my Leeds teammate Brian Flynn's shirt is one of the two Welsh ones I have. Remember my first international against Northern Ireland in 1972, when Terry Neill scored the winner in a drab game at Wembley? I had been taken off with half an hour to go, and was so disappointed at not scoring and being hooked on debut that I was dwelling on it.

When the game was over and everyone gathered on the pitch, I was on the verge of exchanging my shirt. Alf Ramsey saw what I did, came up and grabbed it from me. "You never give away your first international shirt!" he said. Then, he went to the Irish dressing room and swapped the shirts back. Me being me, I was just so embarrassed. Because, me being me, I had never thought about the significance. But it taught me a lesson, and I was so glad that Alf intervened.

17

A LONE RANGER

I needed a move to London, as simple as that. The fact that it meant dropping down a level to QPR wasn't ideal in terms of my career, but for Linda it was a relief after years of depression. For us as a couple it was necessary. And everyone knew because it was all over the newspapers.

But God knows what the Leeds fans who idolised me thought. They didn't need to tell me that I had been their favourite and had given up my first chance of playing in Europe. It was easy to think that I had messed it all up, but short of splitting my family apart I had little option.

I responded to the phone call to speak with Tommy Docherty at Loftus Road and – wouldn't you know it? – signed a blank contract! Rangers were in the Second Division, but I was still an England player and concerned how the status was going to affect my future chances. No wonder the chairman Jim Gregory said: "I like you for signing a blank contract because that shows trust in us."

It did – but it also showed my inability to negotiate my worth. The truth was I avoided the issue because I wanted to get a deal done to help my marriage. I somehow managed to pass the medical, despite arriving on crutches, and the aim was to get on with playing again in, hopefully, a happier and more stable domestic environment.

I had heard during my last year with Leeds that Arsenal were interested in me, but nothing came of it, so things might have worked out very differently. There was no point in dwelling on that and now, given everything that had happened, there was justifiable optimism on my part that things could work out at home.

QPR had as recently as 1975 finished second in the league to Liverpool, boasted great players such as Stan Bowles and Gerry Francis and enjoyed a reputation for entertaining football despite a subsequent relegation.

They still had an aura about them and were regarded as being like Chelsea in the 1970s when the Blues had Peter Osgood and Alan Hudson. Rangers were a fashionable and trendy outfit and also a final and successful destination for some top-end careers that were coming to a close, for men such as Terry Venables and Frank McLintock.

It didn't take a great leap of faith to believe that Loftus Road could well be a stage I could enjoy if things went right on the pitch. It was ironic that they paid £400,000 for me when they could have had me for nothing when I was rejected as a schoolboy, but there was no animosity from me about that now. The initial 10-day stay at the Garth Hotel for Linda, the kids and me cost me a lot of money – no expenses in those days – although it at least was only about 200 yards from my mum in Cricklewood.

Then we lodged in Hendon for a couple of months before moving into a house in Radlett, Boreham Wood, which was a commuter area. It was quite upmarket and my kids went to school with the Shadows' guitarist Hank Marvin's kids. George Michael lived nearby and the England cricket captain Mike Gatting had a shop there.

It has since made me wonder if Leeds had missed a trick by not suggesting I might live in London to ease my domestic issues. At that stage of my career they might have allowed me to train with someone else in London and go up to Leeds for training a couple of days a week in order to keep me. Of course it might have had repercussions with the rest of the squad, plus the travelling would be a pain, so it was a difficult one. But I thought they might have tried something or other, seeing as I had wanted to stay.

The Doc had a great reputation and had managed my team Chelsea in the 1960s, building a young, exciting side. He had unbelievable character and loved a joke, but when it came to the game, he definitely had his serious head on. Tommy was given financial backing as Rangers attempted a quick return to the top division and he used it well to build a good team; David McCreery, Chris Woods, Mickey Walsh, Steve Burke and Steve Wicks were all signed in a year or so as he went for promotion big time.

The injury I brought with me kept me out for the first half-dozen fixtures, including one of the League Cup victories over two legs against Bradford City. It was frustrating for all of us and Docherty even quipped at one stage: "Are you ever going to play for this club?" It was said in a semi-joking way, but it possibly betrayed his own feelings as to whether he might have made a mistake. Either way it didn't exactly make me feel any better.

Years later John Graham, who had been Rangers' physio and became a very good friend, told me an interesting tale of that period when I was unable to shake off the injury. I had been having painkilling injections under Tommy, even for my debut, and in one game I was in such absolute agony I came in at half-time and said: "I don't know what's wrong, but I'm going to have to have another injection if I'm going out again." John told me that the medical staff had injected water into the joint before the game because they thought I was taking the piss. They put the right stuff in at half-time!

The team had lost three of the four league games by the time I made my league debut against Fulham, so a 3-0 home win steadied the ship. And scoring made it a special day for me. I found myself pretty well forward, about 30 yards out, as the ball was chipped straight over my shoulder. It bounced and as it dropped, I volleyed a real dipper over the goalkeeper. Although I had been given a tremendous welcome by the crowd at the start, I was definitely made to feel like the king now!

I had loved the old Loftus Road stadium in the earlier days, about 1971, when there was an open terrace on the far side and a roof behind one goal of another side. Now I had come back as a QPR player, the old ground had virtually all gone and it was more or less as it is now. The capacity was now only about 20,000, but it is a lovely stadium with a great atmosphere which I really enjoyed playing at.

Goddard and Clive Allen got the other goals that day, a clear sign of how important they were to be for us all season. My euphoria was soon dampened, though, because injury and subsequent spin-off injuries intervened and I was in and out of the team until the turn of the year. It was massively frustrating so when the Doc had made that comment about me having treatment so often, it hurt. I wouldn't want my commitment questioned, but I also didn't want confrontation and wouldn't have a go back. So I kept it to myself and got through it.

Missing games through injury also robbed me of the chance to line up more regularly with Stan Bowles, the type of flamboyant, modern player loved by London crowds at that time. It was a real shame because the telepathy was brilliant between two skilful players who knew what each other wanted. Playing with Stan was fun and we became good mates, although he had been there for a while and could occasionally be a bit argumentative. I don't know if that irritated the Doc, but if it did, and with us not doing so well, he might have thought he could let him go. And he did, to Nottingham Forest just before Christmas.

It didn't augur well because we lost four and drew one of the next five and although there was an improvement, we had too many draws in the second half of the season. We were a very decent side and were probably favourites to go up every year, so were disappointed not to manage it as we finished fifth, six points behind the champions Leicester City. In many ways it's baffling that we didn't challenge more closely with what we had at our disposal.

Steve Burke was effective down the left, but we could have done with Martin Busby not being so injury-prone because he was a fantastic player with great vision. Despite being a nervous type on the pitch, Ian Gillard was a solid defender I got on really well with and Steve Wicks was an absolute giant in the air and good with his left peg, in front of a great goalkeeper, Chris Woods.

I have to mention the late Glenn Roeder, who was another top performer who really could read the game. He got nine goals that season and had his own little dummy on the ball that always seemed to work well. When he moved to play at the back, he was even better and in my opinion one of the best in the country. Another genuine bloke, he was in the Alan Hansen mould and I could see even then that he would be manager material.

Up top we were so well-served by Clive Allen – who scored goals wherever he went and led our chart with 28, plus two in the cups – and Paul Goddard, who we called 'Sarge' on account of him being in the Boys' Brigade as a youngster. He still had a slight build and wasn't strong, but Paul was a lovely little player with skills that caused defenders problems and scored 16 goals.

Right-back Don Shanks missed out on being an ever-present only because he didn't play in the final game – but he went better than achieving that by dating Mary Stavin, otherwise known as Miss World. I don't know how he managed it because I went to his flat once and it was so untidy. And by the way she wasn't there!

The only one who did play every fixture was Northern Ireland international David McCreery, who had a long and distinguished career. He was a busy player who went non-stop all game, every game, and you couldn't miss him because he had his shorts hitched up in a distinctive, down-to-business way.

Gary Waddock was starting to establish himself at this time and you would want him in your team because he was brilliant at marking anyone out of a game. Another great mate of mine, he helped to foster a good team spirit that season. Yet despite all that, we seemed to have drifted and faced another season in the second tier.

Did Docherty do enough? I don't know, but we obviously couldn't have gelled as successfully as we thought we should. I didn't feel I was doing badly, especially at home, and I had lost my England squad place by then so I would have been trying my damndest to perform and get back in. After the turn of the year when I had recovered from injury, I missed only one more game.

In an era when clubs were nowhere near as trigger-happy as they are today, Rangers were ruthless and sacked Tommy at the end of the season. Expectations had been so high that anything less than promotion wasn't going to justify the spending on the team, not even fourth place. It seemed harsh enough for a group of players to decide to initiate a meeting with Jim Gregory and ask for the Doc to be reinstated.

Even at 30 years old and a senior player I wouldn't dare have attempted such a move on my own, but Ian Gillard, Glenn Roeder, Steve Wicks, probably a couple of others and I went to Roehampton to Jim's business premises. We tried to convince him that we had a good squad and that we would sort it the following season. I still don't know if Tommy knew about our plea, but I would be very surprised if Gregory didn't tell him and a stay of execution was issued. Tommy stayed on, but fate was to deal him a critical additional blow before too long. And the fickle finger was to pay me a visit, too...

***

The almost inevitable effect of our failure to win promotion occurred in the summer of 1980 when the bigger clubs swooped on our strike-force. Clive Allen was transferred to Arsenal for £1.25m, a move that was hardly surprising after he had scored so many goals, but he left a big hole in our team. What was surprising was that he didn't play a single competitive game for the Gunners before signing soon after for Crystal Palace in a swap deal for defender Kenny Sansom.

With Paul Goddard joining West Ham United for £800,000 as well, our main goals supply had been decimated. QPR's gamble a year earlier hadn't paid off so there had to be a period of financial restraint and cashing in to balance the books. At least that is the way I looked at it because I couldn't see the Doc voluntarily selling the best forward pairing in the division. There were certainly no arrivals who might be regarded as major investments.

One of the universal truths in football is that when goals aren't replaced, you are asking for trouble and it was asking too much of Chelsea recruit Tommy Langley to carry the burden on his own. Allen, like most great goalscorers, was a very selfish and confident player – albeit a gentleman – and a phenomenal finisher; he could head them in, turn with the ball or get on a run to score and I would always back him to get on to things.

To score as often as he did owed not just to skill and assurance, but the fact that he was always thinking about getting a shot in. As a result the move would more or less end with Clive because he would succeed with that ... or lose the ball. But you couldn't knock him because he was worth his weight in gold. Or goals!

Langley worked hard and scored at a one-in-three ratio which made him our joint top scorer, but he had injury issues that season and there was precious little else until Mike Flanagan came in at the end of the year. I was as guilty as anyone else, getting only one goal, although I was pleased to play 31 games either side of an injury that kept me out for most of October and November.

By then, in the League Cup, we had beaten Derby County on penalties – after two 0-0 draws! – and been dumped out in the next round, losing 4-1 at Notts County. With single wins only in each of the first three months the fans, as any other club's would be, were becoming critical and Docherty was sacked again. This time for good.

He'd had a reprieve, but couldn't make it work, as much through circumstance as anything else, and my marriage suffered the same outcome.

After having had depression for so long, my missus had been relieved to get back to London, but I'm not sure it actually helped and our home life didn't get much better. For her anyway.

Living out in Radlett, I really had only Andy King living anywhere nearby for company and we became great pals. It was so sad when I learned he had died from a heart attack in 2017, aged just 58. Before the Doc left, the squad had a weekend in Greece for a friendly or something. I had said to Tommy: "I can't really go because my wife is thinking of divorcing me." He agreed it would be okay that I missed the trip, but nearer the time he changed his mind.

"You're coming," he said. "It'll do you good." In the end I agreed to go – of course I did – and it did help me because, when I rang Linda from Greece, she told me that her mind was made up. I was fortunate to be rooming with Dave McCreery, who I loved to bits. When I told him the news, he was a proper mate and very comforting.

Linda wanted the divorce because basically I think she just didn't want me. I had tried to smooth things over, but she was adamant and I didn't contest it. There was no point. I had done my best, but years of her depression had worn me down, too. By then I believed that the strain was affecting my game a little, although getting on the pitch was something of a release. That's why I think Tommy insisted I went to Greece.

It seemed my life had this constant theme of unravelling running through it; my father walking out, rejection at Chelsea and QPR, Linda's difficulties and now divorce. All those things had weighed heavily and I had no-one behind me to unload on or help. There was no counselling or treatment and although today's players perhaps have additional pressures, there is also more help available, thankfully. That is a big step forward.

The divorce was finalised in early 1981 when our kids were about four, nine and 11 years old. It broke my heart to have to tell them and I went back to live with my mum, having bought Linda and the kids a house just four miles away in Mill Hill. Linda and I continued to talk and although I was bitter, I had proper access and did the school run every day. She remarried eventually and I'm glad that we've since shared numerous Christmases with our kids and my current wife Liz, especially because all three of us were at school together.

Going to live with Mum was convenient and of course it ensured that I wasn't on my own. But it was murder at first because I was kind of grieving and started drinking a bit at home, probably more than I should. Many people use alcohol as a coping mechanism in situations they are struggling with and I did exactly that because I felt sorry for myself.

My life became training, stopping in on my own, drinking and watching television – and that wasn't conducive for an athlete's state of mind. Or anyone's, come to think of it. It just made things worse, mentally and physically.

It wasn't so over the top to start with, but a lack of sleep added to my deterioration and led to Ian Gillard and some of the lads christening me "Minger" because of how I was looking. They weren't being unkind – it was just dressing-room fun and they weren't really aware of how low I was becoming. It was to become much worse by the end of my career.

18

VENABLES THE VISIONARY

You can't spend all your professional career and not come into contact with hun-
•re•s of •ifferent people. An• in football that comprises several roles in a••ition
to players – coaches, chairmen, administrators, fans ... and managers.

To a large extent they tend to merge into one and when I am asked about recalling individuals, it can often come down to remembering the good or the not so good. They both remain memorable, just for very different reasons. The majority, as in any workplace, are ordinary in the best sense as regards doing their jobs, getting on with things in the right way and being approachable. But it does help if you get on as well because it makes life easier and in some cases they can add positive improvements to your own life or career.

I was fortunate to be popular with fans at all my clubs and, I think it's fair to say, with the players, too. Fans and players are the heartbeat of any club and my memories of some of those are mentioned in these pages. Because I seldom mixed with the administrators or board members, that largely leaves football staff. And managers in particular.

They all had their moments, but only a select few commanded my total respect for how they improved me as a player and how they dealt with me on a day-to-day basis. I respected Sir Alf Ramsey hugely, but as my international manager his time with me, and therefore his influence, was bound to be limited. At club level there is really only one candidate because to me he was head and shoulders above the rest.

It was only a matter of timing: no-one could do anything about what dictated that Terry Venables came along so late in my career and I really wish that hadn't been the case. By the time Tommy Docherty left QPR, I

156

most likely was complacent enough to think that I knew the game inside out and certainly wouldn't be envisaging adding new elements to my own performances. After all, you can't teach an old dog new tricks, they say. I couldn't have been more wrong.

I was disappointed that Tommy 'Doc' went because I don't like change, but Terry was a fantastic appointment and for me the best coach and manager I played for at club level. He had been an accomplished ball-playing midfielder at the top level with the "bright-young-thing" aura about him, so it was little surprise that he went into coaching and management in a style that reflected his own way of doing things.

His work at Crystal Palace, where he set about developing a young and exciting team, soon put him on the managerial map and it was a bit of a coup for Rangers to bring him and many of his staff in. The man was by no means one-dimensional either; he recorded a song or two, wrote books and even helped to pen a hit TV crime series, *Hazell*, which fixed him even more firmly in the public eye. Terry was into everything, but more than that he was successful. His man-about-town lifestyle and cheeky personality were refreshing and there might have been a gulf between us with regard to our respective character traits, but we got on like a house on fire.

Tel liked my style of play and he certainly loved Paul Gascoigne when he later managed him for England. It still makes me wonder if I might have won more caps if he'd been in charge of the national team during my earlier career. No-one will convince me that England wouldn't have been more successful if Terry had been manager for many years, which he should have been. I loved the way he managed, coached and spoke to players.

He was always on the training pitch, leading every session and coaching like no other manager I'd ever known. So many others let their coaches do that while they observed and it was massively beneficial – we had no doubt what he wanted and that process forged a connection between him and the players. He was so bloody good at it that there was no chance of anyone not respecting him.

Getting his back-four right was his priority because he loved to play the offside trap, which required discipline and co-ordination. He had me playing wide in a four-man midfield system, which required the two wide midfielders to shove the opposition inside and not down the line.

The aim was to force the opposition into having to play into the congest-ed middle as we pushed up. So we wide midfielders would cop a telling-off if we'd let the ball down the line.

If we pushed up, we might lose a few goals as a result, but still make a big net gain. It worked and I thought it was a great tactic. Under him that team was better prepared and structured than any other I played in. We were tactically aware and disciplined in our shape, but he encouraged flair as well.

Everyone on the training pitch could understand him and knew exact-ly what he wanted straightaway because of how he put it across. Break-ing his ideas down, explaining them and communicating clearly was his gift, but he was relentlessly thorough in repeating it until he was satis-fied. There were no half-measures. No sessions were delivered just for the sake of it without ensuring that the players benefitted. His advanced ideas were new, at least to me, and so different from what I'd ever done before. Other coaches were in comparison all about discipline and or-ganisation, to the almost total exclusion of anything more than the most basic of tactics.

Terry was all fresh ideas, more tactically sophisticated and he affected his team more than any other I'd played for. He made you believe he knew what he was talking about, to have confidence in him. That isn't the be-all and end-all, but it helps. Confidence in yourself is massive for a player and he promoted that, assisted by Alan Harris, Ron's brother, and other ex-Palace staff including physio Dave Butler.

I was 31 years old when Terry came, so he never got the best years of me, but I was still capable of pulling my weight and it was gratifying that he talked to me often about tactics in a way no-one else had. While most of it was him passing information on for the benefit of the team, he wanted us to discuss formations and ideas. He was so receptive and advanced in his thinking, at least in English football circles, and he de-veloped that further by drawing in other people's thoughts before using what he felt appropriate.

Although Sir Alf Ramsey had maintained that Martin Peters had been 10 years ahead of his time – which might have been a bit of a stretch – Tel was a real trailblazer. I don't know if his theories originated in his own head, which wouldn't surprise me, or were learned from the continent. Our national game has picked up so much from beyond our shores; the continentals were training with a ball years before us while we were still prioritising all the running and physical stuff more than technique.

It was eye-opening to be shown different ways of playing. It helped to educate me more about how to go about winning thanks to tactical awareness and what we as a team were setting out to do. Just as crucially that knowledge created our ability to change the plan during a game, should it be necessary. If a problem arose during a match, Venables would spot it and come up with a solution with a tactical or personnel change. He was great at that and never feared making a decision. That owed everything to his natural intelligence, great knowledge of the game and his forensic ability to see what was really going on.

That ability to be reactive was very useful in some games, but Terry's sole focus during the week was on our own structure on the pitch and the way he wanted us to play rather than focusing on the opposition. Elsewhere it was frequently the opposite.

***

QPR's poor start to the season under Docherty led to his dismissal and my two-month absence through injury hadn't helped. Terry breezed in, introduced his staff and set about changing the style and identity of what was to become his team. It happened very quickly.

Gary Waddock was primarily a destroyer, winning tackles all day long, while we had a Samba-style striker with Simon Stainrod up top. Tel's ideas were revolutionary, training was intense and we all listened and trusted him. Results improved rapidly before levelling off for the rest of the campaign, which ended with us in eighth place. How we only drew 3-3 with Shrewsbury and lost 4-0 at Orient I will never know!

Maybe we exposed ourselves at the back because we had so many attacking players and it wasn't that Terry didn't work with the defence; he did to the extent that it could even be a bit boring for some of us to spend an hour on that, first thing, after the warm-up. He was also the first one I knew to get us doing a cool-down for three or four minutes at the end of every session – although we'd still do weights, mainly for the abdominals, afterwards. Sometimes he'd also get us together after training to talk to us, which again was unusual.

John Burridge, who had played under Venables at Palace, was brought in during the season in place of Chris Woods. It was a bit of a shock because Chris was a good goalkeeper. 'Budgie' was an absolute nutcase, a fitness fanatic who would regularly do handstands and stuff, and a non-stop chatterbox. Although a bit short by today's standards, John was decent and there were a lot like that in those days.

Striker Mike Flanagan had come in after Clive Allen had left, but Clive was to later return. Subsequently Flanagan and Allen were partnered in our attack – which was great fun for those who remembered the old music-hall act of the same name! Another character arrived, Barry Silkman, who had a short spell at QPR that season and was always turning up with new shoes, shirts and suits to sell. He played wide left, liked to take people on and was mates with Mickie Most, who was well-known in the music business. Barry took me to see him once. I believe 'Silky' is an agent now, which probably suits his personality down to the ground!

Terry Fenwick and Gerry Francis, both Venables' proteges at Palace, were recruited and although some lads on the fringes such as Steve Burke, Waddo and Gary Micklewhite probably had their noses put out of place, good players were being brought in. Gerry was a great player, but injuries restricted his England career and he didn't stay with us for long in this second spell with the club. He paid me a great compliment by once picking me in his greatest XI on the *Footballers' Football Show*.

I suspect that his body was probably not going to be suited to the plastic pitch which was due to be put down at Loftus Road, and neither was mine really. It was laid in the summer of 1981 when Terry was there because the old pitch was notorious for often being a mud-bath. The River Fleet ran under part of it, or so I was told, and players were apprehensive of the new surface – especially the older ones who were worried about injuries and the largely-unknown general toll on their bodies.

The American manufacturers of Omniturf claimed it would in fact reduce injuries, citing the fact that baseball and American football were played on it as proof. But that wasn't football, when we would be sliding, twisting and turning all the time, so really there was no comparison. Even now football played on astroturf in the MLS is slower paced than the hurly-burly stuff of the 1970s.

Terry wanted it because of the benefits of the even bounce on a perfectly flat surface, which he reasoned would complement our own skills. I can see that – and there was loads of sand on it to deaden the bounce

– but it didn't seem to make much difference. After all, it was laid on concrete, then covered by sheets of carpet and several former teammates have since attributed injuries, or the after-effects of them, to that pitch.

We'd train on it on a Friday to get our touch right and became very confident about it although there was a worry about how less-skilful players would cope. On that surface you needed to play the ball to feet or drop it short so that it ran on to a teammate and not bounce past them. If your passing wasn't accurate, you would end up giving it away a lot. I wanted and received the ball frequently so when passes to me weren't spot on, I had to re-adjust and stretch, which took its toll eventually. The bounce at Loftus Road was much more pronounced than the 'plastics' at Preston, Luton and Oldham, but I have to admit we did play well on it.

We beat almost all our visitors because they came with pre-conditioned doubts about the surface and were beaten before they started. Apart from Watford, ironically. I don't know why, although they were going well at that time. Personally I liked playing on the plastic and soon learned to avoid going to ground; when rugby was given a trial on it soon after the pitch had been laid, there were ambulances coming and going every two minutes because of the burns. It was terrible.

Some of the advantage we gained was nullified by having to keep adapting to grass again when we played away, especially if we had trained on plastic because of a waterlogged training ground. Sometimes Ian Gillard, Gerry Francis or I would say: "Bloody 'ell, I'm knackered" on a Monday or Tuesday, which wouldn't have been the case if we played on grass all the time. But we kept it to ourselves.

Often I couldn't walk properly until Wednesday after a Saturday home game and was once so lethargic that Tel had me back in during the afternoon to run doggies, or shuttle runs, after training! I really was struggling and I don't know if he thought that I had been on the piss, but I wouldn't have done that. I was angry, but wouldn't rock the boat, especially because of my admiration for Tel. He would probably have researched the issues and consequences of using a plastic pitch and considered it worthwhile. The fans? Well, they were okay because we were winning on it.

We had talented players who learned how to play on plastic, but we could see the opposition struggling with the technique required and we probably enjoyed about 70 per cent possession. These days I always moan about players trying to thread balls through instead of using space in the air to get the ball behind defences, but with backspin on the pass. I had to alter my technique accordingly and had pictures in my head about who was receiving the pass and how he needed to receive it. It was a question of being aware of their capabilities.

Overall, injuries apart, I enjoyed the plastic pitch and never thought about it really, although I accept it might have been an issue for players whose game depended more on winning the ball. It must have been hard to learn not to slide in, to stay on your feet or risk a first-degree burn. As a result I think defenders must have improved technically and positionally.

To finish eighth, three places lower than under Docherty, represented respectability after the poor start, but we were way off going up. Venables had lifted us, but in divisional terms it had been a wasted season for me because I wanted to get back in the England team. I had joined QPR expecting them to go up with the signings Tommy had made.

We weren't a team who were going to do well away from home – without Allen and Goddard we didn't have enough to score too many goals – and even with Terry's attention to the defence, we conceded more than once a game. Still I was happy at Rangers, apart from knowing that I would have to wait at least one more year to go up again. At least with Terry in charge, it promised to be an exciting season.

By that point, the divorce was behind me. I felt much better, seeing the kids every day and taking them out at the weekends or bringing them to see Mum, who got on great with them. I was looking forward to a full season on the plastic with Tel, to see what he could do with us, not knowing about the knee and back problems that eventually surfaced later.

The effects of playing on the plastic in terms of injuries were not yet fully understood and I was more concerned with the advantage that familiarity with it would give us. There was no doubting that would be the case and in a way, would affect my normal answer to the question: "Did you enjoy playing at home more than away?"

The easy answer is yes for most players, because you should have more confidence when you have the majority of the support. Therefore, playing away from home becomes a mind thing and it's not unusual for players to go away and question whether they can handle the pressure. We would hear that the home team were good at home and so on, so we needed to impose our own game on them, blah blah, blah. But some players almost wet themselves when they stepped on the pitch.

Can you shut out the crowd? Can you cope with not seeing much of the ball or recover from a mistake to keep your game together? And how do you respond to a noisy crowd if they make you the focus of the attention? I took a lot of stick and I get that, because every club's support delight in baiting the opposition – particularly the highest-profile players.

It only irritated me when they would give it: "Currie doesn't fancy it today," without knowing that I was only 70 per cent fit and pressed into playing. Lots of players would have been the same. Even though I knew that the home fans would pick only on the ones who could have won the game, it did get me down.

Their team might have two men detailed to mark me and it was difficult, but if I was ineffective, it wasn't because it was a mental thing for me or a case of not wanting to do it. I would think: "Shit, this is all my fault" and it would play on my mind. I'm sure that Alan Hudson, Charlie George and Frank Worthington would have felt the same, even if they had been on the piss the day before!

I can honestly say that I absolutely loved it – home or away – especially waving to the crowd and getting a reaction. As a child I loved Charlie Cooke at Chelsea, who seemed to me to be the unluckiest finisher in the world. He would beat about eight men and then hit the post. What a player! Charlie could just jink without moving the ball, leaving defenders on their backsides, and I so wanted to affect the crowd in the way he did me. Home and away, the excitement of performing well and drawing a response from the fans never waned for me.

No team can be sure of how events will pan out in a match and how they will change your mind and attitude, so half-time usually brings the inevitable rethink and tweaks. At Liverpool they would invariably pressure you non-stop, buzzing round and moving the ball so quickly, which was a challenge in itself to combat. Then, if they struggled, the ref would give them a penalty! It's the mental thing again, but it is true that the teams that win things tend to handle it better.

Running out at home was brilliant, knowing most of the crowd was there to watch you and on your side. I do remind myself that I had a fantastic career, taking into account my problems off the field; lying awake at night, divorce, depression, travelling back and forth. And sometimes I even pat myself on the back for getting through that while performing on the field. If we were getting hammered, I would always still try to be the best I could for the team.

I always responded to a bollocking as well, perhaps even more so if I thought I was right. "Sod it," I'd think, "I'll show you what I can do." There were players such as Alan Woodward, Len Badger, Billy Bremner, Trevor Francis and Stan Bowles, to name just a few, who were phenomenal to play with. Then there was Peter Lorimer, who I'd thought initially was just a powerful shooter, Eddie Gray and Allan Clarke. All of them were tremendous and players I would respond to.

I would hear: "Come on, TC, get us moving" from one of them, or Len Badger would chirp up with: "Do us a bit of magic" at Sheffield United. So would Paul Hart, Arthur Graham, Brian Flynn and Trevor Cherry because they knew I could. Home or away.

19

COPING WITH CHANGE

When transfers happen, you never know for sure how they will work out or for how long you will stay in that part of the country. I spent the years between 1981 an• 1986 living at my mum's, which for a man of my age an• profile must have been considered unusual. Especially a footballer on a decent income...

I needed company and some semblance of stability. From a private and personal point of view those years were the most frightening and distressing I have ever known and I am utterly convinced that if I had not been at home, I would have been in an even worse state than I often was. Despite the comfort of having Mum, an aunt and a couple of uncles around, I was depressed. My mind still wasn't right.

A future with new personal relationships seemed a million miles away and the possibility of not being able to see my kids regularly was a worry which happily was to prove unfounded. I also realised that I was the wrong side of 30 and my career was winding down. Everything was very unclear and I didn't have the personal strength or strategies to find positive ways forward. Inevitably I withdrew into myself and tried to mask the fog in my head with cigarettes, alcohol and staying in my room. Just as inevitably, those 'solutions' offered only short-term and false relief.

Feeling sorry for myself, I just wasn't in the right frame of mind for women and there were very few local friends I could lean on for something approaching a social life. I was driving a Ford Granada at that time, but most of the QPR players lived all over the place and I didn't even try to take action which would have given my life some structure. Consequently my existence was simple and potentially destructive.

Mum and her relatives had by then moved to a four-bedroomed detached house because one of my uncles was ill and needed to live downstairs. At least I now had a bedroom of my own. Before the move I was sleeping on a settee in the front room – while playing professional football! At least I was still self-disciplined enough not to have a whisky if there was a midweek game, but otherwise I would. And a smoke as well.

Alan Woo•war• ha• got me on the fags back in 1971 when I was at Sheffiel• United. We twice stayed abroad at Pappandal, a training complex like Lilleshall, for two weeks at a time and it was so boring. That was when we christened ourselves 'Rag-arse Rovers' because Barcelona were there, all decked out in smart stuff while we were in all sorts of raggy, o••, crappy bits of training kit; there were ladders in the socks and our nylon shorts rubbed!

Barca were years ahead of us, training cleverly in formations and looking brilliant. One •ay, travelling back to the hotel, Alan was puffing away at the back of the coach and out of boredom I said: "Give us a drag, Woody." I smoked it, had another and that was it – although I never really regarded myself as a smoker and didn't like people seeing me smoking. There were some at United, such as Woody, Keith Eddy and Colin Franks, who were 'proper' smokers, but I would have two or three at the most. And always in private or on the team bus after a game.

***

Away from training and playing, my priority now was seeing the kids. I'd come home and pick them up later in the afternoon to spend time together before taking them back to Linda's. It wasn't easy speaking with her so sometimes I dropped them at the door. Those sessions did mean I was still seeing family, but I didn't do much new with them to take my mind off things.

My next-door neighbours at Radlett for a year were a stockbroker couple, Jeff and Viv, who had two little girls a bit older than Natalie, and I got on well with them. We would play Yahtzee, a dice game, a couple of nights a week and I sometimes played tennis with Jeff. His company had a hospitality box on the halfway line at Spurs and he used to take me in 1983 when I wasn't playing because of injury. They sort of took me under their wing and I went to places such as Aberystwyth and Lavenham in Suffolk with them. It was a very welcome respite in my life.

I'd accompany them and their friends on the odd night out and go to their New Year's Eve parties, but I wasn't looking for a woman. Just company. Viv's birthday was the same as mine so it was a double celebration. Jeff and I visited the RAC Club in Pall Mall where he was a member and on Thursday nights we'd meet in town after he and his mates, Graham and Barry, had finished work, to play a bit of snooker. I would catch the bus in and Jeff gave me a lift home to Mum's. It was great fun for a couple of years and that relationship was really beneficial for me. None of them was ever going to lead me to drink or dodgy clubs. They were lovely people and I don't exaggerate when I say that, because of the way I was feeling generally, they might well have saved my life.

Still, the feeling of being comfortable back home with my family didn't compare with sharing a home with a wife and kids and I definitely wasn't settled inside my head. I think I needed professional help at that stage. To this day, despite the issues I have had to face, I still haven't tried any.

I was never aware of being depressed during my first marriage because I had my football, but on reflection I now think I was, because of Linda's condition and the trips to London I felt compelled to make. There were so many arguments that I didn't realise that I was suffering as well, because I was trying hard to help with picking the kids up, shopping, doing meals and everything else.

I came to understand that depression is an illness when she was diagnosed – she had tried to adjust to coming up north to live, but seeing her that way was worrying. I didn't want the arguments and subsequent split and I wouldn't have so easily accepted the move further north to Leeds if I hadn't thought that a change of scene at least would be good for her. London would have been better and even an hour further south might have significantly improved our relationship.

***

I don't think Terry needed to change the 1981-82 team much because he had already laid the foundations of a good squad, at least for accumulating points regularly on the plastic. The downside was that, even though we were still predominantly grass players, we still had trouble getting them on away grounds.

The biggest limiting factor was probably that we went out to win matches and left gaps; we scored plenty and were always confident of winning, perhaps too much. We had match-winners and creators and I still can't believe it took four seasons to win promotion. I had fully expected Rangers to go straight up, especially when Venables had built such a good back-four and was so tactically innovative.

Clive Allen even came back from Palace which was a huge fillip. Arsenal had bought him from QPR and not long after swapped him for Kenny Sansom, who was at Palace when Terry was in charge there. I think that was Arsenal's plan all along, but Terry was such a fan of Clive, who guaranteed 20-plus goals a season. He was a lovely lad – selfish at times on the pitch, as most great strikers are, but that's because they have to be on most occasions.

I knew Simon Stainrod from my time at Bramall Lane, but he was then a relative youngster with Keith Edwards and Tony Kenworthy. But he became a great player at Loftus Road, so much so that I told him he was good enough to play for England; he was very skilful and cocky, perhaps too much for his own good on occasions. There was just something lacking in Simon's approach to the game that held him back – I had told Ray Hankin the same about his own game as well when we were at Leeds – but I really enjoyed playing with him.

We had a great understanding and I would play the ball up to him so that he could bring others into the game – he was strong enough to hold off almost the entire back-four. By nature, though, he was more of an individual and, if he felt the game was his stage, he wouldn't hesitate to do his own thing. I loved his confidence and attitude. I'll let you in on a true story about someone else who did his own thing, even if I didn't know him and didn't appreciate him contacting me.

One day I was up at Birkdale College Sports Ground in Greenford, where QPR trained, and picked up my mail as usual. I was opening it all up outside the changing-rooms and in one package was ... a fully-charged condom! Even worse, there was also a photograph of the bloke who sent it, lying back on a bed in an advanced state of arousal, really, er ... saluting me. "I hope you like my photo," a message with it read. "If you want to meet up, when you run out at the next home match, run to the centre-circle, undo your boots and then do them up again."

The letter and contents went into the bin as I went to the changing-rooms to be physically sick and needless to say, I made sure I avoided the centre-circle like the plague for the entire 90 minutes of the next game. In fact, it just occurred to me – maybe he had taken that Alan Birchenall kiss picture too seriously!

DREAMS AND NIGHTMARES

The 1981-82 season – my third for Rangers – was so disjointed for me that it felt as if I was never really to get going for more than half-a-dozen games at a time. An early injury set the tone and my body was now saying it had enough. Ridiculously, though, I was about to achieve a life-long dream ...

I missed the first two games when, after finishing a training session, my knee gave way as I was walking downstairs at Birbeck College Sports Ground. The immediate visit to the hospital and subsequent X-ray revealed that a piece of bone the size of a tooth had chipped off and got into the knee joint. After an operation to remove it, I decided to keep the piece of bone in a jar by my hospital bed. But before long somebody nicked it. I ask: "Why would anyone?"

The loss of some muscle on my thigh was more significant and damaging, even though the surgeons had nicked only a bit off. It was the same left knee I'd had issues with in 1974 and I never got the muscle bulk back to what it had been. To this day I still have problems with that knee.

I was out for much longer than expected and for most of the season I was in and out of the team as other related strains, or maybe the change to a plastic pitch, played their part. I didn't know then that it was to be my last real season even though I struggled on for a few more, trying to get back.

Our patchy away form and an indifferent winter played a big part in keeping us just short of mounting a consistent challenge for promotion. We were always chasing it, but left ourselves too much to do and finished a respectable fifth. But 'respectable' hadn't been our ambition and I had played only 20 games, scoring just once in a 3-2 defeat at Leicester City in March.

Watford had a great season and did for us easily in the League Cup after we had knocked out Portsmouth and Bristol City. But my childhood hopes of playing in an FA Cup final increased with every step we took. We needed a replay to dispose of Middlesbrough after a 1-1 home draw. Stainrod had got our goal and he added two more up there as we won 3-2. My biggest memory about that was being substituted and seeing my replacement, Warren Neill, score as well!

Blackpool held us to a goalless draw in the north-west, but ran into a rampant Clive Allen who grabbed four goals in our 5-1 replay win. Doing well in the competition hadn't been our priority when the season started, but when we were drawn first against Grimsby Town in the fifth round, I was confident of reaching the quarter-finals.

Injury ruled me out, but the 3-1 victory justified my belief in the team. We were a second-tier side and needed the draw to be kind to us which, being honest, it had been so far. And that continued when we were paired with divisional rivals Crystal Palace for a semi-final place.

We had won one and drawn one with them in the league and although they were very close games, with just one goal scored in both, we were very confident at home. When a single Clive Allen goal squeezed us past them, we were in the semis – as far as I had ever been in that famous old competition.

Between that day and the semi-final, our form and results were typically up and down with two wins and three defeats. But a 4-0 victory and a loss by the same scoreline suggested that if we were on our game, we could shock a higher-ranked side. And that's what we got in top-flight West Brom, who we would face at Highbury. I doubt players such as John Wile and my mate and former roommate, Andy King, would appreciate our conviction that it was a winnable game for us despite their status. But so it proved, despite Allen's goal being a block tackle that flew into the net like a rocket!

Glenn Roeder and I had sort of ruled the game so we felt we deserved to go to Wembley for the FA Cup final, which was still the highlight of England's football scene in those days. I was in a final at last and I was absolutely ecstatic, feeling on cloud nine for weeks leading up to the big day. I thought it was my year and I still have photographs of us celebrating in the Highbury bath afterwards, complete with strategically-placed champagne!

The only thing that might put any kind of brake on my huge expectation and excitement was injury. Too many players had experienced that awkward mindset during the weeks leading up to the final; they wanted to impress and cement their place in the team, but were also worried about getting crocked. And, of course, that's how it panned out for me.

A fortnight and four league games later I did my calf in a home win over Shrewsbury Town and was out for the next five matches. Having had such a stop-start season with various niggles during the campaign, I feared the worst. I thought I would miss the big one. Selecting me for that would have represented a big gamble for the manager as well and I don't know whether playing me in the final game before the final, against Cambridge, was really about Terry testing me to find out if I was up to it. It was understandable if he did. But even going into that match, I knew I had missed so much training that I could have been only about 65 per cent fit. Fortunately I didn't break down. The final was only a week later....

Normally I wouldn't have worried about being selected because I knew I was worth my place. But I was worried now. Rest and treatment are so important for healing a calf strain and I hadn't trained for three weeks before the final. Then during the three days before the game, I wanted to make sure I could at least start it.

As a rule the warm-up loosens up the muscle and you get through, but looking back, I must have been holding back a bit every time I put my foot down. The staff and Terry wanted me to play, so I was told to train sensibly. "Don't go mad," they said because they didn't want to take that risk of it popping again after 20 minutes. It was intensive treatment three times a day, but after three successive years of losing at the semi-final stage, I was so desperate to play.

It was a question of proving myself to the physio Dave Butler. He knew a calf strain could happen like a shot going off and if it was bad, I would need six weeks of recovery. But if the injury comes on gradually, you might get back in a week; either way I knew I was on very thin ice. After protecting it to begin with, I had to give it full blast in the end to justify being selected.

It would be selfish not to take into account the emotions and hopes of other players who had their own issues to deal with, especially those on the fringes of the team whose selection was not guaranteed. If I didn't make it, then Gary Micklewhite would probably come in after playing in midfield a few times with Gary Waddock, while Wayne Fereday was another option.

It must have been difficult for them as well as me. All three of us wanted the team to win and our mates to do well, but each of us was desperate to play – and that had to be at someone else's expense. Not being picked is a tricky and uncomfortable scenario, which I could relate to because of my England experiences. And we had to wait until the night before the final before Terry announced the team in the Selsdon Park Hotel. It was agony in the room as we all waited, in varying degrees of expectation and confidence. But I was in.

You can only imagine my relief when my name was read out. Gary, Wayne and I hadn't discussed the situation, but I have no doubt that behind their personal disappointment they would genuinely be pleased for me. It is a huge credit to them, and also the great bunch of players in my Leeds days, because they always wanted me to play – even if it was at their own expense.

I knew that I was some way from being match-fit after being out for basically a month and was worried to death that it would go wrong. But I was just so pleased to be playing out that childhood dream, as we all were. It was a fantastic feeling. I regarded that game as the icing on my career and it had come just in time.

Terry had wanted me in because I was the main creative part of the team and he had been checking on my progress every day. It was an honour to be chosen in what was basically our normal team. Now it was time for me to live out everything that FA Cup final day meant to players of my era and long before – enjoying those hours and moments before a ball is kicked, being watched by millions of people around the country on national TV. It was a genuine showpiece and Spurs fans wouldn't have minded being such big favourites, even though their team had endured a long season as well.

From a media perspective it's fair to say that as the game drew nearer, their previews often suggested that the result would hinge on the contest between Glenn Hoddle and me. Journalists have to be creative to produce articles that will interest their readers and that type of 'story' was standard practice in producing talking-points.

Players are used to that and I benefited from the extra exposure on several occasions. Writers are not always right, but in this case their view had significance for me because of my complete admiration for Hoddle. He is the greatest midfielder I have ever seen and should have been given more than 100 England caps, in my opinion. He would always be first on my teamsheet with Peter Shilton, for one. Top, top players I was privileged to share a football pitch with.

We would see how our battle unfolded on the day. The main thing about playing in an FA Cup final – apart from winning, of course – was extracting every second of enjoyment from it and I'm talking about the sense of occasion. Cup-final suits seemed to be a bit of a thing back then and always attracted attention – we weren't used to turning up for games, even big ones, in matching posh clothes! But it was part of the ritual for Wembley. So was the coach's journey to the stadium, snaking between thousands of fans who showed their support or derision in ways which were easy to understand. Occasionally naughty, but generally good-natured.

Our mood on board was great although I'm sure one or two, as I glanced around, would be suffering a few nerves. We were mates and you inevitably grew to know how they ticked and reacted to different situations. Ian Gillard and Mike Flanagan might have had the odd nervous flutter, while Simon Stainrod would have been thinking: "This is my stage." Glenn Roeder? No problem. As a good captain and fine player, he would be able to handle it. Gary Waddock would just want to get out there and start competing.

I'd already played at Wembley on 10 occasions with England so I was less nervous about that than whether the calf issue might trouble me again. For those too young to remember the old Wembley, it had big dressing-rooms and baths and, although not pristine or modern, it didn't matter to us in the slightest. The overriding emotion was: This is Wembley, and in many cases the greatest day of our lives.

Before it was time to put on our kit, we went on the pitch, walked about looking for friends and family in the crowd and did interviews at 1pm for half an hour. Without wishing to appear too traditionalist or a killjoy, I can't believe that FA Cup finals today can mean as much to the players as they did to us before the football landscape changed in the 1990s. To be fair, they can't.

It was real *Roy of the Rovers* stuff, the biggest game in our club calendar, because it was such an occasion and everyone watched it on television. Live domestic games were almost unheard of back then, but the FA Cup seems to have become much less of a priority in modern times. The gloss has been taken off now there is so much live football and money has become so important in the game. And as a result, our national game has lost so much.

Walking out next to the opposition was fantastic and I recall looking around and being impressed by how much support there was for us. We'd been getting home crowds of about 15,000 and then, all of a sudden, there were 35,000 Rangers fans there. It was so good to see them.

The pitch was in good condition, as it had been for the England fixtures I'd played there in the 1970s. I liked it and, contrary to popular belief, didn't find that it sapped the energy from the legs. Holding that Horse of the Year show was blamed a lot for churning the surface, but the authorities had sorted it all out by that point.

I had family members in the crowd that day, including my mum – who, and you may not believe this, was watching me play professionally for the first time. She now only ever went out to shop and was worried about doing even that in later years. Her suffering with ulcerate• legs eventually require• them being regularly newly-bandaged by visiting nurses.

It meant a lot to both of us that she was at Wembley and it was a great day out for her and lots of relatives and friends. Very unfortunately that couldn't inclu•e my uncle Terry, who was in a ba• way an• not fit enough to atten•. My daughter Natalie was sitting on my mum's lap and told me afterwards that Mum had fallen asleep during the match!

I don't know if my father was there because we weren't in touch then. The last time I ha• seen him was at a QPR v West Ham fixture, when I ha• left tickets for my uncles, Bert and Jim. They intercepted me and explained that there weren't any – before my father turned up with them in his hand. I didn't like that at all, so I had a go at him. It was out of character for me, but as far as I am concerned, you don't take things that are not meant for you – whoever you are.

Afterwards on my way home I drove past him, mackintosh in hand and carrying the Sporting Life. It was the last time I saw him until he was on his •eathbe•. Years before, while with Sheffiel• Unite•, I was aske• by Crystal Palace to contact my father because he owed them money for match tickets. His cheque had bounced, as had others he had given me when he owed me as well. It was a sobering feeling telling Palace that I was sorry, but it was nothing to do with me.

Was he a wrong 'un? Yes and no. He was a womaniser who had walked out of my life when I was four years old and had other kids at the same time. Mum said he'd rather spend a night in jail instead of paying her the quid a week maintenance and he would get money out of auntie Vera and others. Yes, he held down a job but leaving his wife and young family, and the subsequent inappropriate efforts to avoi• financial responsibilities, meant that there was no way I could respect him, let alone have warm feelings towards him.

***

For the first 10 minutes I eased myself in, having made sure I had warmed up properly beforehand. The game didn't start well for us because Clive Allen got injured and had to be substituted later. It was his first Wembley final and such a shame because he loved to play and score goals. I bet he could have cut his own throat in frustration and it was a massive blow to our chances. I was devastated for him and the team because his goals had been getting us good results. Cue another negative thought: "Here we go again… my luck's out."

We were second-best, but managed to get to the final whistle with the scoreline goalless and into extra-time. With only 10 minutes left, Hoddle picked the ball up and I closed him down as he worked a shooting position. I thought I'd blocked his shot, but the ball hit the inside of my thigh and deflected past Peter Hucker in our goal.

Here we go again...

There wasn't long to go now, but we had a throw-in which Stainrod hurled long into the penalty area. Bob Hazell flicked it on at the near post and in came Terry Fenwick to head the ball into the net for 1-1. I don't think I have ever experienced such a shared outpouring of joy as he ran to the corner flag, with the rest of us giving chase to jump on him and celebrate.

We had one more scare before the end came; I think Tony Galvin was just inside our box on the byline and I was not letting him turn. Actually, in my over-enthusiasm, I did shove him with my momentum. Maybe it should have been a penalty, and perhaps a red card. But referee Clive White waved play on. *There is a God …*

Spurs might have won by about three goals in the end, which would have been fair. But we had a replay. They had played well, but missed chances. We'd nullified Glenn a bit, surrounding him en masse, as we'd practised, but he still schemed as only he could. Peter Hucker had been brilliant, deservedly receiving the man-of-the-match award and during an interview straight afterwards I was reminded that Spurs had lifted the trophy the previous year following Ricky Villa's brilliant individual effort. The TV interviewer said: "You've had to work hard for that, TC, against the current cup holders." My attempt at a joke response was: "Well, I've had to roll my sleeves up." I was wearing a short-sleeved shirt...

Terry Venables had been as positive as he always was throughout the lead-up, during the match and afterwards, when he was complimentary to us. He had his tactical plan and although we hadn't bargained for the early disruption because of injury, we were able to maintain it because the score had been 0-0 for so long – we just had to keep playing as we were.

The players didn't receive medals for that first game, although we did go up the steps to meet Princess Anne and FA officials. We had under-performed a bit on the day but Spurs were a very good team, even with Ossie Ardiles and Villa missing because of the Falklands War. The pair were Argentinians, from a country we were at war with and although the players were well-treated and liked over here, I think they decided it best to avoid such a high-profile televised event. It was unfortunate for them that they were caught in the political crossfire, especially as we couldn't help but feel that we would inevitably benefit from their absence.

Their formidable side still included Ray Clemence, Graham Roberts, Paul Miller, Steve Perryman, Steve Archibald and Garth Crooks, though, and they were very experienced in the FA Cup. Yes, they had been the better team on the day, but we were a second-tier side and still alive for another shot. The replay might be a different matter.

We knew Spurs had had a tough season and might be knackered for another game just five days later, back at Wembley. We had grounds for confidence even without Clive and Glenn Roeder, who was suspended. Steve Wicks, our centre-half who had played most of the season, also missed both finals and having had the better of the first game, maybe there would be a nervousness in the Spurs camp, that they hadn't won the cup already? Or could complacency creep in?

So on the night after the final we celebrated as if we had won it anyway at the Royal Garden Hotel, Kensington – where we would have gone if we had lifted the trophy – and the Sunday was spent recovering from the night before!

We then began preparations for the replay; training as normal with meetings and reviews of the first game and what we were going to tweak or put right. Terry had to rejig the team because of the absentees and decided to switch Terry Fenwick to centre-half, bring Warren Neill in at right-back and replace Allen with Gary Micklewhite.

I had protected myself in the final so that my injury didn't flare up again and I felt ready to play the second match. It was doubly pleasing because if I had broken down in the first half-hour or so, I knew I would have failed the manager and my teammates. I felt more confident about getting through the replay, which was played on a Thursday evening.

We stayed overnight at the Royal Lancaster Hotel on Bayswater Road and had to wait all day for the final to start. And not long after it did, fate dealt us another sickening blow.

21

OPPORTUNITIES
SNATCHED AWAY

In everyone's life there are moments so pivotal that, whether the individual has control over them or not, they become milestones along the way and shape their lives. Sometimes destinies are secured because of the actions taken. And on other occasions, actions have little to do with it ...

Clive White blew his whistle. But it wasn't to start the game. I wished so much it had been. He blew it because I had made a desperate challenge.

After only six minutes the referee had seen Spurs' defender Graham Roberts run almost unchallenged through our half and into the penalty area. The danger was obvious to concerned QPR fans, and promising to the Tottenham supporters, but there was also danger in my attempt to stop him from inflicting maximum damage. I had expected a teammate to have blocked him by now and, not really close enough to put in a more orthodox tackle, I lunged, hopefully and desperately, trying to push the ball away from him.

As soon as I failed, but caught him, I knew the inevitable outcome – and recognised that horrible, guilty feeling that thousands of players have known since the game was invented. I knew straightaway that it was a foul, but what made it worse was how it had come about. Not known for his tackling, Hoddle had run 10 yards towards Waddock and flew into a tackle with both feet, leaving him in a pile on the turf.

It should have been a free-kick, but it wasn't given and the ball ran to Roberts in the centre circle. Closest to him, I tracked him all the way to the penalty area at an angle to goal for what must have been close to 35 yards. I was stop/starting most of the way, expecting our defence to step in and deny the space. But it was too late.

Roberts had been given an opportunity and he was going to try his luck. As he went to draw his foot back to shoot, I went to slide in, probably from a yard behind him. I honestly went for the ball and if I had been Bobby Moore, I might have timed it. But it was from a very difficult position to get right. The result was that Spurs got a penalty and Waddock only got treatment from the effects of the 'challenge.' None of us had appealed hard for a foul on Waddock, even though the two-footed tackle was outlawed even then. Maybe we thought that it was so obvious and there was no need.

With Roeder suspended, the honour of captaincy had been handed to me and I had led the team out, unable to avoid thinking that winning the FA Cup that night was meant to be *my moment* after all this time. And I wouldn't care afterwards how long it had taken. But Hoddle, a player I admired so much, sent Peter Hucker the wrong way from the spot and I couldn't help but feel I had let everybody down. I had captained the side on a few occasions during the campaign when Roeder was missing, as I had at all my clubs after leaving Watford, and I did my best to cajole the lads into a renewed effort.

My style was to lead by example rather than to take responsibility for making tactical tweaks. As far as I was concerned, that was what a manager was for, able to see everything from the sideline. I was delighted to get the honour in the cup final, especially knowing that I might soon be walking up the steps to lift the cup.

The early blow may have seen us crumble and roll over, but the reality was far different and it's fair to say that we had much the better of things throughout as Spurs created few chances. We did, on numerous occasions, but just couldn't stick the bloody ball in the net and Stainrod in particular was very disappointed not to get a couple of goals. Tel made us stay in the match and fight throughout and Spurs were so knackered, they almost tottered over the line.

It was a bittersweet experience shaking hands with Glenn Hoddle of all people after what had happened. Waddo shed some tears and in comforting him, I don't know how I didn't as well. At least he had the consolation of swapping shirts with Hoddle. I really wish I had because I hadn't in the first game either. We played both games in red shirts with black shorts and socks and Spurs twice wore all yellow, but I don't know why we both changed because there shouldn't have been a clash. Anyway I now had two red shirts as mementos and neither was Glenn's. Swapping with anyone in particular hadn't been my initial thought after the first game and after the replay I was too late, so… Bollocks!

That defeat was the biggest disappointment in my career, without a doubt. The qualifier against Poland which England lost at Wembley was another, but as it turned out, had we qualified for the World Cup I would have missed the finals because of injury anyway. I was now at the stage in my career when disappointments hurt even more as I realised there may be no more opportunities. That turned out to be true – I certainly didn't get anywhere near further FA Cup glory in later years with Chesham, Torquay and Hendon!

It was a subdued celebration and a very deflating one despite plenty of drink flowing and people sympathising with us. There were a couple of crumbs of comfort; the club made plenty of money from the two games and they had been great occasions for our supporters. Although finishing fifth and reaching the cup final would represent a great season for most clubs in the second tier, we as players had little to show for it.

I was still living with Mum and had no partner, but as far as my football was concerned, I was still under contract at the end of that third year. And Venables stayed on so, if I avoided further injury, I could still be optimistic about that aspect of my life. The trouble was that I was using football to hold myself together and at 32 years of age, that would be only a temporary and fragile lifeline.

Everything was going well until we played a friendly against Wimbledon at Plough Lane, five days before the new season. Needing to get a yard on Glyn Hodges while running with the ball, I dig a drag-back to make him stutter in his stride. But Hodges, ironically a future Sheffield United player, wasn't a textbook tackler. He took the dummy, went for the ball and down I went. I don't think he meant to foul me and it had happened to me before. But on this occasion, as I fell, I felt the medial knee ligament go.

That was game over for me and after having the joint wrapped up in loads of wadding, I got a lift home from Rangers' director Ian Simpson. Being injured is horrible, mentally as well as physically, and during rehab I thought I would be all right. Because I so badly wanted to be all right. I just didn't want to think I might be in trouble for the simple reason that I wanted to play forever. And as daft as it seems, in my head I thought I would.

There is no doubt that the injury was serious and I played only one match all season, a 2-2 draw with Blackburn. Not surprisingly it didn't go well and I got a rocket from Terry, after saying I was fit when I clearly wasn't. I wasn't even 50 per cent fit, and I was turning like a flippin' oil tanker. Despite the rehab I had lost strength in my thigh because of muscle wastage – at least one and a half inches off the diameter. As a result the knee had to take all the extra pounding every time I hit the ground, and then there was the twisting and turning. Without strong muscles around it, the ligament just didn't have the support it needed and might give way at any time. I just couldn't get fully fit.

These days it is still swollen and although it doesn't give way, it is painful and weak. All through my career, like many players, I had a variety of aches and strains and played when not fully fit because I always thought I would be all right in 10 minutes.

Terry was no fool and had seen that I couldn't get around the pitch when I thought I had been hoodwinking him to a certain extent. I was fit enough to run in straight lines, but I knew it wasn't right and the recuperation wasn't being effective enough either. I just couldn't get the muscle back to what it should have been. In today's game I would probably have had six months out, working and waiting to build the muscle bulk back. But in the early 1980s sophisticated scanning systems didn't exist. You just had to get on with it.

It was playing on my mind. I was divorced, living with my mum, had lost an FA Cup final, •rinking more •uring the week, not living with my ki•s an• feeling pretty down most of the time. I was coming to the end of my career and didn't know it was going to get worse...

***

As if to rub further salt into my personal wounds, Rangers went up to the top-flight that season, winning it virtually at a canter from Wolves and Leicester City. The team registered a high number of wins at home, which was expected, but also plenty away, returning a massive positive goal difference.

I hadn't expected to be out for the whole season when I got the injury and had continued to try to build the knee back up, but the team was playing so well that I would have had a struggle anyway. The team seemed to click after the cup final and Terry had built such a good team that things just gelled. To me, in cynical moments, it seemed inevitable after I had dropped out. When I was playing regularly, I generally had control of our possession so, when I wasn't, Tel probably tweaked something to make up for it. My replacement, Mike Fillery, was a fine player and he helped with the inevitable change of style, which I regularly watched from Box Two at Loftus Road.

When QPR were away, I was often at White Hart Lane, in another box on the halfway line belonging to my mate Jeff Lawrence. It was lovely watching Hoddle, Villa, Ardiles and Co. go about their business, but it made me miss playing even more … especially when the FA Cup I had come so close to lifting was always on show there.

Not playing a part that season was difficult to take, but honestly I was pleased about the team's progress as the campaign went on. Some players would rather do well personally than see the team flourish, but as promotion became increasingly likely, I was optimistic enough to start looking forward to the top-flight again. Looking back, I don't really know why. I knew my knee was a bit loose and not yet strong enough to stand up to the challenges it would face.

The treatment I was being given didn't change and although I played a number of games for the reserves, I was getting only gradually better; it wasn't nearly enough, especially for playing on a plastic pitch. In the cold light of day I should have read the signs. But still I thought I'd get another contract. It didn't work out that way, but if I had been a bit more streetwise – or had a modern-day agent – it would have. When we went up, it was the end of my four-year deal and Terry confirmed that my spell there had ended. Perhaps the specialists at QPR had told him that my knee was not going to improve enough. Who knows?

But there was a technicality that would have worked to my benefit if I had been aware of it. I don't know if Terry was either. Apparently at that time, if a player didn't want to move after a four-year contract had ended, his club had to give him at least another year. In effect the player had an option in his favour, but I was too wrapped up with wanting to be left alone to play football to be up to speed on that kind of thing. I didn't learn until years later that I could have stayed on, and maybe benefited from proper treatment.

It knocked me back terribly because I thought I still had something to offer and for the first time since I had turned professional, I felt I wasn't wanted. The immediate thought was that my career was going to be downhill from there and with all his experience Tel must surely have known I wasn't going to make it. His primary responsibility was to his team, who had just been promoted without me. I had never before had to contemplate what I would be doing next in the game, or indeed where.

It was a given that I wanted to continue playing and at that stage I wasn't considering trying anything else. It wasn't as if I had prepared for retirement by, for example, taking my coaching badges. A year or so earlier, when I was playing regularly, Terry had said to me: "Look, you have got to go into coaching when you pack in. 'Cos you see everything."

I was flattered that he thought I was like him, but in my mind there was never a right time to do it. Who knows if I could have made a success of it? But if I had, my life would most likely have taken some very different turns. At this point, though, it wasn't an option and Terry offered me another one instead.

Football was a developing market in different parts of the world and countries were keen to push the game to raise the profile of their own leagues. One popular way of doing that was to make them attractive, especially to experienced overseas players who had a profile that would attract publicity. In the twilight of their careers many great players from around the world spent an enjoyable season or three abroad, the USA being the best example – where they could play in the sunshine, earn a decent few quid and still be fit enough to play competitively.

Tel called me in, told me that there was interest in me from a Canadian club in the freshly formed Canadian Professional Soccer League and suggested that I should consider going over there. I should probably have rung the Professional Footballers' Association for advice, to get a better idea of what it would involve. But, being me, I didn't. There were too many negative thoughts at the forefront of my mind; it wasn't English league football, Canada was too far away and I would be on my own. And surely some clubs in England would be interested in taking me.

But it never entered my head to sound out other English clubs which, given that I knew loads of players, coaches and managers, would have been easy. I was doing my own training, mainly in the park or on grass verges three times a week, sensibly avoiding hard surfaces and waiting for other offers to come my way.

The only attraction to me in joining Toronto Nationals seemed to be that I was in touch with a former teammate of mine at Watford and Sheffield United. Colin Franks was there and we spoke a few times by telephone. We were big mates and he encouraged me to go because he knew I would be an asset, so I told him that I would think about it.

There wasn't any real pushing for an answer and I hadn't discussed it with anyone else. For a few weeks I again dithered about a decision while my mind was in real turmoil. Ninety per cent of me didn't want to go and the other 10 per cent was saying: "Well, it's a game of football." I wasn't a keen flier either. But Colin was there and he wasn't promoting a lifestyle or anything. He just said that I could stay with him and his family for the first month. So I said yes and packed five suitcases for what was meant to be a six-month season. Ahem...

Colin had his own nice, detached house in Burlington, Ontario, and also got me a rental place to move to after the first month spent living with him and his family. Being there on my own didn't appeal at all, although it did mean I could watch baseball on television every night. It was a sport I hadn't really seen before, but I soon loved it, as I did American football. But I hated badminton and especially basketball. I just didn't get the idea of the two teams taking turns to run up the court!

Toronto Nationals were due to play in the first ever Canadian professional league, designed to provide a pathway into senior football that didn't previously exist – before that, promising 16 and 17-year-old players had nowhere to go in terms of a professional structure. The nation wanted the game to grow and it seemed a progressive step. There were only six teams, though – Montreal, Calgary, Edmonton, Toronto, Hamilton and Missisaga – so we were due to play each other twice at home and twice away.

The squad had a training camp not far outside Toronto for about three weeks in pre-season and although the medical wasn't exactly rigorous, I was amazed to pass it. The treatment I was given for my knee went downhill from there – it was a joke, really. There was virtually none. Training, too, was atrocious; basically a bit of running and not much more. One session was held on a massive open field with goals, but no markings. It was about 15-a-side and you could use the whole field, including going round the back of the goals. There seemed to be no aim to it and I wondered what the hell I was doing there.

Naturally there were a few Canadians in the squad, but it was lucky that Colin and I had one or two useful players with us to help to raise the standard, namely a very good German called Heinz-Gunther Nunez. There was also a little Ecuadorian number 10 who could play, but Colin – who had previously played for Toronto Blizzards against some good-quality opposition – knew it was crap.

The standard was probably comparable at that time with the Third Division standard back home and all the teams included some foreigners of a professional standard. Our strip was all light blue, like Coventry City's, and despite my misgiving about much of the experience I was at least enjoying playing my usual role, wearing the number 10 shirt. I still have that, along with various other items including match programmes.

We were a good team at that level, probably the best of the six and looked likely to win the league. I was on the equivalent of £600 per week, but after being paid for the first two weeks, things started to go wrong. Again! Our multi-millionaire owner pulled the plug after our first home game because we drew an attendance of only 1,000 and he needed 5,000. I learned later from Venables that the Nationals had also reneged on a payment to QPR. That surprised me as much as anything because I was supposedly out of contract!

After the wages had dried up, the players voted to carry on playing while the solicitors worked on our behalf in the hope that things might improve. But in two months it had all blown up and we could see the league wasn't going to work. In fact, during our final game we had about half-a-dozen players sent off. With so few teams in the league, losing one would weaken it considerably and others would almost inevitably follow suit. Sure enough, within about two months of the six-month season starting the league folded and I never did receive any more wages.

In hindsight I think the owner had misjudged the potential success of the league. He had probably been convinced by somebody or something that this new venture was going to capture the public's imagination. Had they done any research beforehand – opinion polls maybe? I don't know, but they were daft if they hadn't because they were never going to get 5,000 crowds, at least to begin with. We never met the owner and we didn't know his motivation for taking it on, but our gates were not the exception in the league.

It was also a regret that we never got to play the second-best team, Montreal. The travel distances in Canada are huge compared with England; it's 300 miles to Montreal, which was far enough, but that is dwarfed by the 2,000 miles to Calgary and Edmonton, right next to the Rockies.

I wanted to go to Edmonton because I had become an ice-hockey fan and the legendary Wayne Gretzky was then playing for the Edmonton Oilers, who I had adopted as my team. But I did watch the Boston Bruins play Edmonton in the Stanley Cup final and, on television, Gordon Strachan and Aberdeen winning the European Cup Winners' Cup under Sir Alex Ferguson.

There had been a bit of media interest in me over there and I did a few interviews, also appearing on television as a pundit for the cup final back home. As far as my knee was concerned, I had been able to manage and protect it to get through training easily, while matches were in my comfort zone as well. But I was now realistic enough to realise that it must have been gradually deteriorating.

Colin lived about 40 minutes from the ground and we'd drive there wearing overcoats because it was cold and he had no heater in his car – and this was in June! The food and culture were similar to England and although I didn't get to see much of the Canadian countryside, I am glad to have spent time in Toronto. It really is a lovely city. But it was all over now. It had been a milestone moment for me, because I had dared to try something different, but my inclination was just to dwell on the conclusion that something else had gone wrong in my life. Only two things occupied my mind; I was going home and I had no money. I should have got on the blower to home, letting it be known to the football world that I was back and a free agent. But that just wasn't in me.

Another option I should have considered was moving over the border and playing in America, as Colin had done before. It would have been so easy to have just given my old Sheffield United buddy Alan Woodward a call at the Tulsa Roughnecks, where he had been since 1979. But no. I just decided I was going back home.

The truth was that I really was very lonely, particularly during that second month on my own. Eventually I had enough money to fly home, just two months after arrival. And I couldn't wait.

22

THE FINAL WHISTLE

With successful players today enjoying fabulous wages and the business guid-
ance of their agents, they don't lack the means to make provision for their fu-
tures as their careers wind down. I envy that and don't begrudge it, but my own
experience was painful and inevitable because I couldn't grasp the reality and
take positive action.

Not long after my return to England, I got a break. It maybe
was not at the level I would have wanted, but it was a start
and gave me a bit of a boost. England's World Cup-winning
captain Bobby Moore was by then chief executive at Southend United and made a call, offering to sign me on a monthly contract.
That was fair enough at that stage, but it turned out to be a duff decision
on their part. Two days after I signed, I was due to play my first match
and to say it was a disappointment would be an understatement.

I was running out with the team for the warm-up at 10 to three and as
soon as I stepped over the sideline and put my foot down to push off and
kick a ball, my calf muscle went. Trying to run it off didn't work so I had
no option but to go in and tell the manager, Peter Morris. You can imagine
his reaction. "You must be f****** joking," he said. "I've already put the
teamsheet in, so we'll get fined £1,000 for changing the team for a start!"

I was in his bad books straightaway and he had to get a substitute out of
the stand. For the next three months I travelled the North Circular Road
every morning for training and treatment at 9am. 'Buster' the physio was
a lovely bloke and every morning he got me to keep my ankle in the sea
for 20 minutes which, believe you me, was absolutely freezing. Then it
was back for treatment and home for 1pm.

After I had played a couple of reserve games, I thought I had done well and Morris called me in. "Look," he said. "I don't think you'll ever be right."

I was so disappointed, but just said: "Fair enough," turned round and walked out. In fact, I never went back. Perhaps I should have spoken to Bobby Moore. Then again he might have already spoken to the manager and agreed with him. In hindsight Morris may have been right: who knows? But from then on I wasn't getting any treatment for the knee, or building up my thigh. I didn't have a plan for getting myself healed and fit, or the facilities of a club behind me. With nothing else on the immediate horizon I played a few non-league matches with my brother Paul at Chesham.

My first game was at Tring, north of London in the Chiltern Hills, and I recall that we played in a West Ham-type kit – the newspapers were even there to watch! Southend had been paying me £300 a week, but it was £60 a game for Chesham. Other than that I had absolutely nothing.

I needed the money, but was playing more because I wanted to – even though at that level was a bit frustrating. If I had been a coach, I would have become very frustrated! But I loved playing with those lads and I didn't worry about the surroundings and lack of facilities. As long as the pitch was marked out properly and there was a ball in the middle, I was at least playing and able to lift myself from my personal gloom for a short period.

The crowds were up a bit and I could clearly hear their shouts, but I'd had that at professional level and it was nothing new. I used to shout back sometimes and have a laugh with them. Handling comments from the terraces is a personal thing for any player and although I liked it because it helped to get me going, I know some players didn't. Before very long the manager was sacked, my brother joined Hendon and I packed in there.

I paid Mum 20 quid a week and, needing the money, started taxi-driving for a firm in Kilburn, sometimes for as many as 16 hours a day. I had to use my own car, an oldish blue Opel Rekord, while paying the owner 35 quid a week for the radio and aerial. It got so bad that when I had a nail in a tyre, I had to leave it in. If I took it out, the tyre would have gone down and I couldn't afford a new one. I was earning about £90 a week and paying my wife £60 of that. After the £20 to Mum, there was very little left.

My patch was mainly in north-west Lon•on an• although my figures might not be totally accurate, I was lucky if I got five jobs a •ay. I woul• sit in the office in Kilburn for hours, waiting for fares, an• never got recognise• while I was •riving punters about. On one occasion I took four or five female customers somewhere and afterwards found out they had pissed on the seats. Another bloke put something in my han• to pay an• ran off, leaving me hol•ing a han•ful of shit and bolts. What a horrible time. I was at a very low ebb and gave it up when the automatic gears blew up on me.

Things were just as depressing when I took another £90-a-week job in a video shop just up the road from where I was living. Customers were very, very rare and I was usually on my own in the shop all day long, for another couple of months. That was THE lowest point of my life. I was socialising only with Jeff and Viv and their friends and I would be on the scotch and fags on alternate •ays – I •on't know how I affor•e• it even if I occasionally use• to miss a night or two. Spending most of my time alone in my bedroom, there was no-one seeing it and trying to change it.

Not long after coming back from Canada, Frank Clough, a well-known journalist who covered the England trips, interviewed me at my mum's. His brief was to •o a big article about me playing in the FA Cup final, the injury, the Cana•ian fiasco an• how things ha• •eteriorate•. I was really gla• of the couple of grand I was given for that because it was well-needed, but when the paper was published, the headline ran: 'Broke and Boozed' because I had told him the depths to which I had sunk.

Some of my pals were less than impressed with that slant, although I accept that the writer doesn't write the headline. Frank personally apologised and confirme• that some e•itor at the paper ha• use• the sensationalist hea•line which didn't do the truth of my story justice.

***

A former teammate, Steve Wicks, got me an interview with Jim Smith at QPR to become youth-team coach, but nothing came of it. I was willing to give it a try even though I don't know if I could have handled it. In my heart I knew I would have found it difficult coaching young blokes who couldn't play as I wanted them – largely because I remembered playing and having a go at teammates.

Venables and I had often talked tactics and after seeing me do and say things on the pitch, he thought I had it in me to coach. Personally I don't know if I could have been able to put it over. I never really coached any-where at all, but I really would have loved to be a manager and I think that would have suited me more than coaching.

At one time the then-Sheffield United chairman Reg Brealey rang and arranged a meeting with me over lunch at his offices in Sleaford, Lin-colnshire. It was completely unexpected and I suspected Andy Daykin, United's commercial manager and an old pal, might have put a word in for me. Reg and I sat at opposite ends of the boardroom table, eating a fish salad, while he mentioned a couple of possible avenues that might open up for me. One was some talk of me playing for the reserves at United and helping to bring emerging talent through.

That kind of appealed, but the other idea was a non-starter for me. Brealey was quite a visionary character and mentioned Brunei and an academy he was thinking of setting up over there. Danny Bergara, the former Blades coach, had already been lined up for coaching in the new project so Reg was cracking on with it. As soon as I realised where Bru-nei is – about an inch from Australia on the map! – I politely declined straightaway. That would be far too bold a move for me, whatever trou-ble I was in. Money had never even been mentioned.

Subsequently Reg set up a meeting for me with Blades boss Ian Porter-field, but all I got from him was negativity really. He was the manager and I was still a popular figure with the fans, so did he feel threatened? Was it regarded as just a PR stunt? I don't honestly know, but nothing came of it. I still hadn't attempted to initiate contact with any clubs or managers; both Bobby Moore and Ken Bates had called me with offers. Ken wanted me to bring on the reserves at Chelsea, but even though it was the club I had loved as a kid, it didn't materialise because I didn't get back to him. My head wasn't right again. I was all over the place, couldn't think things through and make a plan and would never throw myself into anything.

A year later my reluctance to do that cost me what would probably have been my best opportunity to get back into the game. Tony Bar-rington, a Sheffield United director when I had been there, offered me the chance to become player-manager at Wigan Athletic.

For someone with no experience in coaching or management I should have snatched his hand off and walked to Wigan. But the place seemed like another planet in terms of distance from where the kids were and I wanted to be closer to them. In the back of my mind I knew my knee wasn't great, but I would have been on the ladder in my mid-thirties. Not taking that job is probably my biggest regret to this day.

God knows why I hadn't got back to Ken Bates because at least that job would have allowed me to stay closer to the children. For me decision-making usually meant putting it off until a 'tomorrow' that never came. The blame is entirely mine because I didn't take responsibility when there were opportunities I had not even had to create through my own efforts. I was now allowing what had happened to me, in terms of injury, to screw me up.

Now I still beat myself up about what I let by back then when I could have taken responsibility for shaping my future. I think: "You idiot. You were seeing the kids every day, but you could have still taken the Wigan job and seen them as often as you could just to get started." Surely I should at least have looked into whether a compromise might have been possible. Nobody owed me a living and I'd had my day. But I couldn't let it go.

I was too involved in drinking at home to be going out, so I had few friends and no new relationships. Things hadn't really improved since I returned from Canada and, when I could see so little hope in the future, I eventually thought of suicide. It got as far as writing goodbye letters to my kids, which horrifies me now. I had them for weeks, but somehow pulled myself together enough to not leave them. I eventually ripped the letters up.

But I still needed some money and out of the blue, in February 1984, the ex-Chelsea defender David Webb called me up from Torquay. "I've got Eddie Kelly down here as a coach," he said, "and you can come here as a player." They were close to the bottom of the old Fourth Division at the time, but David and Eddie were great blokes who I'd played against many times. Eddie even turned out for us as well on a few occasions during what was left of the season – once upon a time that would have been some midfield. My wage was £300 per match and they still owe me for four!

Torquay didn't put me through a medical, which was just as well be-cause I tended to play one match and miss the next two, or play two and miss the third because of the knee. I was doing my own knee-strength-ening exercises and icing it along the way because I had jumped at this chance to give it another go.

I would go by train from Paddington, which took three hours, includ-ing a change at Newton Abbot, on a Thursday ahead of a home game on the Friday night, and then stay overnight in a lovely hotel. Webby made no demands about living in the area or training with them and ensured that I was paid expenses. If we were playing up north, I would use the train or the team coach picked me up just off the North Circular.

They had a good bunch of lads I enjoyed playing with, including striker Stevie Phillips, who was some player. They were all great to me and we had a lot of fun despite not being that successful. I don't really know why – no legs possibly – but whatever I had, I gave it. Plainmoor was okay and I went back for a testimonial there a few years later.

Playing Fourth Division football didn't bother me because it was a game, despite there being plenty of 'targeting' at that level. It was worse than higher up the pyramid and once, I was elbowed off the ball and suffered a depressed fracture. I had seen it coming but, for whatever reason, didn't get out of the way. It wasn't my style to get over-involved with fisticuffs, even though I think I could have comfortably held my own if ever I had to.

Performing on the big stage in front of large crowds was always such a wonderful experience for much of my career and I can't deny I missed it when it was gone. The experience at Torquay was very different, but I really didn't care; the pitch was still the same size, I was still popular with the fans and I played my usual game, spraying the ball about.

The downside was that I was now having to strap the knee ligament up with narrow tape to make my leg feel much more stable than it really was. It did have the double advantage of not looking as serious as bandaging, though, which definitely would have been a tempting target for my opponents.

If the knee was playing up and I couldn't play, I could let the gaffer know and it wouldn't be a problem. Importantly the lads were equally as accommodating about my situation; no-one put me under pressure, which is the way I needed it to be. I would have felt guilty if I had been under contract. The manager wasn't a bully and he knew how to treat players, despite spending so much of his own career at the top level.

Torquay players didn't get paid during the summer and I can't remember if the money from matches might have carried me through those months or whether I was also doing that stint at the video shop. There was never any talk of being offered a permanent contract – although there was a bit of a mention of doing some coaching, which didn't go any further – and when the next season started, the pattern of missing matches was just the same.

The lack of treatment didn't allow me to build up muscle, even though at home I was trying to do that by using a boot weight – probably 'borrowed' from QPR! The knee was becoming arthritic as well and I might well have been weakening the joint anyway by doing the exercises. It just wasn't getting better and results on the field still weren't great, so the writing really was on the wall. My time at Torquay just fizzled out.

My spell there consisted of 16 games in which I scored once, the winner at Hereford, and at least my last goal was a good one. Not long afterwards I played my final ever league match, a 3-1 loss at Bury, and then my last FA Cup fixture when we went to Orient and got stuffed 3-0. Twenty years later David Webb still remembered my time at Torquay and mentioned on a talk show that he had dangled a coaching job for me.

I knew then that my life as a professional footballer was over. The only realistic chance of playing again was in non-league, and I would have to look for another way of making a living if I was to get out of the rut I was in. Almost any team would do. I needed to play for my own sanity as well as for the cash to stay afloat, although even that existence would lack direction and satisfaction. Then Gary Hand, an apprentice with me at Watford in the 1960s, rang and asked me to play for Hendon, where he was manager. I said I would love to. Hendon had been our Wembley as kids growing up in that neck of the woods, so it was a really sentimental experience.

But I was having to strap the knee up even more now to manage my way through, and the cycle of playing and then the joint flaring up continued. I was on about £100 a game and managed only five of those before the knee packed up again. Playing should have been out of the question now and a brief flirtation with Dunstable did none of us any good.

As my football life drained away, my mentality was getting worse; I wasn't going anywhere, had no ambitions and definitely no thoughts about what to do with my life. There was nothing to take my mind off things and I didn't have the drive to lift myself out of the hole I was digging. With no-one to tell me that I still had highs to look forward to if I adopted a different attitude, I wasn't in control of my own life. All I did was feel sorry for myself; my family, wife, career and money were all gone.

BACK UP NORTH

*We are often told we should make our own luck and many of us have the for-
titude to do that. If you possess that quality, I am genuinely envious because it
wasn't in my make-up to adopt that attitude when I was really down. But sometimes luck can give a bloke a helping hand anyway...*

Positive things started to happen for me in 1986. Following an
exploratory operation at Watford General Hospital, I was left
with fluid on my damaged knee; a recurring condition I have
lived with ever since. It needed to be drained and the medical
staff had to perform the procedure about four times before blood appeared, indicating that the fluid had disappeared.

With the swelling reduced I was able to accept an invitation, from
out of the blue, to take part in Tony Kenworthy's testimonial game at
Sheffield United during that summer. Tony was a youngster breaking
into the first-team during my final months at Bramall Lane and an uncompromising central defender who went on to enjoy a long spell with
the Blades. My knee was always going to be a concern so I had to manage
it carefully during the match, but I really enjoyed the occasion and the
chance to play with some wonderful players again.

About that time I was introduced to a young lady called Jane Rowan,
who was helping on the corporate event side of Tony's fundraising year.
Months later we bumped into each other at the Brincliffe Oaks pub in
Sheffield, a meeting-point for the organisers, and subsequently I started seeing her now and then. A local businessman and big Blades fan,
Howard Stephenson, had also very kindly suggested that I should have
a testimonial of my own and offered to front a committee dedicated to
arranging a year of events.

It was music to my ears – not just for the financial benefit that I could definitely have done with, but also because it showed I was still remembered fondly by United fans. It was such a confidence boost when I really needed it the most.

Howard arranged for me to go to see the comedian Freddie Starr at Blackpool with the aim of asking him to play in my own testimonial and Jane accompanied me. Freddie had trained with us at United in the early 1970s when he appeared in cabaret in Sheffield and in return he had arranged tickets for us players to watch his show. This time I went into his dressing-room at Blackpool's Winter Gardens – he had just a robe on – and it was a shame that he had to apologise for being unable to play. Freddie liked a kickabout and would have been a big draw.

As my 'year' got underway, I kept coming up to Sheffield to attend various events that had been arranged for me and Howard would give me £200 expenses to help me out with the cost of travel and everything else. He was helped by a mutual mate, Dave Coxon, who was himself an ex-player at United, and I stayed with him whenever I came up.

I am immensely grateful for the work that those two and the rest of the committee put in on my behalf because it unquestionably turned my life around. They pulled out all the stops for the game in October to put out a fantastic line-up when Dennis Waterman's Showbiz XI took on Sheffield United's promotion-winning 1971 side.

They paid, I think I am right in saying, £1,000 for George Best to travel and the same for Alan Woodward to come over from the USA. Those two were joined by Frank Worthington, Alan Hudson, Allan Clarke, Billy Bremner, Roy McFarland and Archie Gemmill, plus singers Paul Heaton, from *The Housemartins*, and *Def Leppard's* Joe Elliott.

It was so humbling that they appeared so willingly and I was probably unable to express my gratitude as fully as I wanted to because I was very emotional about it all. It was fantastic that George Best came – I was aware that he often didn't show up, although there is a chance that he was put under pressure to do so because his agent wanted to play as well! Organising can be time-consuming and often frustrating work and although some of those players and celebrities were great friends of mine, Howard and Dave did really well to get everyone on board for my big day.

None of us expected the biggest crowd in the world, especially when United's first-team weren't enjoying a good period or pulling in high attendances. We were going to open only the South Stand, but so many kept turning up that they had to open the Kop and then the Bramall Lane stand. In the end well over 20,000 were inside, some without paying, and it was the biggest crowd of the season!

What a tribute and one of the greatest days of my life; 27 degrees and not a cloud in the sky for a 4pm kick-off on a Sunday afternoon. Such a lot had happened to me since leaving the city 10 years earlier and I couldn't have dared hope for such support after being away for so long. But the fans did me proud at a time when I was most in need of a break, an uplift in my spirits. They convinced me that Sheffield United would be a life-long love affair, paving the way for significant changes in my life. This time I was prepared to meet them head-on with new conviction. In all honesty the thought of moving back to Sheffield at that time hadn't occurred to me, but in hindsight a few pieces of the jigsaw were beginning to fall into place.

There was no realisation back then that spending time in the city, re-connecting with people – including supporters – and having something tangible to focus on was soon going to open doors. Howard negotiated a sponsored car for me from Gilders, which was a real boon. I was now easily able to get back and forth for events, including a race night and the testimonial dinner.

The committee's hard work paid off because after expenses I benefited to the tune of £13,000, plus the car valued at about £3,000. It might not sound much now, but it was a long time ago. Maybe we should have charged a higher admission price for the game, but the fans turning up in such numbers meant so much more to me. Partly as a result of the testimonial I was eventually able to put a 25 per cent deposit down on a £40,000 bungalow in Dronfield, just outside Sheffield. My gift of decanters to the committee members seemed a small token in view of what they achieved on my behalf.

When the hullaballoo had eventually died down, Howard, Cocky, their wives, Jane and my kids went on holiday to Los Americas, Tenerife. We had a great time relaxing and reflecting on all that had gone into the previous 12 months. Jane had sometimes babysat for my kids when I had brought them up with me from London, but it was basically the time when we got together. I had virtually given up on my leg at this time, but had one last try with my surgeon, Mr. Sharrard, at the Claremont Hospital in Sheffield. Incidentally he had helped several patients with short or unequal leg length, using screws to balance them out or increase leg length by a couple of inches. He believed he could sort me out somehow by drilling small holes into my knee bone so that every time fluid appeared, it drained away internally.

I hadn't been able to walk properly before the surgery, but things did improve and the knee was the best it had been in a couple of years. My rehabilitation was supervised by the ex-Sheffield Wednesday physio Alan Smith and I give him credit, too, because he did a lot of work with me. I was only 37 and thought I would be able to get through some non-league football. But ultimately it was to prove beyond me.

A few months after the operation I was contacted by my old United room-mate Paddy Buckley, who was managing Goole Town in the Northern Premier League. "Come here and be a player-coach," he said. I took him up on the offer and took training a couple of nights a week. The ground wasn't bad and training was nothing too technical, mainly ball-work. The pitch had a perimeter track and it was a bit like playing in a park, but again it was a game and about 150 to 200 turned up to watch, including a few Blades fans. They paid me £60 a game and the chairman was a butcher, so I got cheap meat as well!

To be fair we had quite the foundation of a decent team in ex-Owl Dave Rushbury, who was good at centre-half; a lively left-winger called Paul Showler – a copper who ended up as a professional at Barnet – and a talented Worksop lad, Paul Cavill, up-front. But the stay didn't last long, probably about half a season, because it was just too much for my knee again. It became a familiar scenario – my heart saying play and my head saying you can't, certainly not in proper competitive football.

Charity games were a different matter and half-a-dozen times a year I would turn out for Johnny Quinn's All-Stars. Johnny was ex-Sheffield Wednesday and for many years he did wonderful work for local fundraising, putting together teams of ex-pros who always drew sizeable crowds. I enjoyed those because people such as Len Badger, Ted Hemsley, Emlyn Hughes, Jack Whitham and so on could still play a bit.

It was a good job because we played against some hard teams, such as Arbourthorne EA, so we really had to make the ball do the work. And I scored loads of goals because, to save me from risking my knee in midfield, I was paired up top with Jack. I recall Alan Woodward – on a visit from the States – Geoff Salmons and I being photographed wearing Sheffield Wednesday shirts after one game. I had a rash for a fortnight! I played for them until my late forties, by which time Emlyn had taken over. Enough had been going right for me at last after that testimonial year that I made what was, for me, the brave move of leaving London and returning permanently to Sheffield. At last, I had come to my senses and done something – and a job offer really gave me courage to go for it.

My relationship with Jane had developed enough for me to consider moving up anyway, but finance would have been an issue – I had no job. Jane was working in Sheffield for Shockers, her uncle's car-suspension parts business, and I also joined the payroll – until a brand new and intriguing opportunity came my way. Jane was 27 years old and I was 13 years her senior when we married in August 1989. We moved into a new house and just about everything was fine. The only fly in the ointment was not seeing my kids as often and as easily, but I could breathe again. I had a future and could start to put my head over the parapet with a bit more dignity than I had for a long time.

Stability and purpose had returned to my life, even if football now seemed a million miles away. But then it reappeared and not in any way I could have predicted. It probably didn't cross my radar when both Manchester clubs, Bolton Wanderers, Bury, Preston North End and Oldham Athletic were named as clubs involved in a pilot scheme in 1986.

The scheme was called Football in the Community and it was to do great work for many years, transforming and initiating connections between professional football clubs and the communities they represented. The head office was in Manchester and the organisation was led by a man called Roger Reade. A year later it was considered successful enough to be rolled out across the rest of the county, including Merseyside. Yorkshire offices quickly followed suit, as did the rest of the country.

Jointly funded by the government and the Professional Footballers' Association, it created jobs for ex-players, forming another tier for them as community officers. In other words, it helped ex-pros transition from being suddenly unemployed at the end of their careers to the world of work that all of us recognise as being more 'normal.' It may not have been every ex-player's cup of tea, but Roger Reade is fond of reminding me occasionally that I once told him: "It may be an exaggeration to say that it saved my life, but there is no doubt it was a lifesaver!"

***

Football in the Community aimed to deliver football coaching and other leisure activities to local schoolchildren and was the brainchild of former Blackpool and Newcastle United striker Mickey Burns. During that pilot year Manchester United hero Brian Kidd became the first community officer, based in Salford, and other one-time professionals including Richard Finney, Ray McHale and Dick Krzywicki were also involved in the embryonic scheme, along with Tommy Spencer.

Most professional clubs came on board gradually over the ensuing years and the help they offered will have varied greatly. They weren't meant to bankroll the scheme, but there was an inevitable disparity in co-operation levels and available facilities, despite there being plenty of scope for mutual and beneficial publicity.

Sheffield United weren't in the first tranche of clubs to join up, but from the outside I was beginning to feel that if and when the job existed, it would appeal to me. Just why I thought that I am not sure, even now, because in many ways it required a skill-set I didn't think I had. And it paid only £105 per week. But it wasn't long before United and the other five local South Yorkshire professional clubs joined at the same time and I did confirm my interest.

I was given the impression that if I applied, it would be more or less mine and I still harbour suspicions that Howard Stephenson may have been influential in that. He knew everybody and was into everything and I would think he helped me towards the top of any list. Again Andy Daykin played a part in getting my name in the hat by dropping it to Derek Dooley, perhaps more successfully this time.

Whatever the procedure behind it, on February 1, 1988 – exactly 20 years to the day that I had signed for United – I was unveiled as their first community officer. As well as her work for Shockers, Jane was a part-time model for a lady called Delyse Humphreys and I'd occasionally ferry the girls around to their modelling jobs. We never talked about having babies and I had more of a social life now after five years on my own – which wouldn't be difficult to achieve! Even living only four doors away from her parents wasn't an issue and my daughter Natalie came up to stay during every school holiday.

It was a very different marriage from my first. Linda's depression was really the cause of my own and that certainly wasn't the case this time round. Jane was very bubbly and outgoing. I now had the car-parts job and my kids were doing all right, but we didn't go to London more than 10 times a year and then only overnight. I should have done more to see mum and the kids. It's possible that Jane didn't want to be down there too long and although it didn't cause any tension, I do regret it now.

The early years had the ingredients for a happy marriage, but I still wasn't as relaxed and content as I should have been, particularly when I was by then back working at Bramall Lane. I remember Jane waking up one night to find me sitting on the bed and asking me what was wrong. "I don't know," I said, "but something's not right."

There wasn't anything obviously wrong that I could put my finger on and think: "This isn't working." We were pretty much like any other married couple, working our way through it with good days and bad days and living our lives normally. It started to change when I received a letter in 1996 from an old school friend I hadn't seen since 1971.

Liz Mullineux had been my first girlfriend at 11 years of age. She was born just three months after me, shortly after her family moved down to London from the Wirral, and had an interesting claim to fame. Her great-great grandfather had been captain of *the Daffodil*, the first ferry across the Mersey. Now married with children of her own and a fund-raiser for a boys' football team, she was asking if I could fix a visit to Shef-field United for the team. I rang the number she had given me and the first thing she asked was whether I still had my hair long! It was entirely innocent, no suggestion of putting out feelers towards a relationship and my reaction was that it would be nice to catch up on our lives. In fact, I went home and told Jane what had happened and asked if she minded If I went to London to meet her. "Not at all," she said, so I took a day off and went down to discuss the idea during Liz's lunch hour.

Arrangements were made, the day was agreed and when the visit hap-pened, I took them all to the Football in the Community's Saturday Club, where her team participated in a mini-tournament. They loved it and the day was rounded off by us all going to the match in the afternoon. That led to Liz and me deciding to arrange a school reunion for March 1997. Because she was in Kent, most of the work fell to her, helped by mutual pal Bob Turpie, while I popped down occasionally for meetings about the progress being made. We ended up with 90 people turning up, mainly from our own year, and it was a fantastic night at Hendon FC who were good enough to let us have the room for free.

The relationship between Liz and I developed from there and Jane and I eventually divorced in 1998. It was inevitable really because I hadn't hidden anything. Seeing Liz again initially had been entirely innocent – I was telling Jane all about it – but when it developed, and Jane questioned me, I had never denied it. It hadn't all been plain sailing until then with Jane, but I wouldn't say that cracks had started to appear, despite the age difference. That had never been an issue, but things came to a head in the end when she told me to get rid of Liz. I did for a month, but then resumed the relationship and understandably that was too much for Jane to take. In retrospect it was just not me to be that way. An affair wasn't in my nature, but it was entirely my fault. And it was the same for Liz.

Neither of us enjoyed hurting people we were so close to. Only two years previously Jane and I had bought Shockers, which hadn't been cheap, and we had put the house up for collateral. But I didn't know that Shockers wasn't in my name, so that proved an expensive mistake. The divorce cost me £14,000 that I didn't have for the solicitor, although the PFA helped me out with a couple of the payments. I had been naive and Jane had done all the paperwork, so I had to give my half of the house to her in settlement when in fact I had put in £10,000 from my testimonial money.

I left well before the divorce and moved in with an old friend and national sports journalist Mike Morgan in Totley, Sheffield, initially for a month. Mike had been the best man at my wedding to Jane and I can still trust him with my life. Liz popped up for weekends when she could, but always ended up going back to London in tears because I still hadn't been able to make the final break to be with her. That must have been really hard for Liz because she knew she would be leaving her kids and she didn't want to hurt her husband – as I didn't with Jane.

So we were both in turmoil, wracked with guilt at what we were doing. At Mike's I was drinking whisky again – and from about 11am. I hadn't been doing that as much with Jane because I wasn't as lonely. To me, saying goodbye is very final so I rarely say it, but I did to Jane when she told me it was all over. Then Liz and I moved in with Mike, where we were sharing a single bed. That's all we had – apart from, in my case, my luggage and a set of cutlery from my testimonial!

24

A GIANT LEAP

Hea•ing up Sheffiel• Unite•'s Football in the Community Scheme was a massive shot in the arm for me after what had gone before. A chance to consolidate my move to Sheffiel• an• reclaim some cre•ibility by buil•ing another career. An• the fear that it may be the last-chance saloon ...

F amily apart, I had never in my life been responsible for directing others and even less helping to shape anyone's future. Daunted? You bet I was – this was a whole lot of stuff I had never had to deal with before. But I was in a much better place, more settled and with something of a support network behind me. And in many ways, I felt I had come home.

As the scheme rolled out, there were lots of meetings to get those of us in the front line up to speed. Our area head office was in Barnsley where I met up again with ex-Miller Tommy Spencer, who I was later to form a close partnership with. We were required to hold the FA prelimi-nary coaching badge and I did mine alongside former Owl Dean Barrick at Staveley, where Kevin Fogg led the course. Kevin later became one of United's youth coaches at the Shirecliffe academy with another top bloke, Ron Reid.

As well as leading practical coaching sessions, I had to sit examinations as part of the preliminary badge. They were never my strong point and so, with examiners watching over me, I was very nervous. Mercifully I got through, but a few years later we were put on a prep course at Nor-ton College in Sheffield for the full badge and a well-known coach was leading it. My God, he really was a bit of a know-it-all and on one occa-sion I, nearing 40 years old, was involved in a game on the old Redgra – or red gravel – pitch with about 20-a-side. I can't remember what he had seen me do to warrant him stopping the session and asking me, almost sneeringly: "Ey, son, what's your name?"

Now I am not a loudmouth or someone who makes a point of letting everyone know who I am, but, come on – you would have thought a football coach would have had an inkling, wouldn't you? "Tony Currie," I almost sheepishly replied. When the realisation dawned, he grimaced, obviously rethinking his strategy as he put his head in his hands. "Okay, then," he said. I thought he was going to give me a dressing down. In fact, I'm sure he was. When I told him who I was, his embarrassment was immediately apparent and I wondered if he had even bothered to look down his list of attendees before starting the session.

None of it went very well, really, and during the preliminary badge course – which incidentally I did alongside Kevin Fogg – I was told not to over-coach. That threw me for a start! Then on the full badge course I didn't take to the lead coach Dave Burnside one little bit and wished I was with Mick Wadsworth, another future Blades coach whom I really liked and rated.

At the venue, Lilleshall, our accommodation was about two miles from the gate so all the lads were in the bar at night or getting advice from the coaches, but that wasn't for me. I just wanted to be in my room, which probably went against me because the others were showing interest and putting themselves about. It wasn't their fault. Just my inhibitions restricting me again, I suppose.

Throughout that episode we each had to take four coaching sessions, each lasting about 20 minutes. With most of the course members being ex-pros or teachers, it was intimidating and each time was probably the longest 20 minutes of my life. The whole fortnight was a nightmare to me and although I ended up with the intermediate badge, I reckoned that they must have felt sorry for me!

I was let down by my weakness at taking exams and by being nervous coaching in front of others. I was good enough to play for England, but not to coach people who weren't! Joking apart, I should stress I understand that there are wonderful coaches who weren't top players themselves and you don't have to look too far these days to find those. In my defence I definitely applied myself fully and put in loads of studying at night, even though I didn't want to do it. I just had to for the new role.

Coaching had never really appealed to me as much as managing, which

I had always fancied more. A coach doesn't have the job of picking a team and deciding how to play, but those are the responsibilities I wanted instead of coaching someone else's beliefs. It was a hard two weeks on that full badge course and during the following two summers I was back at Lilleshall again, doing both parts of my physio courses.

That was three years on the trot of studying and taking examinations and it was murder, real head-banging stuff for me at least. I couldn't concentrate on the classroom stuff, so much so that I came home during the second part, telling Jane that I couldn't handle lectures from 9am to 5pm and studying until late at night. Although I made an effort and did well to catch up a bit to do a re-sit, I didn't get a pass.

The preparation period was quite intense because it covered so many elements I was decidedly sketchy about. Management courses, laminates and overhead projectors, presentations and talk sessions were bloody frightening to my rather private self. All I really knew was playing football and these things were nothing to do with what happens on a football field. They were about organisation, course knowledge, dealing with trainees, book-keeping, first aid, fundraising and so on – essential stuff for what was vital to running a business. I needed plenty of direction, but was probably no more clueless than many of the other 'leaders' in training; most of us were ex-footballers with precious little experience of the working world.

Happily some of the preparation we did was more enjoyable than others, especially a spell spent in the Lake District where we worked in teams on problem solving. That was great fun, especially when we were tasked with building our own rafts and most of us ended up sinking – there were all sorts of cock-ups! It was so chaotic that I wondered how any of us would eventually be deemed capable of taking any responsibility ever again. Anyway we got through and then the real stuff began. Recruiting volunteer staff from the dole was obviously the start in order for us to offer programmes and I didn't know what to expect. Fortunately that first batch of six I got were good and included a lad called Steve Booker, who I still see occasionally all these years later.

I had literally hundreds of staff during my time in the job and they all had to apply before I interviewed them to work out whether they were cut out to work with the public. We didn't turn many down, especially in view of the rising clamour for equal opportunities, and their dole money was paid by the government because they were trained by me with the goal of obtaining their NVQ in recreation and leisure. That accreditation was a step towards better things – permanent employment, somewhere, was their ultimate target.

They were paid their dole money, plus a bit more, and we had targets for helping them to get back into work. That was a key component of the scheme and we were quite proud when we made the top four or five in the country for that. It was often hard to tell who would shine or not, but it was often the older ones – perhaps in their fifties – who got on best with the kids. Generally volunteers reflected different elements in our society, good and bad, and I suppose that is what you would expect because they were out of work for many different reasons. Consequently their attitudes and the amount of dedication they showed varied to a high degree – just like any other workplace, in fact.

One of my volunteers was Toni Minichiello. Honestly he was brilliant because he definitely had a goal, to get into sport and on to the coaching ladder. He wasn't really a footballer, but did his best and could put it across. Tony is a lovely bloke and I was genuinely thrilled to see him emerge a few years later as the coach of Sheffield's world and Olympic champion decathlete Jess Ennis. His success is a clear example of what dedication and drive can do – along with no little ability.

Working on the scheme wasn't for everyone and some of the trainees turned out to be no-shows at some point or another. Some would do their six months and if they failed, would re-apply to try to get their City & Guilds qualification; Tommy Spencer and the ex-Wednesday player Charlie Williamson would examine them to make the decision, but it was also based on the six-month period.

It was so gratifying to see many of them put in the effort and find personal reward later down the line. People such as Andy Keenan went on to a very good job in schools after being a permanent member with us for years. I had two Neil Pearsons achieve something similar, along with Gary Hindley – whose son, Ryan, is doing well in local Sheffield football.

Gary and Tony are great lads who went into decent jobs more or less because of what they had achieved with us. You could see how they would make something of themselves as they were mature and conducted themselves in the right way. It's a pleasure to still be in touch with some of them.

So, I had the staff and now it was time to find the 'customers.' I was given the telephone numbers of every school in Sheffield at all age levels and went from there, ringing and offering to teach their pupils on courses lasting half a term, six weeks. We included specific targeted schools as well, including those for the disabled or for girls, to make sure we were, in more modern parlance, diverse and inclusive.

Devising a timetable that fitted with our resources with the schedule that individual schools wanted wasn't easy logistically; teachers would request specific slots at different times and different days. Often they didn't dovetail kindly for our manpower resources and we would be flying about from one to another. It was a statistical conundrum sometimes and not helpful in trying to appear as professional as we could be.

Most of the kids didn't have many skills – some were tiny five-year-olds and the footballs were almost up to their knees! Today there is more appropriate equipment available, but then we had to use what we had and adapt. Smaller play balls were the answer and they didn't have to be football specific; later there came versions for netball, hockey, tunnel ball and relays. We might have, for example, three groups with three coaches doing 20 minutes at each activity.

Normally I would lead from the start initially and the coaches would pick it up as we went along to give more breadth to what we were doing. Gradually I could then figure out which coaches were best at a specific activity, who to trust and so on. We had some great ones, some average and some rogues, but it was great when any of the most able went on to become permanent staff.

To start with I found it all hard work, but for once I don't think I should beat myself up about that. Compared with a footballer's lifestyle they were long days and the scheme occupied all my time, although I eventually had two job-sharing secretaries, Colleen Fawdry and Paul Miller, to do the bulk of the telephoning and typing. When I first started the ringing around of schools, we had a very good response and were quite booked up.

But we soon had to stop going into secondary schools because, if we were in a predominantly Sheffield Wednesday-supporting area of the city under our United banner, the abuse and swearing were ridiculous. The Owls' scheme must have had a similar experience until we learned to steer clear of each other's patch.

That is the problem with a two-team city and it wouldn't happen any-where near as much in Barnsley or Rotherham. I wasn't happy with it at all, not least as there might be junior-school kids within earshot of our sessions. Even as far away as Worksop, out of our area really, one of our first schools was a bit of an eye-opener. We turned up in our tracksuits to coach some 11-year-olds and one of them said: "What you lot doing here? We don't want you wankers over here!"

"What the hell have we come to here?" I thought. Granted, the teach-ers who would have been taking the classes were always with us during our sessions, mostly in the allotted PE time, but some were better than others at dealing with awkward situations. A lot were female teachers, because we were mainly taking youngsters and as we developed relation-ships with schools during the year, we built up mutual trust.

After establishing a foothold, our programme developed in its scope with projects other than coaching; the hugely-popular Saturday Club, programmes for senior citizens featuring bingo sessions and occasionally outings to the coast. At an old folks' facility on Verdon Street in the city, we borrowed a bingo machine once a week for a session and I went to the local shops to beg, steal and borrow prizes. There were tins of beans, nice cake, cans of pop or soup and I would add my own prizes if we were short of time. They absolutely loved it!

It wasn't always so gratifying. We shared a minibus on a weekly basis with our Sheffield Wednesday counterparts and on one occasion we took the OAPs to Scarborough in two minibuses. As soon as we arrived, one of the old ladies put her foot down and broke her ankle. I had to spend the whole day at the hospital with her and needless to say, we didn't do that again! Happily, although today's health and safety obsession hadn't yet taken root, there was still awareness and cover to ensure precautions were in place. The Saturday Club at Gleadless School and then the Shef-field Works Department complex at Heeley Bank Road lasted a couple of hours for under-13s who would take part in a swap shop and games that we put on. The activities used football to learn geography, for example, by placing teams on a map that had dots for cities, or something similar with rivers or lakes as clues.

It was popular, educational and fun and I spent many an evening doing the preparation for my ideas. The co-operation of the club, who readily supplied tickets when I needed them, enabled us to round off the day by taking all the kids to a game at Bramall Lane in the afternoon. To the public and beneficiaries of what we did, we were "from Sheffield United" and, although the clubs weren't the ones who paid us, there was mutual positive publicity. In return for what we were doing in their name, they donated tickets, allowed use of some of their facilities and encouraged players to attend some of our events.

For player appearances we relied heavily on the attitude of the succession of team managers at Bramall Lane. Dave Bassett and Neil Warnock particularly were always supportive and I believe Chris Wilder was in the same mould. They understood the value of our work, the goodwill it could generate towards the club and its impact on generating supporters of the future. In 1991 a change in the structure of the Football in the Community scheme impacted very heavily on all involved at the sharp end of delivery. Now we were required to become self-sufficient. This would be a whole new ball game because there would now be a black hole where the money to pay us and provide the equipment and staff had been.

After a few years there was change in the air and professional clubs were asked if they wanted to carry on with it. United said yes. The ensuing reorganisation meant a change of name, so we became Sheffield United Football in the Community and that's when Tommy joined me. He had the option of Rotherham or us, chose Sheffield United and we had 16 years together from then on.

Finding funding from somewhere was absolutely essential and raising sponsorship was challenging enough to cause a few sleepless nights. But all the clubs involved were in the same boat. It meant strength in numbers because it presented an opportunity to bring in sponsors who could see the benefit of a nationwide deal.

I went down to London with Roger Reade and the entourage of the PFA and Football in the Community to do a deal with Pizza Hut, then Wagon Wheels and later even Adidas. They offered a fantastic £5million deal to provide the scheme with loads of kit, enhanced by Coca-Cola agreeing to sports-match anything more than £1,000. That also helped enormously. These large, lucrative deals kept us going for two or three years and it was a process much easier than each scheme continually trying to make ends meet with lots of smaller, local links. Although the staff still had to be on minimum wages, they were at least off the dole by virtue of being on an approved scheme.

Because the change had been flagged up in good time, we had time to build up the scheme's reserves of money, while also thinking about how we might tackle it. We needed to make additional changes to be financially viable and yet still attractive enough to generate regular users. When we had started, our soccer schools were offered for free and only one child turned up – a girl, as it happens. That was worrying because we had put it out there with what we thought was adequate advertising. But we slowly built up our reputation until we were doing them throughout the year and during the holidays.

Normally we would attract between 50 and 70 children, but sometimes there would be as many as 130 which meant bringing in extra coaches. There had to be a charge now, but £15 for the five-day course was great value. In summer we also offered a subsidised ground tour of Old Trafford.

Birthday parties did so well that we were doing them five nights a week and had so much interest there could have been two a night. Those parties and soccer schools accounted for about two-thirds of our total income with the rest coming from the Saturday Club and other events. The switch was worrying when it came, but we worked so well together that we made a success of it. I found myself immersed in doing the books, reports, breakdown records of how many kids had attended and all sorts. We were under pressure to deliver, hence monthly appraisals of the staff and me by area managers who would make recommendations of what we needed to focus on.

I was accountable for something not happening on a football pitch for the first time since I was a teenager at the builder's yard. I was responsible for people's lives via processes that I had never previously thought myself capable of. I was coping now in my own way. But there are always turns in the road ahead ...

25

CHANGING TIMES

Nobody and nothing lasts forever. That had been a lesson hard-earned when my playing career ended. Now it was time to acknowledge that other things move on, too, and to learn that the trick was to handle them better than before.

Despite wages not being great, the Football in the Community job was enjoyable enough overall and I devoted almost 20 years to it. I could not have seen that when I was spending those five years at Mum's in virtual solitude and my life had been spiralling downwards. Fast.

In comparison my later years have been infinitely better, despite my mood sometimes darkening when I recall what I lost in terms of playing the game. I appreciate that almost every player has to face his time being called eventually, but my default mindset shut that out. I would wallow in my loss. Nothing could replace being a player and I think I would have been happy to have played football every single day of my life.

And that is why the Football in the Community scheme was so important to me. It was stable, challenging and kept me occupied despite elements of it being relentless or hard work. Tommy Spencer and I weren't on the United payroll, but we were proud of helping to put big numbers on seats, too.

We saw kids at five years old become regular supporters by the time they had grown up. We could recall some of them having a birthday party with us or enrolling year in, year out at a soccer school and coming home with a United shirt. Some will be pushing 40 years old plus now. I still get them coming up to me to ask if I remember them, and that's really nice.

Ben Starosta was seven years old when he first came on our courses and he continued until he was 13. He got his head down, worked his socks off and eventually made the professional grade at Sheffield United as well as playing for Poland under-20s. Jordan Slew and George Long also followed a similar path with us, making the first-team at the Lane before moving on, while Billy Sharp also came to the sessions. And we all know what he went on to achieve in the game, helping his beloved Blades into the Premier League.

We weren't there to make professional players, though, and the real satisfaction came from the number of youngsters who enrolled on the scheme and thoroughly enjoyed themselves at whatever level they could perform. It was equally gratifying if they acquired loyal friends and forged a life-long interest in the great game.

For the first eight years of being in post I was with Jane, but in 1996 we divorced and Liz and I are still together to this day. The circumstances of how we felt the need to divorce caused pain for a lot of people, but we are not the first to have to make such a decision. It's life, isn't it?

Liz is a totally-different personality from me. I am a 'mañana' or leave-it-until-tomorrow type, while she feels that everything should be done yesterday. She's great, basically doing everything for us – including all the post, banking and even gardening, a pastime she really enjoys. I'm not a lazy person and we work together, but not surprisingly I tend to be a labourer.

We are a proper pair in the sense that we go to most events together and, thanks to celebrity golf days in particular, we have met and become friends with a number of comedians, entertainers and sportsmen. It's been fabulous getting to know the real people behind the faces and chatting to them when they have been away from the normal spotlight.

It all started when I stood in for Frank Worthington when he couldn't make one of the golf days in the 1990s. World champion darts player and all-round gem of a bloke Eric Bristow suggested that I should join the celebrity golf tour, which had players from a variety of sports and numerous entertainers on the register.

Not all of us could turn up to every occasion, of course – there were about 35 a year – but I frequently came across Dennis Taylor, John Virgo, John Lowe, Willie Thorne and Keith Deller, a big Ipswich Town fan, from darts. And fellow footballers Phil Neal, Frank Worthington, Trevor Cherry, Willie Morgan – who was a very good golfer – Graeme

Sharp and Roy Evans were regulars, while Tony Hateley subsequently became a great friend of mine.

On that first visit I was predictably very nervous on the opening tee because it was the first time a crowd had ever watched me playing golf. Right on cue I shanked it. Give me a 40,000 crowd and a size-five football any day of the week! But I got through it and gladly signed up, going on to meet a star of stage, film and television, Norman Wisdom, who I was a big fan of, and the lead singer of *The Fortunes*, Shel McRae. Singer-actor Howard Keel was a big international star and came over for the Howard Keel Classic which was organised every year by Willie Morgan. He also made a point of attending the Johnny Mathis Classic in Ireland. Such massive stars!

The black-tie dinners afterwards were always a highlight and helped to swell the charity coffers. Comedian Frank Carson regularly got up to entertain us, as did Stan Boardman – who would often have been up all night, but usually won! Imagine playing golf to raise money, meeting friends, having dinner and then listening to Howard Keel and Johnny Mathis sing to you? They were such great days which have been sorely missed since 2008 by all who played in them.

For some of the lads who had been retired from their sports for some time, the golf tour and get-togethers had become a big part of their lives. They looked forward to them and it was heart-wrenching when it had to finish. The 2008 financial crash forced many big companies to limit their sponsorship budgets and, after a few years of hanging on, the celebs had to pack it in. Although Liz didn't actually play the game herself, we were both equally upset.

My wife is a total people person who loves to chat and I regard that as a good thing because it nicely balances my shyness. I liked the fact that she really talked in depth to my mum for five years before she died – now she knows more about my family than I do. Regretfully I hadn't done that and should have spoken to her more, particularly about my father and her relationship with him. Needless to say I should have asked questions on plenty of occasions during my life, most notably during my football career.

Life was trundling along on an even keel until a major upheaval in 2007. An organisation attached to the PFA and called the Footballers Further Education and Vocational Training Society started to play a major part in the restructuring of what we were doing. It had been supporting footballers who were at the end of their careers, or who hadn't made it, and from 2004 it had become clear that they were interested in developing their own club community schemes.

By 2007 they – and the Premier League – had started throwing a lot of money into clubs, which meant they grew and developed quickly. The sums outweighed those that the original Football in the Community had been able to provide and, in return for their increased funding, the Premier League understandably wanted more control.

Although the aims were basically the same in terms of supporting clubs, the Premier League felt that there was scope for more inclusive work. The result was a foundation-based system at clubs whose charitable arms became either trusts or foundations, both doing good for local people. The reorganisation did not mean individual officers such as Tommy and me would automatically keep our jobs when the transition was made. And although the programmes were about to become more cash-rich to help them to run, there would be some redundancies at top level, which meant officers didn't have their trusted colleagues to call on.

I remember a meeting at a restaurant on Ecclesall Road when Tommy and I were wondering what was happening to us. We knew our jobs were finishing and learned that the former Blades player Mark Todd would be appointed leader of the United foundation. He wasn't unfamiliar with the Football in the Community scheme because he had been with Rotherham United's for several years and there had been signs in recent years that something such as this was going to happen because some clubs had taken over their own schemes, operating them in a bigger way while remaining under the national Football in the Community umbrella.

At Sheffield United one of our staff, Sue Beeley, was really the one whose diligent groundwork began to sort out the reorganisation and new thinking made it obvious that it was going to be very different. Numerous staple elements of our original timetable were stopped and many new initiatives were started – all made possible by the extra funding on the table. The foundation had more bodies involved in working on the project. It was better-resourced and able to involve individuals who had expertise in key areas regarded as essential within the new model.

The new emphasis was more on education and there was money and staff to deliver it, a development that shaped my own point of view; it would have been great if Tommy and I had been able to access the additional funding and staffing we needed to build on our very successful birthday parties and soccer schools.

Fortunately in the early days when money was tight and we had to find sponsorship, I had somebody to do that for us. I wasn't a negotiator by any means; if I was, I would have been on 10 grand a week when I was playing!

So that was that; my second career had come to an end. It gives me satisfaction to look back at how that scheme developed during the years and selfishly, maybe on this occasion, how I coped and grew with it. Despite, or maybe because of the ups and downs, it was a great personal development period for me.

My self-confidence grew enormously, not just in learning new skills, but also in how to relate to people. Even simply talking to parents at the prize-giving at the end of each soccer school was something I'd had to push myself to do initially after I'd doubted my ability to carry it off.

It didn't make me rich – I went from £105 per week through various small rises until I reached about £400 when I finished – but it was infinitely better than being on nothing at all when I came back. And when all is said and done, I had held a responsible job for 20 years, stayed married this time and got my life back on track.

Once again, I found myself in the position of having no idea about what would come next. But I knew one thing for sure – for better or worse, I was in a much better position to deal with whatever it was this time round.

26

WHAT A FINISH!

Tommy an♦ I both nee♦e♦ to work an♦ offere♦ to carry on, but I think we both knew that we'♦ fin♦ a♦juste♦ roles in the foun♦ation ♦ifficult to a♦apt to. We'♦ ♦one our stint an♦ in the en♦ Tommy accepte♦ a pay-off. Me? Well, I can still scarcely believe all the things that have happened to me since ...

Before I'd had much time to draw breath, I was invited to a private meeting over lunch with Simon Argall, then United's head of operations. If the proverbial feather had been in his hand, he could have knocked me down with it when he asked if I would consider being Sheffield United's first ever club ambassador, on pretty much the same money I was then being paid.

Bloody 'ell! It didn't take long for me to see it as a role I should be honoured to accept, one that had been created especially for me. I began to understand that the club really did appreciate my service and time at Bramall Lane and were prepared to entrust me with a brand new and important job.

It would be a big change, but was perfect and meant a timely end to the five-day week treadmill of reaching targets and so on. I would still have responsibilities, but it felt made for me and wasn't anywhere near as intense and demanding. I was getting older, after all! I was even offered an office, but declined because I didn't want a nine-to-five job sitting at a desk with a computer, even though I was on call 24 hours per day. It really was just the ticket, allowing me to do officially what I'd always done – meeting the public, talking to them here and there and doing whatever the club wanted me to do.

For starters there was variation and a lack of routine that was refreshing. Usually I wouldn't know from day to day, or at least week to week, what was coming up. I could take a morning call asking me to go and represent Sheffield United at a dinner, or to make a presentation or visit someone in hospital, plus the occasional more high-profile event with the club's hierarchy.

It was a mutually-beneficial arrangement; the club had a designated representative to wheel out whenever appropriate and I supplied the profile as a recognisable face the fans could relate to. However much of a failure I might have felt in my personal life, I was reminded that I had made a significant impact for United on and off the field and was not being allowed to forget how highly-regarded I actually was by the club and the fantastic fans. There were such levels of recognition afforded me that it is overwhelming to recall them all here. But here goes!

The *Sheffiel• Star,* the city's long-established newspaper, added a new category to their local professional football awards, an annual event that attracts all the players, managers and journalists from the South Yorkshire region. So it was a pleasure to be remembered and become the first person inducted into the awards' hall of fame among prizewinners from the current great and good of football and media in the area.

At about the same time I was appointed club ambassador, one of the hospitality suites on the John Street side of the ground was dedicated to me. That was fantastic and a total surprise because I wasn't told until the large room, which has large windows overlooking the pitch, was close to being rebranded. The Tony Currie Suite, open to diners on matchdays, was opened with Sky TV in attendance.

So it was a shock a few years later when the then-chief executive called me in to see him one day. After about 20 minutes of hyping me up about being a great player, he said: "I'm thinking of changing the name of your room although I haven't decided yet what to call it. Perhaps 'Ambassadors.' What do you think about that?"

"How the f**k do you think I feel about it?" I thought to myself. But my response had to be more considered. "Whatever is best for the club," I said. I left it at that and eventually it became TC10 on matchdays, which wasn't a bad name, and The Ambassadors' Suite during the rest of the week when they were trying to sell it for non-football functions. I think there were occasions when it had been difficult to sell the room out, whatever it was called, but, as I pointed out, we were in League One – the third tier – at the time and consequently putting bums on any seats was difficult.

Really it was a victim of circumstance. If we had been in the Premier League, it would have sold itself. Anyway the room is now at all times called the Tony Currie Restaurant, thanks, I think, to the efforts of people such as former chairman Chris Steer and Martin Green, a director, who have always supported me well for many years.

Not all footballers are bigheads, but I'm pretty certain that all of them experience at least a warm glow of satisfaction when they are given recognition purely for their performances on the field. We are all a bit that way surely, whatever type of work we undertake, so I am massively privileged to talk about this next event.

In 2014 United were celebrating their 125th season with a series of events during the year. Unfortunately it was about the time a round of redundancies were in the air at Bramall Lane and the chief executive, Julian Winter, told me I was being offered half the hours and much less than half the wages. I was so humiliated that I decided to accept the redundancy and was told that I didn't even have to work that current week out. That hurt, I can tell you.

But someone of obvious influence then suggested that announcing me as the winner of the planned poll for Sheffield United's greatest ever player – while making me redundant – might not be the smartest PR move, however much the club were hamstrung by financial problems. Soon afterwards the joint chairman Kevin McCabe pulled me aside on a matchday, slapped me playfully around the cheeks and said: "I've only just heard about this, TC. I'm going into the boardroom now to sort it out."

Then he talked me into taking a part-time role – with a bonus – and I was touched that he did. I didn't want to leave the club that had been my life and more importantly everybody likes to feel wanted, especially by their chairman. I had been bruised, no doubt about that, so Kevin talking me back was a big part of why I changed my mind – it wasn't just to preserve an income.

I didn't know I would win the poll, even though a lot of people had predicted that I would, hands down, and I did take the precaution of writing a speech just in case. The evening certainly was a lavish affair in the huge function room at Ponds Forge and there were so many current and ex-players, staff and distinguished guests in the room it was mind-boggling. The evening was brilliantly organised and befitting of a wonderful celebration of a fabulous club.

I am the first to concede that choosing one player as the best when hundreds have played with distinction is, frankly, impossible. Everyone, including me, has a favourite and so many will have been just as deserving – and I am not being modest for the sake of it.

Believe it or not, there was a time when Sheffield United were the best team in England, but none of those players were shortlisted for our big night. You can understand why. It was about the time when football was in its relative infancy and the year 1900 was ticking round. Nobody in 2014 would vote for them because they would never have seen them play and to a point, the same would be true of other heroes who followed them.

I am unbelievably and sincerely proud to have been given the accolade, but realistic enough to acknowledge that it is perhaps one that nobody should win. I think I was fortunate enough to be still rated nearly 40 years after leaving, never mind the poor buggers from 125 years ago! It's inevitable that players from the much more recent past would still be fresh in the minds of the voters.

Phil Jagielka was second and Brian Deane finished third in the voting. They were two great players, without a doubt, but can you believe that Alan Woodward came only fifth? He should have been first or second in my eyes. But then again I didn't see our 1899 league championship-winning team either!

It was the most cherished of titles and two most important factors made it possible: my teammates – to this day still my best friends – and the backing of the supporters, who have never ceased to acknowledge my own contribution to their club. That is why I was so thrilled that more of them were able to be present when my next honour came along.

In 2018 it had been 50 years since I had signed for Sheffield United as an 18-year-old straight up from London. I had been elsewhere for some of the intervening years of course, but the club very kindly arranged several events during the year to help me to celebrate. I knew nothing about the 'big one' in advance although there were a few signs leading up to it – hushed phone calls and hurriedly-concluded conversations that didn't include me.

But all I had to go on was being told there was something I had to turn up to on the night at the Lane. Liz did not tell me anything, which must have been mighty difficult for her, especially when she had been part of the committee who set up a brilliantly-produced *This is your Life* evening.

What a mind-blowing night it was – just phenomenal and right up there with one of my top five ever. Bramall Lane's Platinum Suite looked fabulous, the ticket-only dinner event was easily sold out well in advance and the only downside was that more fans weren't able to join me. The crowds mean everything to footballers and those supporters with tickets really enjoyed the format. It unashamedly and faithfully replicated the television version, which in itself was a treat – to me, it was most definitely the real thing. Right down to being brought into the packed room to the familiar music and opening announcement: "Tony Currie, this is your life." Spine-tingling stuff.

I think I was in a daze as I made my way to the stage, initially recognising only the odd face in the audience on the way and being unable to take in everything that was going on. Liz sat by my side and at least I was able to spot my relatives taking pride of place in my eyeline on the front table. Even then I wasn't prepared for what was to unfold and just how many characters were sitting there waiting to come up and speak. Others who were unable to be there on the night had done video messages which were played on large screens or via audio recordings. It made me feel 10 feet tall.

My old teammates had their say – which was always going to make me nervous! – and it was just great to have Allan Clarke and Mick Jones from Leeds and Peter Hucker from QPR, too. Since my Watford days I had stayed in occasional touch with my fellow Hornets apprentice Mickey Packer, but I didn't expect him to be there in person, as with Tommy Docherty. The Doc seemed as if he wanted to sit on stage and talk all night!

My first roommate in Sheffield, Paddy Buckley, sent a video message, which really meant a lot after all those years, and imagine my reaction when the great international athlete Dave Bedford came on stage. I couldn't outrun him at school and I certainly couldn't now! The show went like clockwork and overran, but nobody was leaving.

BBC icon John Motson contributed a video of his account of commentating on "a quality goal" while singers and Blades fans Paul Heaton, of *The Beautiful South* and *The Housemartins*, and *Def Leppard's* Joe Elliott followed suit with their own memories, too. The actor Sean Bean and

QPR's Glenn Roeder couldn't be there either, but went to the trouble of sending video recorded messages. Keith Edwards amused us as usual and it was wonderful to hear Toni Minichiello, now a world-renowned coach in his own right in athletics.

When I was in my heyday at United, our matchday announcer Ian Ramsey hit on the idea of playing the *Limmy & Family Cookin* chart hit *You Can Do Magic* at every game and it became regarded by our fans as my own personal theme tune. On the night Ian received some recognition for the idea, which was a nice touch. It was tremendously nostalgic to hear it again on the night with Ian there as well.

Apologies to anyone whom I may have missed out, but I will mention one more because of the effort he made to be there – and the fact that I can't resist another opportunity to mention *Coronation Street.* Chris Gascoyne, a Blades fan who plays Peter Barlow, had to be delayed because of his filming schedules, but insisted on driving over from Lancashire to be with us. I wish he hadn't – when he came in halfway through, he was virtually mobbed and more popular than I was!

Liz and I are big *Corrie* fans and we stayed in touch with Chris after he had arranged for us to meet the cast. Apologies in advance if you are not familiar with the *Corrie* cast or plots, but I once texted him to say that the nasty murderer Pat Phelan had to go. Chris messaged back: "Don't worry, I'm on it."

He must have been because not long afterwards the actor who played Phelan sent me a video. Adopting the menacing manner of his *Corrie* persona, he warned: "Tony, I've heard you've been talking about me," before then making threats about what he was going to do to me by way of reprisal. It was as good as playing for England for me, that was!

I won't ever forget the effort, love and commitment put in by friends, colleagues and supporters to make the night happen for my benefit and it goes a hell of a long way towards rebalancing my mood if I slip into one of my lingering darker moments.

During his chairmanship of United Kevin McCabe had been a supporter of mine and I respected the fact that he is a genuine fan from the terraces who achieved his dream of owning United. So when he and subsequent co-owner, Prince Abdullah bin Mosaad bin Abdulaziz Al Saud, eventually took to the courts to settle a dispute as to who should become sole owner, there was an understandable uncertainty for everyone. I have to say that the new regime have subsequently been absolutely brilliant to me.

Liz and I were in a garden centre in Barlborough when Kevin rang me in the summer of 2018 and his suggestion knocked me for six. "We'd like you to become a director," he said.

Yes, that's right – a director!

"You're joking?!" I spluttered. It was so unexpected I almost wondered if I had heard correctly.

"No, I'm deadly serious," he replied.

I don't recall taking long to consider the offer and its implications before my mouth took over of its own accord. "Thank you very much," I said. "Of course I will."

It's not the sort of proposal you get every day, is it? I had been in the game for such a long time, but never in a million years did I even think about such a thing happening to me. My acceptance was immediate and without real thought, but I knew it couldn't be anything to do with me putting in any funding or offering any business expertise. I had none of either really.

Instead I felt I would have a contribution to make in some areas even though it would never extend to influencing the playing side. And nor should it have done. But it was considered useful to have another voice from someone who had been in the game and was still connected to United. And I was excited to be asked.

I thoroughly enjoyed the whole experience of being Tony Currie, Sheffield United FC director and ambassador. I was so proud. It was wonderful and it is amazing how being a director attracts so much respect, mainly from people inside the club, even though I had been there for so many years.

Few directors work on anything like a daily basis at clubs and consequently I continued to fulfil my ambassador role for 99 per cent of the time. When we signed players, I might make the odd comment to the media – such a weirdly-pleasing thing to be able to do after being asked to speak as a player during my own transfers.

The ownership issues rolled on during my year in post and really overshadowed most other matters that might have been dealt with as a board. It was so intense and important that there were just two board meetings, one a conference call and the other down in London. How ironic that I should have to go back 'home' for a board meeting for my club up north!

My stint had to end when Kevin McCabe lost the verdict and I was duty-bound to resign because he had initiated my induction in the first place. Happily for me the Prince and his regime ensured that my association with the club didn't end there, saying to me: "Look, we know and appreciate that you've been friends with Kevin, but we still want you to continue being an ambassador. You have been here a long time; you mean a lot to the fans and we know the club means a lot to you."

That was great news and, I suppose, largely unexpected given the politics involved. They put me on a good weekly wage, which I was equally appreciative of, and things worked out very well for me personally during a turbulent period for the club. I was chuffed about still being wanted and being able to retain some of the privileges of being a director. I respected them for that.

The Covid-19 pandemic, which began in the United Kingdom in 2020, severely restricted some of my normal ambassadorial duties because of the social-distancing limit on numbers. It also prevented me from attending supporters' funerals, chatting to fans in the shop, visiting hospitals and supporting the various charities I work with. But it was important for me to replace some of that contact by recording video messages for people I couldn't get in to see in hospital or keeping in touch through Zoom and telephone calls. No doubt that was appreciated even more in such troubled, lonely times.

I help out when wanted in an official capacity at St Luke's Hospice, Bluebell Wood Children's Hospice, Weston Park Cancer Centre and Sheffield Children's Hospital. When December comes around, we visit as many places as we are able to and the players give out Christmas presents on behalf of Sheffield United.

The charity I was longest associated with is situated only a long goal-kick away from Bramall Lane. St Wilfrid's Centre for the homeless and vulnerable truly does wonderful work and is indebted to Kevin Bradley, who was head of the organisation for well over 20 years and always 100 per cent committed to it. My special connection started when I was in Football in the Community and invited by Kevin to have a look round. I got more involved, maybe twice a week to help out with some of the sporting activities, and was drawn in by bittersweet stories and experiences of the people who were using the place.

Honestly, they often broke my heart with equal measures of joy and sadness, but St Wilfrid's was inevitably a place of sanctuary and understanding for them all. It got to the stage when I would never dream of turning down any request to help out and imagine what a thrill it was for them when I brought along players and managers, including Neil Warnock and Rob Hulse, to join them for their Christmas dinners. On one occasion Ted Hemsley, Len Badger, Mark Todd and I took part in their annual Blades v Owls cricket match on a field across the road. How on earth Kevin managed to get the high commissioner of Pakistan along as a guest, I will never know!

A regular football Steel City derby took place among the clients and when Liz and I or some other football figure were due to present medals, they would look forward to it for ages. And for us visitors, the way they regarded the whole process as their Wembley was very touching. Running a charity is hard work and fundraising is central to its existence. Kevin conducted a question-and-answer session with me at the ground to help out when St Wilf's needed £6million of funds to go towards building a mini-hotel for those who needed beds for the short term. Reaching the target was a big achievement and going along to its eventual opening was brilliant.

Kevin and his staff did an absolutely wonderful, selfless job that was a genuine community benefit right on Sheffield United's doorstep. Going there undoubtedly affected me in a good way and changed me for the better – and if that sounds cheesy, I don't care because there is goodness going both ways in that building.

27

THE ULTIMATE ACCOLADE

Everybody loves a happy ending, especially in football when your team scores a last-minute winner. An♦ for Sheffiel♦ Unite♦ – my club – to pay me such a great compliment so far into our long association just fills me with pri♦e an♦ gratitude.

A s a professional footballer it is inevitable that you grow attached to your home ground. It's your place of work, playing out what you have done on the training ground, and a 'safe place' where your supporters urge you on. Mostly! You get to know it inside-out; the camber of the pitch, how it is affected by bad weather, how its dimensions might dictate how you play, where most of the noise comes from. But most of all, it's home.

Logic dictates that you win more matches there than away, so you're more likely to have the most successful and vivid memories. More of your fans are there, urging you on, and it becomes a very different and inspiring experience than playing on someone else's patch. It's almost impossible not to grow attached to your own ground.

Supporters who follow their team for years, often with relatively-little experience of other stadiums, surely feel an even stronger attachment. They regard their ground as something of a shrine, which produces a sense of excitement and anticipation that I still feel myself.

Obviously the longer you play with a club the stronger the familiarity, so Vicarage Road, Bramall Lane, Elland Road and Loftus Road all have a special place in my heart. Those grounds have changed a great deal since I played there and no-one can argue that today's facilities for players and fans alike are massively improved.

But while the changes were needed, I still have a few sentimental pangs of regret about the passing of the characterful old grounds I remember clearly. Today's pitches are really what I envy about the current game. Well, maybe the wages as well...

Bramall Lane is without doubt one of the most historic and unique in the world and not just as a football ground. It has been used for one thing or another since the mid-19th century and there is good reason to believe that it is the oldest sports stadium in continuous use across the globe, having staged numerous other sports and events in the past.

Bruce Springsteen, the evangelist Billy Graham and world championship boxing have all been put on there since I arrived in 1968. Yorkshire still played cricket there for another five years and I recall being amazed at how big the Lane was. My God, how it has changed since my debut!

Two statues now stand in the car-park outside the main stand on Cherry Street; leading appearance-maker Joe Shaw, a classy centre-half and captain in the 1950s and 1960s, and Derek Dooley, a man of steel in every sense who served both city clubs in different capacities. It took a long time – and a chairman such as Kevin McCabe, with real empathy for the club – to make the decision to honour two of the Blades' most influential figures in such a physical and permanent form.

I was always taken by the picture of Tom Finney, the great man retaining his balance while sliding through a plume of water on the turf, which won the sports photograph of the year award in the 1950s and was used as the basis of his statue at Preston's Deepdale ground. West Ham have one of Bobby Moore, Geoff Hurst and Martin Peters, their World Cup heroes from 1966, and Bill Shankly looms large at Anfield. Alf Ramsey, Jock Stein, Peter Osgood, Billy Bremner and Johnny Haynes are other examples at other clubs.

The statues help to define a ground, give it an identity and I think that is important. Spectators enjoy the variation and feel of different venues – it all adds to the day out. Unfortunately rebuilding or upgrading our stadiums often results in them being modern, clean and safe, but lacking the quirky elements that made their predecessors so special.

You knew you were at The Dell at Southampton, at the Baseball Ground, Derby, or White Hart Lane – and countless others – because of the floodlights, the stands, their design or some specific landmark in them. I find the modern ones striking in a different way, but with less individuality. Perhaps you had to be there to know what I mean, but I can't deny that progress was well overdue.

Some people will remember that Burnley chairman Bob Lord even named a stand after himself at Turf Moor after pushing through a major reconstruction of the ground. Stand-naming has become a popular feature for clubs to pay tribute to former players or managers, a name very visible from both inside and outside the ground so thousands of fans are aware of it at every game.

I admit I regarded those players lucky enough to be honoured that way with more envy than I should admit, but not in a jealous way. I certainly didn't begrudge them. It just looked like such an honour, to have your name on obvious display as close to the fans as it can get. It can't get much better for a former player to be held in such esteem. So imagine my emotions when I was afforded that privilege at Bramall Lane.

At one time the club considered naming the Bramall Lane stand after me, while Kevin McCabe tried to persuade Sheffield City Council to have the road outside the ground renamed in my honour. "You don't want a statue," he pointed out to me reasonably, "because you'd have to be dead." It was a good point that I was happy to be on board with!

Now the Tony Currie Stand, the south stand which was built while I was at United as a player, is the biggest in the ground and can be seen clearly from the three other sides. First branded in pre-season 2018 for a friendly against Inter Milan, the stand-naming is absolutely right up there with all the wonderful things that have been bestowed on me by Sheffield United, the city and the world of football in general.

28

SO MANY BLESSINGS

I have worke• for Sheffiel• Unite• for more than 40 years in total an• the last 12 years have been packed with some really kind gestures. But I have often said to people that sticking around gets you somewhere and although I was born in London, I've been an adopted Yorkshireman for well over half my life.

Believe me, I am sincerely grateful for all the fabulous things that I have enjoyed about my career. Playing football professionally is the dream of millions across the world and doing so gave me such immense pleasure, but – and it is a monumental 'but' – there has been a nagging consequence.

My overwhelming passion just to be on a pitch playing, along with the frustration when I couldn't, affected my ability to think clearly about how to handle other elements of my life. I loved the routines and the highs, but couldn't handle the lows and what went with them. I clung to the instinctive attitude that if I was playing, then everything would be okay. It was head-in-the-sand stuff really and resulted only in further damage.

No-one can solve their problems and overcome life's challenges just by being on a football pitch for evermore. I'm not looking for sympathy or claiming I have been dealt a bad hand – that would be insulting. But we are all different and have our own strengths and weaknesses, physically, mentally and emotionally. Sometimes our impressions of others don't match how they really are.

Perhaps God got a bit confused on the day he doled out my abilities. Too much of one and not enough of others! There are still mental demons related to the stress problem I've carried for years, part of which was down to trying to convince everyone that I was still fit enough to play. The way I had to leave Leeds and the divorce which followed it began the process of mulling over it all, which I still do today. My mental state is frequently fragile and unpredictable, which is no fun for Liz either.

At about 2pm on the afternoon of July 24, 1991, when I was 41 years old, I suffered a stress attack at work which left me sweating from virtually every pore. An ambulance was called to take me to hospital and an electrocardiogram helped to make the diagnosis. After a day off work I went back to my job, but the incident had been mistakenly reported as a heart attack on *Radio Hallam*. My son Ryan, who had read it in *The Sun*, had been frightened to death – and it made me aware of how being wrapped in my own negative thoughts could affect me. I have been on medication ever since.

During the intervening years a lengthy list of well-intentioned friends advised me to seek help, but I never have. I have handled it on my own, admittedly not very well. Why have I not taken sensible advice? It couldn't do any harm. There is no logical explanation and while I wish I had sought professional help, I don't know if I ever will. That is just the man I am... one who could make things happen on a football pitch in his sleep, but too often was indecisive away from it.

Most of the time in public I put on an act and when I tell people I am an introvert, they laugh. It's like living a double life and the most harmful part is how it can affect the people I love the most when brooding takes a hold. Feeling totally incapable of overcoming my nagging emotions adds to the frustration when I am not being a better version of myself for them.

It's a gloomy picture, but thankfully not the whole story and I still have numerous blessings to count. My family, friends and Sheffield United are my life and despite the turmoil I am as happy as I can be. I owe them all for support, patience and encouragement that have got me to a relative state of calm and contentment.

I am still an introvert and going out a lot isn't my scene, although I really love being in close touch with my ex-United teammates. It is well over 40 years since we played together, but we are like brothers who never tire of talking about the old days. And there are many others I played with or against I am still thrilled to talk to or bump into occasionally. It's a very special band of people who have shared the extraordinary life of a professional footballer.

Not all my childhood dreams were achieved in the game and I would have loved to have won some silverware and more England caps. But I'm thankful for what I did achieve because there are some players who were better than I was, but never played at Wembley or for England.

Being 'rescued' by the fans who organised my testimonial was undoubtedly significant in what opened up for me later at Sheffield United and I have a good deal to thank the club for. It would have been even more memorable if Darren, my brother Paul's son, had also got to play for us. It wasn't to be in the end, but he did answer the call in 2021 and have a spell with us on the other side of the touchline.

Darren was a very talented midfielder and we had him on trial for a month when he was a youth really, but wasn't offered a contract. Within a month he had started as an apprentice at West Ham United and following a loan at Shrewsbury, he played for Wycombe and Barnet. Joe Royle absolutely loved him at Ipswich and although I may be guilty of a bit of family bias, I'd say Darren was the best dead-ball taker around after David Beckham. The only things he lacked were the perceived levels of pace and aggression required at the top level.

To me Darren and Mark Duffy represent a breed of very skilful and perceptive players. They never really scaled the heights they should have hit because big clubs couldn't see past their weaker attributes. I can't help but relate to that sort of lazy labelling because it had been thrown at me years earlier.

Liz and I are very big on family and are enormously proud of the five kids we have between us and the way in which they have made lives for themselves. I have two daughters and a son – Sharon, 52, lives near Wycombe and has three grown-up children, Kieran, Aidan and Niamh. After being a dental nurse for many years she now travels up to London and works with my other daughter Natalie.

Middle child Ryan had trials with Sheffield United in his mid-teens, but had to stop playing because of weak ankles. Now 50, he lives in Norwich and is such a good car salesman I reckon he could sell anyone a car in five minutes – God knows where he got that from! He also has three grown-up children, Sebastian, Charlotte and Lily.

Then there is my youngest at 43, Natalie, married to Bradley – a master carpenter and an 'appy 'Ammer! Although they live in Romford with Sadie, Nat owns her visual merchandising business in Oxford Street and with two grandchildren on Liz's side, we have a total of nine grandies. As any parent will agree, children and their kids are always to be worried about!

Liz's son Matthew, a computer analyst, is in his thirties and lives in Sidcup with wife, Lisa. They have Olivia and Imogen, but there has been a lot of worry and concern about Olivia. She had a brain tumour on her optic nerve, which made her virtually lose her sight. Hopefully one day, through new technology, she may regain partial sight.

And finally Liz's daughter, Grace, is in her early thirties, lives in Maidstone and is an events manager. I love them all and we are a very close-knit bunch who really had to pull together when little Olivia's condition was deteriorating. It truly was a traumatic experience for us all and it taught me a lesson or two about dealing with a tough time.

During the coronavirus lockdowns our family visits were affected because most of our relatives are two-and-a-half hours away in the London area. Seeing them was almost impossible and we were in the same boat as millions of others, trying to cope and hold on to the things that matter most.

With flying badly affected, seeing former United secretary from the 1990s, Dave Capper and his family, was also put on hold. For a large part of the year he and Tina always lived in their house in Spain and for the last dozen or so years Liz and I have visited them in Mazarron, a small sea port in Murcia. The local ex-UK residents formed a supporters' club for Mazarron FC, who play at a standard probably equivalent to the Northern League in England.

Every year Dave organises three fundraising events for the football club – a gala dinner, golf day and race night – and does a great job in bringing in guest speakers as high profile as Dave Bassett, Joe Royle, Jan Mølby, Steve Kindon, Steve Daly, Alan Kennedy, Duncan McKenzie and Alvin Martin. We have become very close with Dave, Tina and their family and Mazarron kindly made me an overseas ambassador, which is a good excuse for getting over there when we can.

Talking of family and my sentimental nature, friends were surprised quite a while ago when we got a dog. I had never wanted one; I had seen my brother, Paul, go through pain three times when he was mourning his. Then in 2008 after Liz had nagged me for a year to have one, I gave in. We homed a rescued German Shepherd and within two days, I was in love. We called him Hendon after where I am from. He came everywhere with us, everyone loved him and he was virtually the club mascot!

Hendon was with us for seven years and I made a couple of good friends because of his daily walks. One, Malcolm Smith, is now a Senior Blade member in his eighties. He went to school with Alan Hodgkinson, my former teammate at United, and also knows another former Blades international in Mick Jones, who lives nearby. The other, Richard Bates, has been a Blades fan since time began. I still see both of them, even though Hendon is no longer with us. We miss him so much, even now. Family and pets, eh?

Although we live in a four-bedroomed house in a nice, secluded spot in the Worksop area, it is likely that we will go back to London one day to be with family. We haven't spoken about it recently, but if the time comes, it will be a real wrench to leave the north. I definitely wouldn't have believed that when I made the opposite journey at 18 years old.

Thank you, Sheffield United, teammates, staff and your supporters – you gave me strength to pull through when I needed it most. Wherever I am, I know I will be able to draw on some fantastic memories of you all. I shared so many of the best hours of my life with supporters and fellow players at Watford, United, Leeds and QPR. This special game draws us all in and inspires our hopes and dreams, in many cases for lifetimes. Nothing can take them away from us.

It has taken me a long time to understand it, and to learn how to use memories in a positive way for myself. I appreciate more now how regrets and dwelling on what might have been can eat away at you, even destroying your life while you live it. Football gave me the opportunity to make good memories and good friends – and not just for myself. It's a privilege to have been able to do that, and I want to enjoy making sure they have been worth making.

MY ENGLAND TEAM

Most of us will have attempted to choose our own all-time greatest football XIs and I have always found that to be an impossible task, whether at club or international level. There are just too many players to choose from – how on earth can you compare a player from, say, the 1950s, with one playing now? Different eras, different conditions, different developments in kit, boots, pitches, tactics, fitness ... the list goes on.

And, of course, everybody is utterly convinced that the game and the players were "better in my day!" It is really a harmless bit of fun to be enjoyed and discussed and left at that. After all, no-one is going to be right or wrong. Opinions will always differ and that's the way it should be.

So I give you what would be my own England XI comprising players I have watched and, in many cases, played alongside for our national team. Just settling on a system to accommodate some I really want to include is difficult enough and favours some players over others. But, in 4-4-2 formation, here goes ...

Peter Shilton

For me our greatest ever, especially when you consider his longevity at the top. Obviously Gordon Banks was right up there and I also enjoyed watching Peter Bonetti, who was so good when I used to watch him for Chelsea. Since then David Seaman and Joe Hart played with distinction but, considering Peter faced challenges from Joe Corrigan, Phil Parkes and Ray Clemence, he definitely had the extra edge.

His training was second to none and his handling was just brilliant, although I have to say he was crap on penalties! If he was around now, and also encouraged to use his feet to make blocks, he would be even better. Although I appreciate how difficult the modern, lighter, swerving ball can be these days, I still see far too many goals let in at the near post for my liking.

Shilts was a talker, as all goalkeepers ought to be, and communication was definitely one of his strong points. I agree that there have been some excellent goalkeepers in the current era – such as Manuel Neuer, Peter Schmeichel, Petr Cech, Ed de Goey and Thibaut Courtois – which has been something of a changeover.

Until about the 1980s, continental 'keepers were, in this country at least, regarded as a bit of a joke. Not so now. They have improved massively and overtaken our own.

Paul Madeley

A teammate at Leeds whom I was forced to appreciate much more when we played together. He was a tall, thoroughbred athlete who was versatile enough to play almost anywhere. Make no mistake, despite not being the greatest passer of a ball, he could really play and nobody got past him because he moved so well and read the game so astutely. And that was despite having eventually to do 20 minutes work with a pulley before games because of a bad back. I put him ahead of Jimmy Armfield, George Cohen and Gary Neville.

Roy McFarland

A central defender, but a real footballer who could score goals for you. Ray was a lovely man, not massive, but great in the air, very solid and a superb timer of a tackle. I can picture him now, bringing the ball out of trouble with an assured left foot and a calmness reminiscent of the man next up ...

Bobby Moore (captain)

The nicest bloke you could ever meet. You couldn't help but admire and respect someone who was attentive in conversation, who always really listened to you and who would give good advice while looking you straight in the eye.
Bobby was slower than I was, but never got exposed for it because his positioning and football brain were amazing. I maintain it was a natural

talent because it enabled him to maintain that same air of calmness off the pitch when things went against him. Who could forget the Bogota incident at the 1970 World Cup? I just couldn't not make him captain, could I?

Emlyn Hughes

His fierce winning attitude helped to shape a fantastic career, during which he also captained his country. To some Emlyn might not always have been the nicest bloke in the world – at times he was a bit of an alpha male – but I got on with him great and we roomed together on England duty on many occasions.

He had two good feet, could play centre-half, left-back and in midfield, so in my book his versatility puts him ahead of Ray Wilson, Kenny Sansom and Terry Cooper. We were good friends – apart from when we were on opposite teams, because he put everything into being a winner! But that was what helped Liverpool and Leeds to win so often in those days.

Colin Bell

His nickname of 'Nijinsky' just couldn't be more appropriate. For the uninitiated Nijinsky was a classic winning racehorse of the time and when Colin showed power and elegance when he surged up and down the pitch, the comparison was easy to make. His energy and drive were insatiable and his fitness was undeniable, even in some pretty sapping conditions at times. Colin, modest and quiet, had a great all-round game – he was decent in the air, a good tackler and he could finish with confidence. No wonder he was so popular within the game, and not just with his own supporters.

Paul Gascoigne

Okay, I'm stepping out of my era just this once because Gazza would probably have been one of the top three greatest of all time if hadn't been an idiot. Which, of course, he couldn't help. His skills were fantastic, he was a great dribbler and he had a quick brain. Across 10 yards he was easily quick enough to make things happen and although he wasn't as two-footed as some, his vision was great.

It's frightening to think how much better he would have been if it wasn't for his personal issues and some of the people he mixed with. I watched Italian football just because he went over there, but he wasn't the same player after his FA Cup final injury in 1991. What an entertainer.

Bobby Charlton

What can I say that people haven't heard before? Just one of this country's all-time greats. What makes him extra special is how he overcame the Munich tragedy to forge a terrific career while remaining humble and modest beyond his playing days. Bobby could play with both feet and was an explosive finisher.

Apparently as a left-winger when he was young, his shooting was very erratic, but when he moved into midfield, it was brilliant because he added control to his power. He couldn't tackle to save his life, but what a player and to see video footage of him even now still excites football fans all over the country; the feint as he veered past people at speed was just a joy. He obviously wasn't slow and if he saw space beyond his marker, he would do his thing and leave defenders powerless in his wake.

Glenn Hoddle

You'll know by now my view on this man. I rate him the very best passer of a ball with both feet, a great scorer and maker of goals; in short, the world's best midfield player ever. Glenn was so easy on the ball and although he couldn't tackle his breakfast, who gives a shit? I'm talking here about classic midfield players who can demand the ball, see passes and deliver them. That is not to say I don't respect the ability of the modern greats such as Lionel Messi, but I regard them almost as strikers in comparison.

Jimmy Greaves

My idol. As a kid I first watched him play for Chelsea in 1958 and although the passage of time can magnify the brilliance of players in the memory, I really can't think there has been anyone quite like him. He scored so many goals in England in the top-flight and although I never saw him over there, I still don't know why he failed in Italy.

Moving abroad then was surely more difficult than now and maybe he didn't settle or adapt to the style of football. On his return he quickly became his old self again and was the Messi of the 1960s, going past people with so little effort.

Jimmy was a genius at what he did and how he did it, building a phenomenally-high goal-to-games ratio. He always seemed to know where the ball would be and many times I saw him ghost through defences from the halfway line without seeming to do much. Again there were signs of what was to come with Messi when Jimmy would produce a little dink at just the right time to leave the goalkeeper on his backside as the ball rolled into the net. He was so unlucky to miss out on playing a major role in England's 1966 World Cup victory.

Allan Clarke

Another one with a great nickname that perfectly fitted his attributes. Sniffer was fantastic to play with for one season at Leeds, plus several outings with England. To be honest he was a dirty sod, a niggly player who never shirked and wasn't scared of anybody. He couldn't be intimidated, which really used to wind up opponents who thought they could put him off his game. The irony is that he could have eaten for England and despite his skinny frame he never put an ounce on. And he's still the same!

Allan is very opinionated and I loved him as a player and as a friend. I bought a house near him when I was at Leeds and we got on great. Sniffer could always find space and was a great goalscorer. Martin Chivers, Mick Channon, Wayne Rooney, Kevin Keegan, Gary Lineker – all great players. But I go with Clarke.

I know, you probably don't agree. My team doesn't include wonderful players from then and now such as Roger Hunt, Geoff Hurst, Frank Lampard, Steven Gerrard and Paul Scholes, whose passing and vision reflect what I think were my own two best assets. But you can't pick everybody and at least it provokes enjoyable discussion.

I didn't want to leave out Alan Hudson, who should have had 50 England caps, or Gerry Francis. But at least I wasn't struggling to narrow down my vote as to who should manage my team ...

Alf Ramsey. Without a doubt.

ACKNOWLEDGEMENTS

Putting together this book was a process that resulted in experiencing and reliving a lifetime of contrasting emotions. When initial discussions began about how it should be written and what to include, I was clear about wanting it to be an account of my life in its entirety ... ups, downs, highs, lows and everything in between.

After all, these days a series of accounts of 90-minute football matches are relatively easy to find, and they alone won't tell you anything like the full story anyway. It's the decisions, anxieties, disappointments, and personal reflections that form the background to them that stay with me just as much.

You will now know I am by no means perfect, but what I have achieved has been in no small measure down to help from dozens of people in a variety of ways. I apologise in advance that I can't mention all of them, but here are just some who helped me along the way....

Les Hill, whose enthusiasm, humour and discipline gave me purpose and the opportunity to start believing I might make it as a sportsman. Catching up with him after I left school has always been a thrill and a pleasure. My Watford youth coach, Frank Grimes, took things a step further after seeing me play at Regents Park before arranging a trial for me at my first club. And selling me my first car!

I am grateful that Ken Furphy gave me my first contract and debut in the professional game, and that John Harris took the chance not long after to bring me north to a city that I have called home for so many years.

The staff, coaches, players and fans of all my clubs have invariably treated me well, but I must mention Len Badger and Ted Hemsley who immediately took me under their wing as soon as I nervously signed for Sheffield United. They and all our teammates became a real band of brothers. It is a friendship I treasure to this day.

At Leeds some great players and fans welcomed me to their club where I was to play some of my best football, and it was a privilege to spend three years of my career amongst them all.

Sir Alf Ramsey made one of my dreams come true by giving me my England debut and I hold him in the highest esteem.

Tommy 'The Doc' Docherty finally caught up with me – after six years of trying! – when he brought me to QPR and I am so glad that I was able to represent a London club.

A sincere thank you to Terry Venables – whose innovative coaching methods were eye-opening to me, even as an established player – and to the players who helped me achieve another dream by appearing in an FA Cup final. Jeff and Viv were lovely, selfless people whose friendship helped me through a dark time, and journalist Mike Morgan – Scoop! – was the most honest reporter I have ever met, and a good friend in an hour of need.

I made so many friends at Bramall Lane during my years as a player and later in different capacities. There are definitely too many to mention, but you know who you are. I worked closely with John Garrett for many years, and he and Kevin Cookson took turns to both help me out and take the mickey!

My longest associate there – commercial director Andy Daykin – was an invaluable and reliable help to me with so many projects. He became a close family friend as a result.

I couldn't have succeeded in my work with the Football in the Community Scheme were it not for Roger Reade, Richard Finney, Dick Krzywicki and Tommy Spencer. We became great pals and had a great working relationship for over 20 years.

The Professional Footballers' Association, often in the guise of then-chairman Gordon Taylor, looked after me for many years, granting me financial support when I needed it, or medical help with injury issues.

My sincere thanks to the regimes of Kevin McCabe and latterly Prince Abdullah, plus chief executive Stephen Bettis, for using me in an ambassadorial role which is simply a job I love, at the club I love. Most Sheffield United team managers supported me with my community work but the Dave Bassett, Neil Warnock and Chris Wilder squads were especially helpful during my various roles.

It is fair to say that I didn't fully appreciate all that would be involved in the process of publishing this book. It made things easier that I was working with – and opening up – to Andy Pack, who I had known for many years in his media role at United.

Sheffield-based journalist and publisher, Danny Hall, was a logical choice for guidance and help throughout the process, and I must say it was an experience I didn't realise I would enjoy so much!

Andrew Kirkham was an invaluable source of statistics from my playing career, while David Bond also helped with proofreading. Thanks, too, to Glenn Ashley, Steve Ellis, Simon Bellis at Sportimage, Sheffield Newspapers and Joe Bamford for supplying photographs. It was also an honour to include some images taken by the late Martyn Harrison, who is sadly missed at Bramall Lane.

The last couple of years has seen the sad loss of a number of former teammates at all my clubs. I send my deepest sympathies and best wishes to their loved ones. And finally, I acknowledge the late Jimmy Greaves – the greatest – for giving me the inspiration to become a footballer.